MAN AND THE EARTH

MAN AND THE EARTH

Patrick Duncan

Towards an Ethic to Transform
Our Impact on the Planet

YouCaxton Publications
Oxford and Shrewsbury

Copyright © Patrick Duncan Jr. 2015

First published in 1974 by Volturna Press, Peterhead, Scotland

Published in 2015 by YouCaxton Publications

ISBN 978-1-909644-79-3

CONTENTS

DEDICATION

To my wife
without whose help
I should have made
many more
mistakes

ILLUSTRATIONS

A MESSAGE FROM SIR PETER SCOTT

Patrick Duncan's book is to be recommended to all who are concerned at the way in which man despoils and degrades the surface of our planet in the process of fostering his own, narrowly conceived, interests, and treats all other species as expendable in so far as they are not of "material use" to his own species. This book puts mankind into a wider context, as part of the whole complex of life-forms, both past and present, and of the planet itself which is to be our home for as long as we can foresee, and perhaps for as long as our species can survive. It suggests an ethical approach which might serve to unite humanity in the task of doing what must be done, and done urgently. I hope it will have that effect, and that it will be read by all those who believe that the present philosophy of maximisation must be replaced by a new concept of high quality human living, by a new respect for environment and by a new reverence for our earth.

Peter Scott

THE AUTHOR

Patrick Duncan, son of a former Governor-General of South Africa, was born in Johannesburg in 1918. He was educated at Winchester and Balliol College, Oxford and was in South Africa when the 1939 war broke out. He went back to England and tried to join the forces but was turned down because of an old injury which had left him, since the age of eleven, with a stiff leg. He worked on the Times and then joined the Colonial Service and was sent at his own request to what was then Basutoland, one of the three High Commission Territories. While there he published, in 1943, a small book called *The Enemy*[1] about the dangers of soil erosion.

From Basutoland he was seconded to Pretoria for three years to be private secretary to the High Commissioner, Sir Evelyn Baring (later Lord Howick).

On his return to Basutoland he became Judicial Commissioner and later published a book, *Sotho Laws and Customs*, based on decided cases.

Throughout these years, and particularly after the Nationalist victory in 1948, he became increasingly concerned with political events in his native land and in 1952 he resigned from the Colonial Service and moved to the Orange Free State.

His first political act was to join the Defiance Campaign that year, and he led a protest march of whites and non-whites into Germiston location, on the outskirts of Johannesburg. Those who marched with him included the late Manilal Gandhi, son of the Mahatma. Patrick Duncan was convicted and given the alternative

---

1   *The Enemy* is in fact a passionate, broad analysis of the devastating impact of people on our environment, and a clarion call to society for mobilisation, after the War, to work together for Utopia. Its scope is as wide in time and space as Man and the Earth. 'The Enemy' is the impact of people on the earth, and this work can be seen as a first step towards the ideas developed in Man and the Earth. *Editors.*

of a fine or a prison sentence with compulsory labour. He chose to go to prison.

He later joined the Liberal Party and became its national organiser and in 1958 founded and edited *Contact*, a political fortnightly magazine.

His political activities, which included attending the All Africa People's Conference in Accra in 1958 as delegate of the Liberal Party, and standing as Liberal candidate in the Cape provincial elections in 1959, brought him two more prison sentences.

In 1962 he was confined to Cape Town for five years but he escaped to Lesotho. While there he resigned from the Liberal Party and became the first white member of the Pan-Africanist Congress. He worked for the Pan-Africanist Congress in the United States and in Britain and then as North African representative living in Algeria. He later worked there for an international relief organisation.

After his burning desire to help build a non-racial South Africa, conservation was his greatest interest. He wrote *Man and the Earth* while he was in Algeria and was still working on it two days before he died at the age of 48.

His biography was written by C.J.Driver 'Patrick Duncan: South African and Pan-African'. James Currey (2000)

See also:

wikipedia.org/wiki/Patrick_Duncan_(anti-apartheid_activist)

PREFATORY REMARKS

by Dr. Douglas M.C.MacEwan,
Founder, Conservation Society

I first started a correspondence with the author of this book while I was doing research in Spain, and he was working in Algeria. He then let me know he was engaged on a book, and sent me the draft of his manuscript.

An immediate chord of sympathy was struck. I seemed to find in the book many of my own thoughts, but expressed with more skill than I could manage. He saw many imperfections in the book, but I encouraged him to finish it.

What I did not know, and what he did no more than hint at, was that he was dying, of an obscure blood disease, and had to go fairly frequently to England for hospital treatment. The revision of his book was carried out, against time, by working often enough around the clock. Finally, he had the revision more or less done, and it was arranged that we should meet in England in the summer of 1967. I arrived in London only to be confronted with the news that he had died in hospital there.

I had undertaken to publish his book, and I regret very much that I was unable to do so quickly. When I finally contemplated publication this year, I had to look through the book again, fearing very much that I would find a great deal of it dated. In fact, I do not think this has happened overmuch. Even the Viet-Nam war, alas, is still with us, and the Roman Catholic Church has still not made up its mind to admit contraception. The one thing that has changed, of course, is that far more people would now be willing to accept the rightness of much of what Patrick Duncan says (at the time when he first wrote me, I was trying to get the Conservation Society started, and he then provided much encouragement).

So what then is the point of producing yet another book to

prove that man is outbreeding his resources? If that were all that is in this book, the answer would be "very little". In fact, I would not be publishing it were I not convinced that it contains an important and unique message for all concerned with the terrible problems facing our generation. What the author proposes here is nothing less than a new basis for ethics which could, just conceivably, unite the human race with all its squabbling and vicious factions, in time to forestall catastrophe. But the time is short, the message is urgent. I have, alas, little hope that it will be heeded. None the less, I do emphatically think that the book should be read, and pondered, and discussed, especially by the young, who may be able to shake off the prejudices of their tradition, to consider dispassionately the dilemma we are in, and the possibility of salvation which Patrick Duncan's suggestion offers.

There is another respect in which this book differs from many popular books on the environmental crisis. This is that it is a typically African production. Patrick Duncan considered himself an African, and this book is instinct with his feeling for the beauty and freedom of Africa's open spaces, for their unsullied purity in the pre-European era, and for their richness of animal life. It is full of fury for what man is doing to the animals. It recalls Swift in its total rejection of human ideas of superiority.

There are in fact few authors - Swift is one, and in Patrick Duncan we have another - who have adequately expressed the contempt which a sensitive person must often feel for the human race as a whole, in all its absurd pretentions to superior ethical values, accompanied invariably as they are by savagery and ruthlessness in behavior. Just possibly it is from this feeling that some men might derive the humility necessary (similar to that, perhaps, that animated the early Christians) to set in motion a change in the whole course of human history.

SOME SAVING CLAUSES

Human affairs - even on the scale of the individual - are so complex that it is scarcely possible to make any positive statement that is both valuable and completely true. It is even more difficult to make general statements without important saving clauses. On the world-scale the difficulty is still greater. Many of the situations are not quantifiable, nor computable, and can only be illuminated by intuitive flashes of insight.

It is therefore necessary, at the beginning of this book which has a somewhat wide scope in time and space, to utter a caution: all generalisations in this book which are not based on statistics are to be taken as intuitive judgments, statements which, in my opinion, are as near to the truth as possible; statements made in the knowledge that in making them one creates many exceptions. They are to be taken as statements which, despite this necessary inaccuracy, I feel to be valuable and true enough to be worth making.

Another point: there is much in this book that is critical of, and even hostile to the human race. I do not wish it thought that I am condemning from an imaginary judgment-throne with myself immune from condemnation. No, these criticisms are directed as much against myself as against my fellow-men. I do not feel myself morally superior to my fellow-men, rather the contrary. What the reader will, I hope, find in this book is judgment as free as can be from considerations of self. Nothing else is worthy of the scientific method. In the final resort little else in any field deserves to be written or read.

AUTHOR'S FOREWORD

In the advanced countries the traditional systems of religion and ethics are crumbling before the progress of science, and for the first time in human history an older generation is sending out a younger generation into the world with almost no guidelines.

Can society survive in the absence of generally accepted guidelines? No more surely, than a game of football can be played if each player takes the right to make up the rules. As the less advanced countries follow the example of the more advanced countries, nothing less than a worldwide social breakdown is threatened. This breakdown is one of the three major dangers that we face at the present time.

The second is the danger that Man will destroy his environment through the recent increases in his numbers and his power, and that in destroying his environment the day of world-starvation will be brought nearer.

The third danger is that of destruction through nuclear warfare. Perhaps this danger is the most acute of the three, yet I shall not touch on it in this book. Many other minds have sought to find a safe way around it and a whole literature, to which I feel I have little to contribute, is growing up. But the other two dangers: the danger of an ethical collapse and the danger of the destruction of the environment, are less in the public eye than they deserve to be. To the discussion of ways around them I feel I have something to contribute. And, who knows, in their solution may be found one of the clues to the nuclear enigma?

Each of these three "super-dangers" is without precedent. Never before has Man had the power to destroy the world in a fiery doomsday. Never before has Man had the power to annihilate other competing forms of life and to degrade the soils and waters of the world. And never before has an older generation failed to hand on to a younger generation guidelines to help it through life. Our decision-making powers seem to have been paralysed by the need to react constructively to so many, so great dangers; not surprisingly, there is no generally-accepted consensus on how to meet these dangers. Let us attempt to visualise the predicament in which Man finds himself. Let us take as the setting for a parable a vast and hardly-penetrable forest. Somewhere in the recesses of this forest is a procession. It is composed of Man and the other forms of life. The point of entry into the forest was the point at which life began, some two to three billion years ago. The point of exit is hidden in impenetrable mists. On the long march to the present many animals have already strayed and perished, since extinction is the penalty for losing the way. The lesson of the dinosaurs is that even the most powerful and the most numerous may have to pay the penalty.

Until recently, the column moved slowly, led by a sort of instinct, the instinct to search for food and for a place in which to live, a search that led to the process that we call natural selection. Living forms searched for "niches," or, as Darwin called them, "places in the economy of Nature," and these forms proceeded to adapt themselves slowly to fill these places fully, and to multiply within them to the greatest possible extent.[1]

In our time the power of Man is already so great that this instinctive, evolutionary law is being repealed. For non-human life it is already Man that is in command, Man that legislates how, and even whether subordinate forms of life are to be allowed to occupy their niches. And for human life, whose niche is now the whole world, the process is beginning by which the unthinking law of indefinite multiplication is being replaced by a more rational law of restraint. Unfortunately the growth of the law of restraint is exceedingly slow.

Unfortunately, also, Man cannot any longer continue to follow the old evolutionary law of expansion. His power is too great for this. If he continues to follow this old law he will destroy himself by nuclear war. The need to abandon it increases the paralysis of the pathfinders. We are lost indeed in the depths of this forest, and the procession is turning into a mob. The leaders of the traditional faiths try to give a direction, but are no longer listened to. Many new voices are also raised but do no more than increase the confusion and the shouting.

A new direction is nevertheless necessary, for the signs that we have strayed from the right path are unmistakeable, In the advanced countries, whose example is now unquestioningly followed by the poorer countries, there is an ever-increasing volume of juvenile delinquency and crime, as society is menaced with dissolution; and of suicide and mental illness, as the human personality is similarly menaced. Waves of hatred sweep back and forth between nation and nation, and political hysteria has reached levels hitherto unknown. Some nations are suffering from overeating, while in others children die of hunger. Urbanisation is proceeding rapidly, yet never before have so many lived in urban squalor. Wars and massacres have never been so cruel or so vast.

At the same time as our wars and our crimes are growing, the advance of science proceeds faster than ever before. We seem to have strayed from the path of goodness at the same time as we have found the right path in knowledge. Is it possible that we have here an inverse law, that as knowledge increases, goodness decreases? I shall seek to show that this is indeed the case, and that the scientific horrors of Belsen are symbolic of the whole of Man's ascent. I shall seek to show that the fears of George Orwell, Aldous Huxley, and a whole generation of science fiction writers are justified, and that unless we change direction we shall land up in an appalling future of immensely powerful and inhuman tyrannies.

If the progress of knowledge and goodness are in fact in inverse ratio, does this mean that we ought somehow to muzzle the scientists? Or, even, to lock science up in a new Pandora's Box which should never, like the old one, be opened? Surely not, because science is now illuminating the path behind us with a new, brilliant light. And out of a clearer knowledge of whence we have come must arise a clearer understanding of whither we will go. Surely not, because we have a sacred duty to know the truth, and only through the scientific method can we approach the truth. Surely not because the scientist's contribution, as I shall attempt to show is a sine qua non for a new ethical system.

Science has so far not initiated an ethical system, but - as shown in the collapse of the traditional religions - science has acquired an absolute veto over any systems which are in contradiction with its discoveries. Any new direction that is proposed must henceforth be in harmony with science. And any new direction that is proposed must come to be widely accepted, for otherwise it will be without power.

Herein lies a great dilemma. It seems that the final exit out of the forest is - at least for a long period into the future - going to be unknowable, and that therefore the long-term direction forward from where we now stand cannot be agreed upon. Yet without a direction which is generally acceptable no ethical system can be erected which is equally generally acceptable. And without such an ethical system it will be difficult to avoid widespread social breakdown and chaos. Is there then no way out of this predicament? If we accept that the long-term direction must for the present remain unknowable is there no shorter-term direction on which a majority of humanity might agree, a direction in accordance with which a generally acceptable system of ethics might be erected? Such an aim would, of course, make no claim to be absolute, and might not suffice for more than a few generations. Yet would not the time gained be of the utmost value? To return to our parable of the forest, is it not possible to find some nearby vantage-point, not necessarily lying in the long-term direction, yet from which the past might be more accurately surveyed, and from which perhaps a path might be charted into the longer-range future? If the direction in which this vantage-point lay were in harmony with science, and generally in the interests of all men it might suffice, for some time, to unify the march forward.

The purpose of this book is to argue that such a vantage-point does indeed exist, and that our path towards it might be generally acceptable to humanity as a whole. The very novelty of the idea might indeed serve to bypass some of the more bitter quarrels which at present divide men from men. This vantage-point, I shall seek to show, is the establishment of a new system of ethics based on a new harmony between Man and his environment, which in our times has become the whole surface of the world.

Such a harmony would be firmly based on science and such an ethic would be powered by a strengthened love of the world.

Probably the establishment of this harmony is generations away. But if, in our times, most people could accept it as desirable then all moves by humanity towards the establishment of this harmony would be in a meaningful direction. And when the stream of life regains a meaningful direction, then an ethical system again becomes a possibility since once again it becomes possible to interrelate small, daily acts to other small acts and to a great tidal direction.

Earlier I used the word 'love'. This is the key word. Love is at the heart of any system of ethics. If an ethic is to be potent and acceptable, it is not enough that it be described in books or that it form the subject of teaching. It must be absorbed in the earliest days by the tiny child from its mother. Man is a social animal, and the normal, human baby is born with a built-in pole of attraction and also with a pole of repulsion. Society is formed by the attachment of the pole of attraction to other members of that society and to objects approved of by that society. Similarly the pole of repulsion must be attached to objects and persons disapproved of by that society. Such attachments are best formed in the first few years of life, and the major factor in the creation of the child's attitude is the attitude of the mother as shown by her smile, her frown, and the tone of her voice.

That the language of love is the language of ethics is shown by the icons, images and stories of heroes and prophets told in the traditional religions. In a religious age the final answer to the central question of ethics "Why should I do what is right?" is "Because what is right pleases God, and we love God." But God's spokesmen are unheard at this time. The revelations of Buddha, Moses, Christ, and Mohamed, and the pantheons of Greece, Rome, and India, though they had many lovely and valuable features, have collapsed, and their ruin is probably irreparable. One day, I believe, the road between God and Man will be reopened, and the reopening will perhaps owe as much to these earlier revelations as it will to science. But this possibility lies far away in the future, and we are still left with the need for a potent ethical system in the present, an ethical system that can be based only on Man's love for the world.

From a different standpoint, too, Man's love for the world is equally necessary. By the growth of his numbers and power, Man has begun to destroy the soils and waters, the seas and the atmosphere. In order to feed and clothe himself he is clearing the forests and turning the wilderness into one great farm. Already he has exterminated the great majority of wild animals. Unwilling or unable to restrain adequately his numbers, he is pillaging the irreplaceable stores of fossil fuels. The destruction must become much more serious as the human populations double and quadruple. One trembles to think of the appalling world that we are bequeathing to our children and grandchildren. One can hardly bear to think of the damage that is now unavoidable by the first third of the twenty-first century. One can hardly bear to think of the disturbances that world-hunger is now fated to cause, as vast throngs of ill-educated people swarm over the globe. Unless in our time the parents of these throngs learn to deepen their love of the world, this paradise that we inherited from our parents will have become an irredeemable slag-heap.

The thesis of this book, then, is that these two greatest needs, the conservation of the biosphere and the establishment of a generally acceptable ethical system for the human race can both be met by one development: the growth of Man's love for the world.

Fig. 1. "Desirable piece of real estate" The Earth from Gemini IV
(Courtesy NASA).

1 Eden

WE ARE living in the most terrible and the most wonderful age of all ages since the beginning of the world. In one short burst of creative energy, short as seen on the geological scale, Man has fought his way out of the caves which he had shared with the animals, and into the scientific age. To-day he creates new elements, and transmutes old elements, and lights fires hotter than the sun itself. His stars ride the night skies. His instruments may be beginning to record the songs sung by the elements at the moment of creation, the first radiation emitted by the newly-born universe.[1]

Such powers, if they could have been imagined in previous ages, would have been called divine. To rearrange somewhat the words of chapters 2 and 3 of Genesis, Man "did eat of the fruit of the tree of knowledge of good and evil and has become as one of us (the Gods)."

You who read this book have eaten of this tree of knowledge. It is exhilarating to know that the advance of knowledge is proceeding faster than ever, and that, in our time, mind has been connected with mind, to produce the intangible, invisible, spherical web of thought that clothes mankind as the atmosphere clothes the terrestrial globe.

Yet it is not in knowledge alone that there has been this increase: there is increase too in the size of the problems that face us, and if the readers of this book allow themselves to be uplifted at the thought of the increase of knowledge, they must also feel the unprecedented weight of tremendous problems on their shoulders. In our time choices must be made that will affect the lives of billions of men and animals for far into the future.

Unfortunately rulers as well as ordinary people seem to be bewildered, and there is no generally accepted response to the predicament of Man.

Sometimes when one is bewildered, it is helpful to take a new look at the problem, and to try to see it from a new angle. Thanks to the development of space travel, it has become possible to do this. Perhaps if we imagine that we have followed Yuri Gagarin and the other cosmonauts into space we may discover elements of a solution in the distance and the beauty of the world, and in the harsh inhospitality of space.[2]

Familiarity breeds contempt, and through habit we take things for granted. Of no object is this more true than the earth we tread upon. For billions of years living things have moved about on its surface and each of us as an individual was born into it and accepts it as naturally as the air we breathe. And so its uniqueness, its beauty, its hospitality to life, its protective atmospheric blanket, its softness, its moisture, its equable temperature are qualities that we rarely give a thought to. Yet the cosmonauts, only a few hundred kilometres away from the surface, are exposed to vacuum, atrocious cold, radio-active dangers, excessive heats. And the space probes are beginning to bring us news of the other bodies in the solar system, and all this news is of environments no less inhospitable than is the surface of the moon.

This world is probably the most desirable chunk of real estate reachable by Man for many centuries, for at the speed of our present space ships it would take many years to reach Jupiter and Saturn, many months to reach Mars and Venus, and 120,000 years to reach the nearest star which, just possibly, might have planets circling it.

The lesson is clear: let us treasure this world, for there is literally nowhere else for us to go to. There is no replacement awaiting our colonisation if we overpopulate this world, or if we damage it irreparably. With all its faults, it's our home.

But the cosmonauts must have felt more than mere toleration for the world. Some of them have brought us back coloured photographs, and have enabled us to share some of the sights they saw. They looked down on brilliantly blue seas, on green forests and brown deserts, all haloed by the brilliant blue gauzy film of the atmosphere. They must have felt like the Jehovah of the Bible. When he had finished creating the world he looked down on the sixth day and "God saw everything that he had made and behold it was very good."(3) If ever these brave men felt fear in the "eternal silences of these infinite spaces" of Pascal, they must have felt happy to know that their return to the earth-paradise had been carefully planned.

"Paradise" is a good word for what they saw. The word was taken from the Persian by the ancient Greeks to describe the pleasaunces built and walled by the powerful satraps of Darius and Xerxes, enclosures of lush greenery protected by high walls from the desert. So, when one thinks of earth's incredible variety of life, and of the marvellous way in which this life is protected from the deadly heats and colds, and radiation-fluxes of space, one sees the parallel with those old Persian garden-paradises.

One hour, surely, in the earth-paradise would be worth a lifetime on the hideous surface of the moon. If we remember this we shall never again take the world for granted, and we shall continually be thankful for the privilege that we have of contemplating and enjoying it during the whole of our life-span.

It is the thesis of this book that the key to the bewildering problems that beset us lies in our seeing the world from this new angle, and in re-thinking our relationship with the world, so as always to remember its uniqueness and its beauty. This uniqueness and beauty exist quite independently of the existence of Man and the world has no need of Man for this uniqueness and beauty to exist. Man, of course, depends entirely on the world for his existence.

This is no place to attempt a universal history, yet for the relationship between Man and the world to be examined, it is necessary for us to look backwards to a few great turning-points or events in the genesis of the world and of life. In doing so we may be less likely to take the world for granted.

At the present time there is some very exciting work being done in fundamental research. One line, which does not concern us here, is research into the smallest particles of matter. Another is into the genesis of the universe and of the world, and this does concern us.

There are several theories of cosmogony, the science of the birth of the universe. Perhaps the simplest is one which is widely supported. It is the theory that the universe began with a big bang. On this theory, in the beginning, all the matter of the universe was contained in one body, the primordial atom, or "ylem". The act of creation was an explosion which shattered this atom, and sent its fragments speeding outwards at relativistic speeds, that is to say speeds approaching the speed of light. The big bang involved temperatures and energies that exceeded anything that has occurred since. Since then, these temperatures and energies have been cooling down and running down. The "big bang" theory is supported by a good deal of evidence, though other evidence supports other theories. In support of the "big bang" theory it seems that the galaxies which form the universe are, indeed, speeding outwards and receding from us at tremendous speeds, the furthest ones at relativistic speeds. It also seems that the general temperature of the universe is cooling, and radio astronomers have even estimated what this temperature is. It seems to be about three degrees above absolute zero, or -270°C.[4]

Such research, by radio astronomers, by astronomers, as well as by geologists and petrologists, is beginning to throw light on the question of the age of the universe and of the world. Their answers are of the same order of magnitude: ten billion years, plus or minus five billion years for the universe, and about 4.5 billion years for the earth.[5] This estimate of the earth's age strangely echoes ancient Hindu mythology, according to which a *kalpa*, "a day and a night of Brahmnâ… or the whole duration of time from the creation to the destruction of the world"was believed to endure for 4,320 million years.[6]

Many millions of years passed before the earth could harbour life. For most of this time the surface was too hot even to allow the oceans to condense, and the 1,345 million cubic kilometres of water that are now in the oceans and the ice-caps must then have formed a cloud mantle some 2000km deep. If there had been any outside observers the earth must then have looked as white as does Venus to-day. One can imagine, as the earth slowly cooled, how these clouds must have condensed again and again on to the surface, only for the water to have boiled off on contact with the red-hot ground, returning upwards again. One can imagine how this process must have been repeated, in an almost endless repetition. Yet not quite endless, for there came a day when the ground was not hot enough to boil it all back, and some of the water must have remained. At this stage there must have occurred unimaginable rains, for the more it rained, the more the ground was cooled, and the faster the rain must have come. It must have rained for hundreds of years, as the oceans literally poured out of the sky on to the surface. The land, bare, lacking all vegetation, must have eroded rapidly as waterfalls of silt moved rocks and sand by the cubic kilometre, grinding and gouging the surface daily into new shapes. "Every valley" in those days must have been "exalted and every mountain and hill made low."[7] For these hundreds of rainy years nothing of course could have been visible on the surface, for no light could have penetrated the clouds.

And then, finally, the clouds began to clear, "and there was light" and 'for the first time the sun shone on a world recognisably like the world we know, a world of mountains, plains and seas, rivers and lakes.[8] There was, of course, no vegetation, nor any other form of life. But the planet must have seemed alive itself, for surely each day brought its convulsive earthquake or eruption; each day must have seen new islands born steaming in the seas, perhaps to be swamped the next day as the boiling seas swept away their foundations, as we are witnessing at this time on a small scale with the birth of the new volcanic island of Surtsey; each day the air must have been rent by the roaring and groaning of the earth in labour.

Slowly the temperature must have fallen till it was comparable to present-day temperatures, and till life could appear, two to three billion years ago.[9]

Living organisms are organisms that are self-reproducing under the control of the nucleic acids DNA and RNA. Yet there is no sharp boundary between non-life and life. No one has yet defined life in a manner acceptable to a consensus of scientists. For instance Professor J. D. Bernal has defined life as "a partial, continuous, progressive, multiform and conditionally interactive self-realisation of the potentialities of atomic electron states."[10] Yet no sooner had this definition of his been published than it was attacked by other scientists, one of whom pointed out that this definition would also cover a crystal or a sun-spot. And the molecular biologist and Nobel prize-winner, John Kendrew has written that "certain arguments are only important if one supposes that there is a fundamental distinction between living things and non-living things, some kind of boundary on one side or the other of which everything must be placed. Personally I do not think that there is any evidence of such a boundary... and I think most molecular-biologists would share this view." [11]

Yet, even if Kendrew is right, it is still possible to speak of living things, and indeed the very title of his book from which the above quotation comes is THE THREAD OF LIFE. Perhaps life is like the red in the rainbow: it shades imperceptibly into the orange, yet it is discrete enough for one to be able to speak about it as one of the colours of the rainbow. What is important to us here is that living things do have in common a tendency to increase in number and complexity, leading through the evolutionary process, to increases in awareness, organisation, and consciousness.

What are these nucleic acids under the control of which life reproduces itself? DNA (deoxyribonucleic acid) and RNA (ribonucleic acid) are long thread-like molecules which are found in every cell of living tissue, which carry the genetic message, and which play the major part in the synthesis of proteins, the manufacture within the cell of the cell's specific product.

To give an idea of the complexity of these molecules, in each of the billions of cells in a single human being there is about a metre's length of DNA, yet many of these cells are only two thousandths of a centimetre across. And "all the DNA in a single human being would reach right across the solar system."[12]

So would the DNA in other higher mammals: just as there seems to be no hard and fast boundary between Man and the animals. We have come a long way since the days when the human race imputed to itself a semi-divine status "a little lower than the angels", since the seventeenth century seriously argued that animals (and not men) were machines, and since men accepted the religious teaching that men had souls in a sense that animals did not.

DNA (and in a few primitive living things RNA) carries the genetic message. The message is coded on to the thread-like molecules in an alphabet of four "letters", the bases thymine, cytosine, adenine, and guanine, which are attached to the thread-like molecules of DNA in "words" or codons of three letters. In recent years some of the world's most gifted scientists have cracked this code, the last letters being "read" in 1966 by the team at the Molecular Biology Laboratory in Cambridge, England.

It seems that the alphabet, and the language and the triplet words, are common to all life, right down to the simplest virus: another link that shows the fundamental unity of all life. The molecules themselves are objects of astonishing beauty and simplicity: they are shaped like a spiral ladder, or the old type of spiral electric flex, with the bases forming the rungs of the ladder, each rung being made of two of the bases that meet in the centre of the rung.

When DNA makes more DNA, what happens is that the double helix, the spiral flex, uncoils and each rung splits allowing one of the bases to go with each half of the double helix. Out of the substances in the cell each half-helix takes new bases to build on itself another half identical to the half that has split off. The identity is preserved in a manner which is simple and elegant: to make a rung the bases must make pairs, but adenine can only fit on to thymine, and cytosine with guanine. Thus, instead of one molecule of DNA, we now have two, identical with the first.

Each self-reproducing cell in the human body, or in any other living organism, contains DNA or RNA molecules which carry the complete information which describes the organism. In a man the amount of information present in each such cell is not less than that contained in eighty 24-volume sets of the Encyclopedia Britannica. For simpler forms of life there is much less information.

These facts awaken one's numinous feelings, the sense that one is very near to the secret of the universe. One is irresistibly reminded of the words of the opening verses of the Gospel according to St. John: "In the beginning was the word, and the word was with God, and the word was God… In him was life and the life was the light of men".

Each year we seem to be given a new translation of the Bible. We may yet live to read, in place of the above words:

"In the beginning was the codon…"

In the cell, this information is used by the cell nucleus to manage the community of molecules that forms the cell, and to synthesise, out of the cellular "soup" the proteins which form the body of the organism. The process is too complex for inclusion here, but the basis is that the DNA message is only switched on in a certain form of cell for such information as concerns that type of cell. This message is "printed" on to the simpler RNA molecules, which are removed from the control-room of the nucleus to the cytoplasm where they are read by small pear-shaped bodies called ribosomes, just as a tape-recorder reads a tape. The ribosome "walks" along the RNA, and as it reads a codon it assembles chain-like amino-acid molecules which are later folded up in complex ways to form protein molecules. These then become the substances which it is the cell's duty to manufacture.

The code is technical, yet its importance as the language of life is so great that it is included here.

TABLE 1.1

The Genetic Code

When DNA hands on its information to DNA for replication it uses the bases: adenine, cytosine, thymine, and guanine. When DNA hands on its information to RNA for protein synthesis the thymine is replaced by uracil: otherwise the code is identical. There are thus on the RNA molecules, four "letters": cytosine (which' we may here call C), adenine (A), guanine (G), and uracil (U). Out of these four letters codons of three letters are the words in which the code is written.

In the left-hand column below are the letters representing the first letter of a codon; the second letter is shown along the top of the table, while the third letter appears in the final column. There are twenty amino-acids, abbreviated as shown below. The table shows which amino-acids are synthesised by which codons.

Amino-acids:					
Phenylalanine	Phe	Threonine	Thr	Glumatic acid	Gly
Leucine	Leu	Alanine	Ala	Aspastic acid	Asp
Isoleucine	Ileu	Tyrosine	Tyr	Lysine	Lys
Methionine	Met	Glycine	Gly	Asparagine	Aspn
Valine	Val	Arginine	Arg	Glutamine	Glun
Serine	Ser	Tryptophan	Tryp	Histidine	His
Proline	Pro	Cysteine	Cys		

Table showing which codons of the Genetic Code apply to which amino-acids:

First position	Second position				Third position
	U	C	A	G	
U	Phe	Ser	Tyr	Cys	U
	Phe	Ser	Tyr	Cys	C
	Leu	Ser	Normal full-stop	Tryp	A
	Leu	Ser	less common full-stop	Tryp	G
C	Leu	Pro	His	Arg	U
	Leu	Pro	His	Arg	C
	Leu	Pro	Glun	Arg	A
	Leu	Pro	Glun	Arg	G
A	Ileu	Thr	As pn	Ser	U
	Ileu	Thr	Aspn	Ser	C
	Ileu ?	Thr	Lys	Arg	A
	Met (also capital letter)	Thr	Lys	Arg	G
G	Val	Ala	Asp	Gly	U
	Val	Ala	Asp	Gly	C
	Val	Ala	Glu	Gly	A
	Val	Ala	Glu	Gly	G

This table appeared in *New Scientist* of 12 May 1966, announcing that the last "letter", the "capital letter" beginning a message, had been decoded by the Molecular Biology Laboratory at Cambridge.

With Man, to understand is to wish to control; and no sooner had the language of life been decoded than ideas began to appear that the conscious remoulding of living forms was now within our grasp, that Man might now become a creator of life, and that in future the very processes of evolution might be consciously guided.

Such ideas will be treated later. For now it is enough to record that, in this most marvellous of all ages, the discovery of life's language is perhaps the most marvellous of all discoveries; and to say so is not to disparage those who are researching into the smallest particles, those who invented atomic fission, who are searching the almost infinite depths of the universe , who are exploring the world's billions of years of history, who have daringly erected hypotheses such as that of relativity, who have invented space flight, the flight of heavier-than-air machines, and radio; and countless other inventions and discoveries. Let us merely register the fact that, next to to-day's high noon of knowledge and understanding, the greatest scientific glories of the renaissance are no more than a straggling and watery sunshaft, such as barely breaks through heavy clouds at dawn.

And so, two or three billions of years ago, the long molecules with their encoded messages appeared, created the earliest forms of life, perhaps simple, virus-like forms, reproduced themselves, and began the long pilgrimage of evolution that has brought life and the world to where it stands to-day. The law of evolution was and is that each form of life multiplies to fill the available living space, "niches" in territory and in the available food-supply, or, as Darwin called them, "places in the economy of Nature."[13] Thereafter, changes may come: either the environment may change, or mutations may change the form of life that is filling the niche. Most such changes will be harmful to the living form, but occasionally, by chance, a change will occur that makes the living form more able to thrive. Then the fecundity that life shows at every level enables the form of life to multiply further, to colonise new living space, to press anew against the retaining-walls of its niche.

A mutation is a change in the hereditary information encoded in the DNA molecules. Often this change is caused by a direct hit by ionising radiation, and often it is caused by some other damage. It is changes such as these, multiplied many thousands of billions of times, over a period of two to three billion years, that, according to the biologists, have allowed all the changes of evolution. It is changes such as these that have filled the valleys with forests of lush greenery, the seas with their coral gardens, and the forests with brightly-coloured birds and jewel-like insects, that have produced, in all, three million species of living forms.[14]

All this beauty was created long before Man appeared:
And other eyes than ours
Were made to look on flowers
Eyes of small birds and insects small:
The deep sun-blushing rose
Round which the prickles close
Opens her bosom to them all.

The tiniest living thing
That soars on living wing
Or crawls among the long grass out of sight
Has just as good a right
To its appointed portion of delight
As any King.[15]

This non-human world owes nothing to Man. On the contrary his intrusion has been the greatest and most deadly disaster that ever befell it.

Perhaps, the best way to understand and assess the pre-human world is to visit one of the larger African national parks and to watch the animals living their lives free of nearly all human predation and Interference. Obviously, for all animals except the predators, death was constantly present, and to an English speaking reader will probably occur the phrase about Nature being red in tooth and claw. But, even if this is so, it does not mean that the animals spend miserable lives in continual fear of being eaten. After all, domestic cattle face death as constantly, and no one would suspect them of living in continual fear. And, in the wild, herbivores seem to ignore the predators unless they know that the hunt is on against themselves. In a developed country human beings know that to travel on the highway, or to light up a cigarette, involves an increase in the statistical probability of an unpleasant death, yet how many are deterred or live in fear for these reasons?[16] Finally, we know that to be hunted and, pulled down by a predator can be a process free of fear or pain. There is a remarkable passage in Dr. David Livingstone's account of his explorations in the interior of Africa which testifies to this fact. He was in Botswana and was attacked by a large lion which knocked him down. "Growling horribly close to my ear, he shook me as a terrier dog does a rat. The shock produced a stupor similar to that which seems to felt by a mouse after the first shake of the cat. It caused a sort of dreaminess, in which there was no sense of pain nor feeling of terror, though quite conscious (sic) of all that was happening. It was like what patients partially under the influence of chloroform describe… The shake annihilated fear and allowed no sense of horror in looking round at the beast…" [17] The lion proceeded to maul the explorer's shoulder seriously before other men came up and shot him, but this mauling produced no feeling of pain.

For these reasons I do not think that the fear of being hunted and eaten did much, in the pre-human world, to cause unhappiness among the animals. Despite the constant presence of death, the vigour and variety of animal life carries its own justification. To be born into sun and shade, with fresh food, water and air to hand, to live with one's own kind under the blue skies, to win a mate, to reproduce, to race untrammelled across the limitless plains, to sleep and to die: what antelope would not choose this if the choice were this or the nothingness of limbo? Surely if ever there were a paradise the world was that paradise in the pre-human ages. It was a paradise, and its trade-mark was beauty, a word to which we will return later in this chapter. In the almost Man-free environment of the great national parks, especially in Africa, this sense of beauty is so powerful that it is almost numinous, and one can feel, in such places, very close to the secret of the universe.

Man's presence, thus, is in no wise necessary to the existence of a world of great beauty and variety. Yet beauty and variety are not the sole values attaching to the pre-human world. It is becoming clear that it was a world rich in personality and intelligence too. Anyone who knows animals knows that their personalities vary as richly as do human personalities. And in the last few years patient research is beginning to show us that non-human intelligence is a reality in the most widely separated species.

Some of the best-known researchers are Karl von Frisch, August Krogh, Wolfgang Steche and Harold Esch for their work on the language of the bees *(Apis mellifera);* John C. Lilly whose speciality is the investigation of the language of the dolphin *Tursiops truncatus;* and Konrad Lorenz who perhaps more than any other modern writer has alerted men to the reality of animal personality, morality, and intelligence.

Von Frisch experimented for many years before publishing his findings in the late 1940's to an astounded world. He showed - and recent research has confirmed and added to his findings - that bees could communicate, both by dances and by sounds, that they could measure, and communicate to each other, information on angles and distances and the nature of the honeyflow. Since life inside the hive is complex, and since it is so difficult to decode the language of the bees, it is probable that the language is even more complex than has yet been discovered. For instance the queen mates once in her life, in the course of a nuptial flight high above the hive. If there is a mid-air bee epithalamion it may be generations before we record and understand it. Likewise if there is a bee cultural tradition, if knowledge is handed on by language, it may take Man longer to decode such words than it took to read the Egyptian hieroglyphics.

Tursiops truncatus, the bottle-nosed dolphin, is one of the 110 known species of dolphin. This family consists of marine, warm-blooded, streamlined, air-breathing animals.[18] Many of the species in this family are about as large as a man, and some are larger. They communicate with each other by emitting clicks and whistles. They are close cousins of the other cetaceans such as the whales, and, as may be seen in the build of the walrus, they are probably distant relatives of the bears: it is thought that many millions of years ago a land animal somewhat like the bears took to the sea, and slowly evolved into these lovely cetaceans.

Dr. Lilly showed that *Tursiops truncatus* is an animal of high intelligence, and that its language, which he and other investigators are recording and trying to decode, is a true language. An interesting account of some of Dr. Lilly's work appeared in 1965. The article described the sonar system of these dolphins, the system of high-pitched clicks that echo off objects in the sea, and in echoing give the animal a picture of its surroundings somewhat as does radar on the radar-screen. "These clicks", said the article, "are not the only emissions of these marine animals. They are, in fact, different from and independent of the means of communication used by the dolphins. These means of communication are basically composed of modulated whistlings. The human ear easily distinguishes between the clicks which are the animal's system of echolocation, and a whistled signal which always has a psychological and social value: courting, calling, maintaining the group, and so on. The language of the dolphins has already been the subject of several projects of research: in spite of this we have information, partial information only, on only about fifteen out of the 110 known species…

"In order to understand the meaning of these sounds it is necessary to study the behaviour of the animals at the time that the sounds are emitted. However, recordings are difficult to make in the open sea, and it is true to say that all recordings have been made in the aquaria in which the animals were being trained…" [19].

Dr. Lilly carried out experiments on dolphins by placing electrodes in various parts of the animals' brains. Certain areas of the brains in which these electrodes were implanted were pleasure areas, and the pleasure derived by the animals from electrical stimuli in these areas was intense. Lilly noted that, sometimes when the animals were deprived of these stimuli, they would "emit audible sounds which were extremely rich and varied".

The size of the dolphin brain, compared with the size of the animal, is approximately equal to that of Man, "and in its complexity, its numerous convolutions, its morphology it is similar to that of Man. This suggests the possibility of great intelligence." [20]

In his affectionate respect for the dolphin Dr. Lilly is in agreement with the views of the Greco-Roman world. The Greeks and Romans knew that dolphins were intelligent and friendly to Man. There was the legend of the musician Arion whose ship foundered in a storm, but who played his lyre so beautifully that an appreciative dolphin carried him to safety on his back. Then there was the story, probably true, told by both Plinies, of a dolphin which befriended a boy at Hippo Diarrhytus (now Bizerta in Tunisia) and became his seagoing steed. In the same way, in the nineteen-fifties, two dolphins befriended bathers at Fish Hoek, near Cape Town, South Africa, and played delightfully with them over a period of many months. There was also the much more famous Pelorus Jack, a beakless Risso's dolphin *(Grampus griseus)* who in 1888 appointed himself the companion for ships travelling between North Island, New Zealand, and South Island, between Wellington and Nelson. For 23 years he scarcely missed a sailing, to the delight of all New Zealanders. In 1911 he died, and there is more than a suspicion that he was shot. [21]

Apart from their intelligence, beauty and friendliness dolphins have astonishing physical abilities. They are able to sound at speed to a depth of four hundred metres, to withstand there a pressure of 40kg per cm^2 and to surface at speed without suffering any ill effects. They have also learned to slide resistlessly through the water and to attain great speeds with little expenditure of energy. Somehow they are able to maximise laminar flow and thus to avoid eddy or boundary turbulence in the water that rushes past them, a secret quite unknown to human swimmers or to the designers of submarines. Perhaps the most striking fact in Dr. Lilly's book is that although the dolphins were often harmed and sometimes killed in the experiments, they for their part never made any attempt to hurt the experimenters. [22] Yet their great jaws, armed with dozens of sharp, conical teeth, could easily have torn off a human limb. Is it possible that in the dolphin we have a natural pacifist, a being with a high morality? Certainly in their family life dolphins behave admirably, and they are quick to succour any of their kind that are wounded or unconscious.

Non-human intelligence is by no means limited to the cetaceans. One of the most astonishing stories comes from South Africa, where a legless railwayman at Uitenhage, Cape Colony, trained a baboon to operate the points and signals from his signal box. Jack, as the baboon was called, became his master's ever-present helper at home, on the way to work when he used to push a trolley along the rails, and at work. And recently it has been reported that an ape has been trained in Australia as a satisfactory tractor-driver. These examples are random, and it is clear that all our experiments and researches have only scratched the surface of this vast field, the field of non-human intelligence, communication and language.

Some of this intelligence is acquired by cultural transfer, and some of it is inherited genetically. For instance the weaver-bird's knowledge of how to build its intricate nest is transmitted from generation to generation and must be encoded on the DNA molecules. This was shown by the great South African naturalist J. A. Marais who brought up several generations of weaver-birds by having their eggs hatched by canaries and not allowing them any contact with their own kind: the nests that they built could not be distinguished from those built in the wilds. It is customary to despise such knowledge and to call it instinct, but it is difficult to understand why, if it is genetically handed down, it is any less marvellous than knowledge culturally handed down.

Take also the spider-wasp, that black and brown insect that paralyses spiders and preserves them for its young in little clay houses, and that never sees its own parents. All its skills are necessarily inherited. Here is an interesting account of its intelligent habits by a French naturalist: "This spider-wasp *(Pompilida)* frequents human dwellings in the south of France (in August). However, it is not there to look for, or to share, Man's foodstuffs. It hunts for spiders with which to feed its young. The whole process of building a home for its eggs is determined by the need to make it a real larder. Why, then, does this wasp go to our houses? Simply because, despite its French name (mason-wasp) this builder cannot produce a mortar that is rain-resistant, and it uses only water-soluble clays. The wasp therefore needs a sheltered spot for the building of its pretty cells… Near a brook, using its jaws, the *pompilida* collects a grain of mud as large as a peppercorn. This grain of mud is worked into a paste with the wasp's saliva. Then, grasping the little ball of clay firmly in its mandibles, the wasp flies to the site which it has chosen with great care. Just like a good potter, the wasp flattens the first ball against the supporting wall to the extent of making it disc-shaped. It then adds the second ball making a curve with the first ball. At the same time, with its mandibles and its front legs, it "draws the dough", making a foundation 4-5mm in height. Soon a small cylinder is seen… Each time, after laying a course, the wasp pushes its head into the pot to check the state of the work and to be quite sure that the cell is taking on the exact proportions that are desired.

"Throughout the work of modelling the clay, the wasp gives out its characteristic sound. Is this an ultra-sonic emission which is intended to speed up the hardening of the clay? Is it simply a noise produced by friction?… It takes about 15-20 journeys to bring enough clay for one cell… The cell's measurements are about 30mm high and 5mm internal diameter."

"The, wasp is not merely a potter, nor merely a mason. Its work implies that it is also a hunter. When the last course is in place the cell has an opening a little smaller than the base. It is now necessary for each cell to be furnished with about 15 spiders, pre-paralysed by a few well-placed stings. The wasp's young (on hatching in the following year) will eat only fresh meat. First a spider is placed in the cell. Then the wasp lays an egg in the cell, and then adds other victims until the cell is full. When there is no more room the wasp becomes a potter again and seals the cell with one ball of clay. One wasp can make l5-20 such cells side by side…"[23]

There are, of course, many other animals that show a niceness of judgement and a foresight that one can only characterise as intelligent. Among invertebrates we have already mentioned the bees. But it is well known how complex and well-governed are the commonwealths of ants and termites, how expert is the spider in building her web, and how exact is her understanding of the strength of the materials which she uses. Beavers show an understanding of hydraulics, and migrating birds show a capacity to navigate with reference to the stars and sun that is almost the equal of human sailors until two hundred years ago. Commenting on facts like these, Professor Kalmus of University College, London, has stated that such animals are able to think in terms of arithmetic, geometry, cosmography, and statistics.[24]

The pre-human world was not only happy and intelligent, varied and beautiful: it was self-cleansing. Nearly all wastes were re-cycled to provide the basis for new life. No sooner did a great tree collapse in the forest, than a thousand insects began to tunnel into it, admitting moisture, fungus spores, bacteria, yeasts and all the other billions of micro-fauna and micro-flora which all, as if in concert, worked to remove the dead wood from the living forest. No sooner did an elephant die in the savannah than vultures, jackals, maggots and microscopic agents of putrefaction appeared to remove the evil-smelling flesh from the sweet-smelling air. Dung was removed by dung-beetles, and buried for the benefit of the new generation of dung-beetles and of the roots of plants.

All these activities of course go on to-day, but the beauty, simplicity and economy of this cycle of life owe nothing to Man. Land and sea, forest, desert and grassland all possess natural systems of garbage-removal from which Man, the messiest of the animals, could learn much. As it is said in the Edward VI version of the *Anglican Book of Common Prayer:* "I commend thy… body to the grounde, earth to earth, ashes to ashes, dust to dust…" Here, sanctified, we have the principle of the compost-heap, or of the layers of leaf-mould in the forest to remind us of *Homer's* line:

οἴη περ φύλλων γενεή, τοίη δε και ανδρών ('As with leaves, so with men.')

An army of micro-flora and micro-fauna, no less varied or interesting than the fauna and flora of an African national park, work to remove rotting flesh and decaying vegetation, to remove the ugliness and evil smells of death, and to transform it into sweet-smelling mould and new fertility for the soil. In one mm one million such beings can subsist, and it is they that make the soil the living thing, the source of life that it is. It is they that turn death into new life.

Earlier in this chapter I said that the pre-human world was, above all, beautiful. But what is beauty? Natural beauty is the essence of life, the quality of being in harmony with the direction taken by life. It is the quality seen when the phenotype (organism) is able to grow into the shape predicted by its own genotype (inherited information), avoiding environmental and social distortions. In addition, natural beauty is a language to which, at a profound level of consciousness, different forms of life are able to respond. It therefore draws together, into a whole, species which are, in evolutionary terms, sometime very remote from each other. For instance many forms of beauty were created for the specific purposes of one species, yet they carry significance for other species. It is, for instance, hundreds of millions of years since our forebears lived in the sea. Yet we carry in our bloodstream a saline memory of those days, and we still are thrilled by the sounds and sight of a breaking wave though we no longer need it for our food and oxygen as do our remote cousins the sea-urchins and sea-anemones. Another example is the green of the forest which is a source of delight to many forms of life, yet its chlorophyll was evolved for the very practical and workaday purpose of photosynthesis, the transformation of sun-energy into carbohydrates, the basic food of the plant. The dappled shadows bring together in delight the preening bird, the cicadas, butterflies and other insects the "panting hart", the lion heated by his hunting, and men, whether they be holiday-makers or poets or members of Robin Hood's company. "A green thought in a green shade"[25] is a thought common to the language of many species from widely differing genera. The scent, the form, the colour and the nectar of a rose, created as part of a business relationship between the rose-bush and the bee, speak a language that men can understand, sometimes with an almost unbearable rush of pain as such scents awaken old memories with vividness and one senses the gap between "what is" and "what might have been".

The golden hive of the aeon-old bee, designed to satisfy the economic needs of its makers, speaks of a perfected form of life, a form of life which, perhaps 280 million years before Man was thought of reached its present pinnacle of beauty, a life animated and held together by philadelphia, the love of the siblings for each other. Though Man was not there when the beehive, was perfected he is nevertheless able to understand something of the aesthetic message of the hive, its scent and colour, its loving ethics, and, as we have already seen, something of its language.

The song of birds is a language which is directed at birds of the same species as that of the songster. Yet, in the orient as in the occident, this song can enchant human listeners separated though they are by a vast evolutionary chasm from the birds. The visual beauty of birds is also part of this inter-general language of beauty, for the brilliant reds, blues and yellows of the macaw were surely not meant only for other macaws.

This common sensitivity to beauty on the part of Man and of other widely separate species has not only stimulated the poets and philosophers: it has also evoked comment from among the scientists. One of them has written as follows: "But there is a final fact which inevitably strikes the observer of the habits of insects: the constant presence of that which we call beauty. In the case of Man, the sense of beauty doubtless originated in direct contact with Nature… Direct contact with Nature is the lot of all living beings, even of the simplest beings. Is it not possible that, in this continual exchange between the living being and the world that surrounds it, there developed a more subtle relationship, more mysterious than those which our human science has measured and analysed?… We know that their (the insects') sensory system is prodigiously well-developed. Is it so surprising that their works, in the astonishing perfection of their structure, should touch us by aspects of their beauty?"[26]

Right through the story of life, right up to the age of Man, it seems that the world had evolved into a garden of variety and beauty, a garden in which evolution continued to operate and in which evolution was facilitated by this very variety. Man's domination of the non-human world has greatly reduced the variety of life, and has distorted in many ways the direction in which non-human life is developing. Is it possible to deduce where the pre-human world was going? Is it possible to isolate, in the history of those two to three billion years, any trends which seem to be constant? For if we could, if we could know the point on the horizon from which non-human life had taken its course, we should know something about the deepest nature of this life - and also, since we spring from it, about ourselves. Now that we have seized control of so much of non-human life, now that the very processes of evolution are coming into our hands, we might know clearly the point on the horizon of the future towards which we ought to steer.

The trends in non-human life that seem to be constant seem to be that life has tended to become more highly organised, more complex, more varied, more conscious, and more beautiful. Some of these trends have been greatly strengthened and speeded in the development of human life. For instance there is no doubt that with the advent of Man life has become even more highly-organised, more complex, and more conscious. Does this mean that it is in harmony with the total development of all life, non-human as well as human, that Man ought to replace all competing forms of life? Surely not, for human life lacks variety and beauty when compared with non-human life, and these two qualities seem to have been necessary for the maximisation of the purposes of evolution.

We cannot know, to-day, the final state towards which non-human life was tending, nor towards which all life ought to tend. But it is probable that a great reduction in the number of species would hinder the evolutionary process by reducing the opportunities for the evolving of new species. And it is also probable that it would reduce the sum-total of beauty. But we do not know, and in our state of ignorance all that we can do is to act as faithful stewards by handing on to the future all that the past has handed on to us.

The question is of paramount importance, more important even than the survival of the human race. It is possible, and we can see it happening before our eyes, for Man to destroy the biosphere, the thin spherical envelope round the world in which all life has its being. It is possible for Man to exterminate all life that surrounds him. At the present rate at which species are becoming extinct the day of universal extinction is not far away. It would also be possible for Man to continue to live in this aseptic, animal-free world, living on synthetic foods. This possibility too is being rapidly approached. Indeed, at present rates of population growth there will not be room for men and animals, and it will be necessary for machines to replace the cow, the pig and the whale as food factories.

It is also possible for Man to wipe himself off the face of the earth. Many thousands of scientists and military men, and many trillions of dollars are in fact being spent to bring nearer the day when the human race commits suicide.

Of all these horrors the worst and most final would be the extermination of the three million species of non-human life, for thus the raw material of evolution would be destroyed. We know enough to know that, if all men died, the processes of evolution would very likely again produce an intelligent being with culture and knowledge. But they could probably only produce this being if there remained a stock of animals from which to work. It is the thesis of this book, therefore, that the preservation of the biosphere and all its life is the most important priority of all, however great the importance of the human race might seem to be. Later we shall examine the need for a new ethic: this ethic will have as its base this axiom, that the world and the biosphere are the supreme value on which the whole system is founded, and that Man's importance comes second.

Fig. 2. "A dead world, a stony, sandy desert without air, water or life".
Copernicus from Lunar Orbiter (Courtesy United Press International, UK,
Ltd).

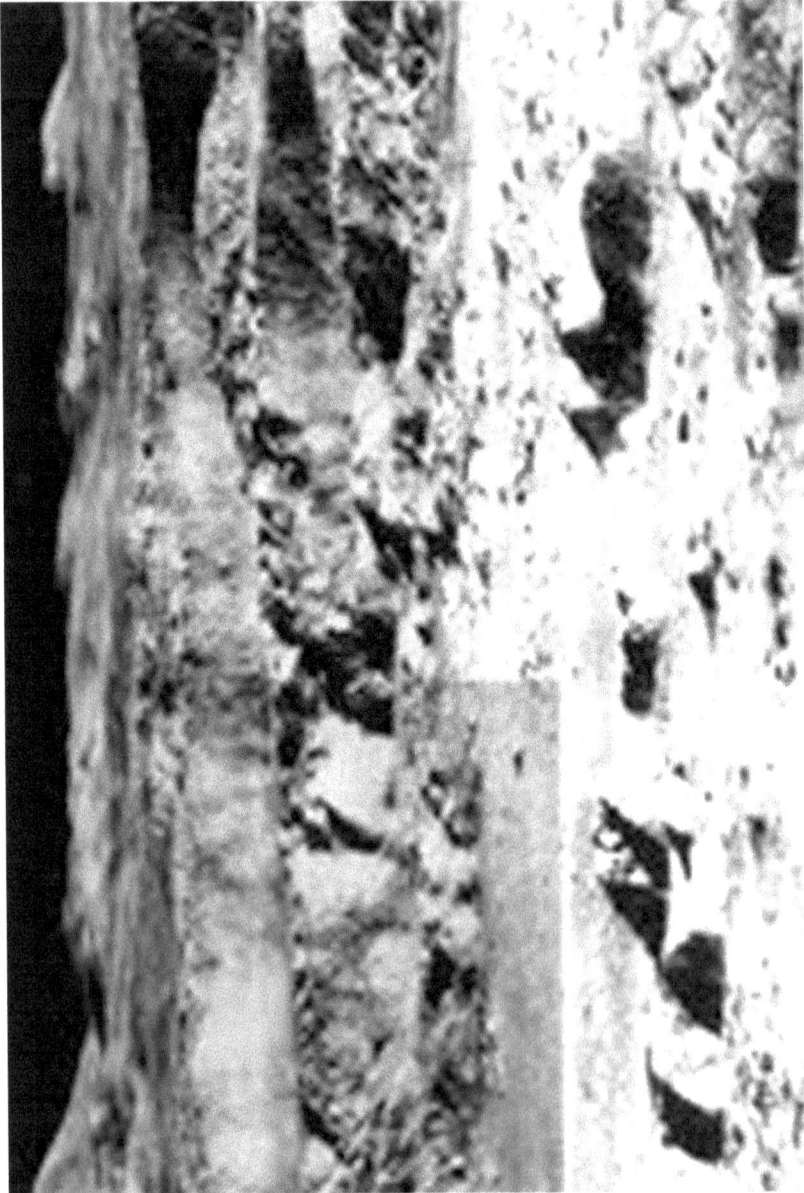

From the above flows the need for the total conservation of all forms of life now in existence. It is possible that, one day, with fuller knowledge, we may come to know with certitude that certain species are irredeemably hostile to other forms of life, and that they are incompatible with the main trends of evolution and the direction in which life ought to be moving. It is possible that, in the light of such knowledge, it may be right in the future to order the total extermination of such forms of life. Likely candidates for this list are the pathogenic micro-organisms and certain flies and parasites. But to-day our knowledge of the totality of life, its inter-relationships, its ecology, its direction and the direction which we ought to take in the long term is so incomplete that any such execution-list is premature. No one now knows: one day even the most troublesome parasite may be needed. One only has to think of the immense contribution of that Mediterranean fruit-fly, *Drosophila,* to the study of genetics, while outside the laboratory it costs the human race millions of dollars a year in damage. One day other forms of life which trouble us to-day may be needed, and extinction is an irreversible act.

Life is so familiar that many of us take it for granted, and see its vivid, various forms with glazed eyes from which the light of wonder has gone. Let us try to look at all this beauty from a new angle, so that we may cease taking it all for granted. Let us imagine that we are looking at it from one of the sister planets of our solar system. We are fast learning what the surface of our own satellite, the Moon, is like. It is clearly a dead world, a stony sandy desert without air, water, or life. When the sun shines on it the heat reaches 120°C, plus or minus 8°C, far higher than the highest temperature to which the sun ever heats the surface of the Earth. But when the sun sets (after a "day" of two weeks), the temperature drops to -185°C, far colder than the earth's coldest spot. Furthermore, as there is no atmosphere, there is no barrier to the deadly sort of ultra-violet rays, and as there is no magnetic field a deadly flux of radiation sweeps the landscape every time there is a magnetic storm on the sun. The Moon's surface is gloomily coloured, in tones of grey-brown. Perhaps to an observer on its surface the only visible object with any colour is our own Earth, hanging in the black sky like a huge globe. It is possible that its colour varies with the terrestrial weather and with the turning of the continents and oceans that face the Moon.

We know much less about Mars, but the more we learn about it the more Moon-like does it come to appear. There is a thin atmosphere (equal in pressure to ours at about 30,000 metres altitude). There is a little hoar-frost which clings to the higher mountains and to the poles. It is one and a half times as far from the Sun as we are, so the rays of the Sun must warm Mars with a frigidly distant heat, giving Mars a night even colder than is that of the Moon. Saturn and Jupiter, not to mention Uranus, Neptune and Pluto are far further out into the night, Saturn being nearly ten times as far from the Sun as we are, and therefore receiving one hundredth of the heat we receive. The most acceptable hypothesis about Jupiter is that its atmosphere is an atmosphere of frozen ammonia, possibly in the form of vapour or even of frozen dust.

If the outer planets seem too far away from the source of light and life to be tolerable for life, what about the inner planets? Some information, admittedly of problematical accuracy, has lately been got from a radar examination of Mercury, the little (4,800km diameter) planet that circles only 57 million km away from the sun, or less than half the earth-distance. According to this information, the temperature on the surface of this planet is 450°C[27], or more than 100°C hotter than the melting point of lead. Venus, between Mercury and us, 108 million km distant from the Sun, or about two-thirds our own distance, our sister planet about the same size as we are, is perhaps the best bet for life. But Venus is shrouded in thick clouds of nitrogen and carbon dioxide that produce a super-heating effect at the surface. Deductions from the intensity of radio emissions from this planet indicate a temperature of 327°C, and a surface pressure of 130 atmospheres.[28]

When one considers these appalling worlds, worlds that make the medieval idea of hell quite cosy, and when one compares them to this Earth, even as it is after 8,500 years of human spoliation and pollution, is it not immediately clear that we have had the fortune to have been born into a demi-paradise, a demi-paradise that once, before we dominated it, was a paradise? Is it not clear that this Earth, in its life-giving mildness, softness and humidity, is the most precious of all known objects? Imagine a sentient being who had been marooned on Mars or the Moon, yet able to observe life on our planet. Surely he would feel that one hour in such a paradise would be worth a lifetime elsewhere. This paradise was the Eden into which Man was born, and which he now controls with such indifferent wisdom. Even if Man is not so valuable as is the totality of the biosphere, he is now powerful enough to control it *de facto*, and for better or for worse all life now depends on Man's innermost character. Whence comes this extraordinary being, so powerful yet so unpleasant and cruel? Science has lately begun to open the book, the rocky filing cabinets in which are preserved the records of Man's appearance. We are learning fast how Man became Man without thereby ceasing to be an animal. It is a stranger and more wonderful story than our grandfathers would have imagined, and it is a story whose essentials are necessary if we are to know the means and the road by which we have reached the here and the now.

And unless we know these essentials we cannot know whither we go and whither we ought to go.

REFERENCES

(1)   cf. 1. 6.

(2)   The 'Russians call their space travellers cosmonauts, from the Greek words for universe and sailor. The Americans call theirs astronauts, *aster* being the Greek for star. The Russian word is to be preferred, for the nearest star is 120,000 years away at present space-ship speeds. Also the Russians did get into space first and the use of 'cosmonaut' gracefully commemorates their priority.

(3)   *Genesis* 1. xxxi.

(4)   Absolute zero is -273. 16°C. Two scientists of the Bell Telephone Laboratories, Arno A. Penzias and R. W. Wilson, discovered in 1965 that there is a cosmic background radiation with a wavelength of 7.3 cm , which seems to come from all directions in space. This radiation corresponds

with the output of a black-body radiator which is at a temperature of 3.5°K. - see *Scientific American* of May 1966 where there is also a report of confirmatory findings by Roll and Wilkinson of Princeton, and Field of the University of California.

(5)   Allan R. Sandage of the Palomar observatory: "7-13 billion years": see *Newsweek.* 31 October 1966.

(6)   *Dictionary of Phrase and Fable.* E. C. Brewer; Cassell, about 1920,

(7)   *Isaiah;* 40: iv.

(8)   *Genesis;* 1: iii.

(9)   *New Scientist,* 19th May, 1966 - What are believed to be the oldest life-derived forms of fossil microorganisms (Eobacterium isolatum) discovered by E.S. Barghoorn and J. W.Schopf in 3 billion-year old cherts in the Transvaal - but see *Scientific American* January 1967, page 39, for a dissenting view.

(10) *New Scientist,* 5 and 12 January, 1967.

(11) *The Thread of Life,* by John Kendrew, London, G. Bell & Sons, 1966; p. 91.

(12) Ibid. p. 63.

(13) *Origin of Species,* 6th edn. , p.64.

(14) There are 200,000 genera of animals. This would run into three million species or more: (There are 60,000 described species of weevils - Haldane called them God's favourite animal!) and then there are the plants, with many more species than the animals.

(15) Christina Rossetti, from "To what Purpose this Waste?" , quoted in *Animal Anthology,* by Diana Spearman, John Baker, London 1966.

(16) For a man of 41 years of age in England in 1966 the expectation of life is 6 years longer for a non-smoker than for a man who smokes 21 cigarettes a day.

(17) *Missionary Travels and Researches,* p. 12, 1857

(18) With the exception of one or two species which are riverine.

(19) *Sciences et Avenir.* No. 223, September 1965; my translation.

(20) Ibid.

(21) This and many other delightful stories appear in *Dolphin,* by Anthony Alpers.

(22) *Man and Dolphin;* by John C. Lilly, London 1962.

(23) "Les grands urbanistes de la Nature" , by lb Schmedes, *Sciences et Avenir.* No. 223, September, 1965; my translation.

(24) *Sciences et Avenir.* No. 228, February 1966.

(25) From "Thoughts in a Garden", by Andrew Marvell (1621-1678).

(26) "Les grands urbanistes de la Nature" , by Ib Schmedes, *Sciences et Avenir.* No. 223, September, 1965; my translation.

(27) *El Moudjahid.* Algiers, 7 September 1965.

(28) "The Planet Venus", by R. Jastrow and S.I. Rasool, *Science Journal,* July 1966.

2 Development of the weapon

"Man is but a great mischievous Baboon"
- William Harvey [1]

"We cannot get away from the fact that we are still animals"
- Professor J. W.S. Pringle, FRS [2]

THERE WAS no exact moment of time when it could have been said: "Till now there have not been men, but from to-day men exist." The human category, like the colours of the rainbow, has no hard and fast boundary, and it shades imperceptibly into that of the animals. The way we class some primates as human and others as pre-human is quite arbitrary. Yet it is nevertheless a classification that must be made. Among other criteria, such a classification is based on the shape of the bones, on the use of tools, on culture, and on social organisation.

Yet, even if no day can ever be recorded as having been the day when Man became Man, this "super-event" in history nevertheless did occur. It seems now that it must have occurred about a million years ago, when some of our ape ancestors learned to dominate other animals in a new way. By dominating other animals these ancestors enlarged their own living-space, the territorial and alimentary boundaries on their lives [3] their *lebensraum,* or, as we say nowadays, their niches. And they enlarged them to an extent so great in quantity that the change became qualitative.

There is a thesis which was brilliantly propounded by a South African scientist named Raymond Dart, and brilliantly expounded by an American author named Robert Ardrey, [4] that what made Man's emergence possible was the invention of the weapon. Robert Ardrey is a dramatist turned palaeontologist, and his book has all the drama of a detective-story.

Let me put the central thesis in Ardrey's own words: "What Dart put forward in his piece was the simple thesis that Man had emerged from the anthropoid background for one reason only: because he was a killer. Long ago, perhaps many millions of years ago, a line of killer apes branched off from the non-aggressive primate background. For reasons of environmental necessity, the line adopted the predatory way. For reasons of predatory necessity, the line advanced. We learned to stand erect in the first place as a necessity of the hunting life. We learned to run in our pursuit of game across the yellowing African savannah. Our hands freed for the mauling and the hauling, we had no further use for a snout; and so it retreated. And lacking fighting teeth or claws, we took recourse by necessity to the weapon.

"A rock, a stick, a heavy bone - to our ancestral killer ape meant the margin of survival. But the use of the weapon meant new and multiplying demands on the nervous system for the co-ordination of muscle and touch and sight. And so at last came the enlarged brain; so at last came Man."[5]

Ardrey describes, and rejects, the theory widely held since the time of Darwin that "the human family had arisen from the neutral, non-aggressive, vegetarian forest ape, or from some common ancestral primate more or less in his likeness. But now we had *Australopithecus*, and he was a carnivore and a predator.[6] And we had the newest claim, that he was armed.

Ardrey describes, with the skill in building tension of his earlier craft, how this thesis of Dr. Dart's had been opposed, and sometimes even sabotaged by his fellow-scientists, and how confirmatory evidence was found in all sorts of unexpected places. From every page breathes the authentic spirit of wonder, and it is a book that is essential reading for those interested in human origins.

It is not necessary to accept every detail of Ardrey's exposition of the Dart thesis. Yet the central claim compels acceptance. We see, then, that the mark of Cain, the biblical killer of his brother, the son of Adam, is indeed on all of us, for, as Ardrey says: "the first recognisably human assertion has been the capacity for murder." Here again the Jewish creation-myth corresponds remarkably with the record which we are learning to read from the strata-pages of the Book of the Rocks.

We are no fallen angels. We became Man because we learned to kill our brother-animals and our human brothers too. And, as we have become civilised, we have learned to kill in greater quantities. As Ardrey puts it: "I regard it as anything but a coincidence that the rate of civilisation's rise has corresponded so closely with man's ascendant capacity to kill. Civilisation is a compensatory consequence of our killing imperative; the one could not exist without the other."[7]

It is the thesis of this book that the whole of human development has followed faithfully the pattern of the beginning, and that with each advance in knowledge and power has come an advance in cruelty and unpleasantness, that the graphs of human power and human evil march together up the page. Ardrey's view that Man is the murdering animal confirms at least the earliest period of my thesis.

Ardrey argues that Man's emergence took place near Lake Victoria in East Africa which has "three times in the last million years... brimmed and twice been reduced to a swamp."[8] Here, I sense, Ardrey is reading too much into the tentative evidence which we have before us. Only a few African sites have yet been explored, and the most famous, at Olduvai, was only found because, by chance, a relatively recent ravine cut through the deposits, thus laying bare the record of the rocks. How many similar deposits lie undiscovered in Africa, or in other continents? Yet it is not necessary for one to accept all such details for the main thesis to be acceptable.

It is nevertheless interesting to note a fact probably unknown to Ardrey , that the Sotho-Tswana peoples of South Africa have always believed that Man originated in a huge reedbed called Ntsoanatsatsi, far to the north of Southern Africa. And it has been believed for about a century that this reedbed Ntsoanatsatsi could only be Lake Victoria.

Acquiring the capacity to use weapons had a double effect: on the one hand, by enabling Man to dominate the animals, the weapon vastly expanded the living-space of the human populations, in accordance with the primeval evolutionary law under which each form of life tends to fill its living- space until it is checked by the territorial and nutritional boundaries of competing forms of life. The weapon enabled Man to push back the defensive boundaries of the animals, and to seize their living-space.

On the other hand Man used his weapons, not only against other animals, but also against men. And so it became necessary for the size of the human group to be increased. War has thus led to a growth in the size and complexity of human society. As society grew, it became necessary for intra-group communications to be improved, War has thus also helped to develop human language and culture.

In our time, too, it has become a truism that war stimulates the pace of invention. War is the most characteristic activity of the human species. Animals, with one exception, do not levy war on their own species, killing male and female, adults and children in an indiscriminate slaughter. This unpleasant animal is the Fire-ant, *(Solenopsis saevissima)*. The other animals, as we shall see, have formalised and stylised their intra-specific fighting and normally do not kill each other. There are thus two species, Man and the fire-ant, that make war, and three million species that are naturally pacifist.

The Greeks and Romans knew that Mars, the god of war, and Venus, the goddess of love, were mystically united, and so it has proved in human history, for since Man emerged his populations have grown steadily.

At first the growth was slow. Perhaps the first million years saw the total creeping to the five million mark, which was possibly reached eight thousand years ago.[9]

A world population of five million hunters, armed with stone, wood and bone weapons, was probably fairly evenly-matched against the wild animals. They were obviously afraid of the lions and tigers, just as these must have become afraid of our ancestors. But, slowly, brain must have told against brute strength, and slowly Man must have won the upper hand in this life-and-death struggle.

He exterminated some of the animals, such as the sabre-toothed tiger and the North American mammoth, and he was not himself exterminated. His power grew, and his skills grew, until, as we shall see in the next chapter, a second "super-event" occurred, the development of agriculture.

Yet, even before the development of agriculture, society and the first towns appeared, and there was no doubt that a new and devastatingly powerful fact was at work in the world: the human intelligence.

Human intelligence has hoisted us into the space age. Will it be powerful enough to recognise the truth about Man: that his cruelty has grown with his knowledge, and that he is the greatest murderer and predator that the world has ever contained? Will it be wise enough for us to make in time a radical change of direction?

REFERENCES

(1)   William Harvey, the discoverer of the circulation of the blood, was wont to say this - in approximately 1630 - see *Aubrey's Brief Lives,* by O. L. Dick, Penguin Books, 1962; page 213.

(2)   Professor of Zoology at Oxford: "Biological Responsibility in a Technological Society" , from *Biology and Human Affairs* Vol. 30, No.3. Summer, 1965.

(3)   See Foreword, p. xvii. Darwin used the phrase: "Places in the economy of nature". Hitler used the concept in politics and used the word "lebensraum" claiming that the German people needed all the lebensraum from the Atlantic to the Urals.

(4)   *African Genesis,* Collins, London, 1961.

(5)   *African Genesis,* page 29.

(6)   The South African fossil erect ape discovered by Robert Broom and Dr. Raymond Dart.

(7)   *African Genesis,* page 348.

(8)   Ibid, page 275.

(9)   Estimate of the Population Reference Bureau, 1755 Massachusetts Avenue N. W. Washington, D.C. 20036, U.S.A.

3 Development of Agriculture & Civilisation

"Les forêts précèdent les peuples; les déserts les suivent."[1]
François René, Vicomte de Châteaubriand.

FOR PERHAPS a million years after Man became Man, he lived in Eden as a hunter and as a gatherer of wild foods. His ascendancy over the wild animals grew slowly, as we have seen, and he was probably able to exterminate some species, but on the whole Man and the wild animals must have lived in considerable fear of each other.[2]

Total domination, the overwhelming victory of Man over the animals, had to await the development of agriculture. This development is the second "super-event" in human history. So far as can be judged, it happened at about the same time in the Middle East and in Central America, about 8,500 years ago.[3] From these two centres the practice of arable and pastoral farming made its irresistible way around the world. To-day only a handful of tiny communities of men live without agriculture, a few in the forests of Amazonia, a few in New Guinea and the pygmies of Southern and Central Africa.

The progress of agriculture was irresistible because farmers are more productive than hunters and are able to produce considerably more than their own families need. On this surplus has been built the whole vast edifice of human civilisation.

Until recently it was believed that the building of towns came after the development of agriculture, but some of the newest excavations show that this was not universally the case. Both at Tell Mureybat (dating back to 7,500 BC), near the Euphrates river some 320km north-east of Damascus in Syria[3a], and at Munhata in the

Jordan valley, south of the Sea of Galilee, it is fairly clear that small towns were built by hunters before animals were domesticated or crops sown.[4] It nevertheless seems clear that, even if in some cases towns were built before farms, it is generally true to say that the opposite was the rule, and that the town and the city have been built on the surplus created by the farmer. In the Middle East, in perhaps 7,500 BC, someone learned to make the wild foods grow in a field, and someone learned to domesticate cows, goats and sheep. Evidence of this change is not lacking. For instance, in another Syrian village, Tel Ramad 25km south west of Damascus, there is evidence of the change-over from hunting to agriculture. Here "a Franco-Syrian… expedition has discovered an 8,500 year old village which tells much about the critical time when Man changed from a nomadic hunter to a farmer… This development was the great turning-point which set mankind on the course of civilised progress, according to Henri de Contenson… who heads the joint expedition. The discovery - the best-preserved settlement of its time found in the Middle East - was made beneath a deserted hill called Tel Ramad…"[5]

Once agriculture was developed, it spread rapidly through the "fertile crescent" the lands of the Euphrates valley and the Jordan valley with their apex at Palmyra. It spread because it permitted the division of labour, and on the division of labour grew political power, and on political power the populations multiplied. On the farmer's surplus arose other classes, the classes of merchants, soldiers, and rulers. In this way were established the kingdoms of Mesopotamia, Egypt, and Anatolia.

On the development of agriculture is based the culture of the world. Let us never forget that the word "culture" stems from the same origin as does the word "coulter", and that the original meaning of "civilised" was urbanised.

No longer was Man just one among predators. The power achieved by the most primitive agricultural kingdoms quickly gave Man victory over the wild animals, and enabled him to dispose as he wished of the forests and grasslands. No longer did our forebears live in subjection to, and therefore necessarily in harmony with their environment. Henceforward, to an ever growing extent, they were able to bend this environment to their wills. With his new power Man thrust aside the animals, and claimed all their living-space. He filled all this living-space with his own children, and his numbers began their spectacular increase.

By fire and axe Man cleared the forests that lodged the wild animals that survived. By fire he cleared the forest to make farms. By the axe he took those trees that he needed for his buildings and his ships. Two vivid descriptions of how the forests were exploited about a thousand years before Christ have come down to us. The first occurs in THE EPIC OF GILGAMESH.[6]

It describes how important to the kingdoms of Mesopotamia were the cedar forests that grew at that time on the mountains that border the valleys of the Tigris and the Euphrates, and how "the exploitation of these forests was a royal prerogative jealously guarded by the kings.

The second is in the Bible: "And Solomon determined to build an house for the name of the LORD… And Solomon sent out threescore and ten thousand men to bear the burdens and fourscore thousand to hew in the mountain, and three thousand six hundred to oversee them… "Then he made an agreement with King Huram of Tyre, and sent him certain requests. King Huram replied favourably, "and" he said in his message to King Solomon, "we will cut wood out of Lebanon as much as thou shalt need: and we will bring it to thee in floats by sea to Joppa; and thou shalt carry it up to Jerusalem."[7]

From those days, in many other lands, men "did cut wood out… as much as they did need", till in our times the last remaining natural forests are being felled at unprecedented speed by armies of mechanised woodcutters. Many of the grandest forests have already gone, and in many lands "the consequence has been the erosion of the associated soils and the drying up of their waters: the island of Madeira, to take one small example, has lost all its indigenous forest. Yet its very name means "timber" for when it was discovered it was altogether covered with forest trees.

But all the Earth was not covered by indigenous forest in the days before Man became Man. Much of the surface was grassland and savannah. Over the millions of years these grasslands and savannahs had, to a degree almost equal to that achieved in the high-canopy forests, achieved an ecological balance. Over the millions of years a cycle of fertility, and a water-cycle, and reserves of fertility had been built up by an incredibly complex community of trees and bushes, grasses and micro-organisms. At the same time as Solomon was cutting out timber from Lebanon with his counterpart Huram, men, as we have seen, were ploughing up an ever-increasing area of grassland and savannah round the world. And as these first, ignorant ploughmen turned over the grasslands they mined the stores of its fertility in a few years, destroying the water-cycles, damaging the micro-fauna and micro-flora, and loosening the soil, and letting the rains wash it off and carry it down as useless mud to the sea.

In order to tame the wilderness and make it into farms Man had to intensify his war on the other animals. No longer was his aim merely to eat the wildlife: now he fought the animals back because he knew that he could not plough while watching for attacking lions over his shoulder. The hunting grounds of the great cats and bears were a landuse incompatible with the farms of men. Yet in this war against the wild beasts the axe and the plough and fire were even more potent weapons in the hand of Man than were the spear and the sword, for they destroyed the habitat on which the wildlife depended. The panthers, lions, tigers and gazelles have retreated as much because they could not adjust their lives to Man's farming, as because they were directly threatened by the hunt.

Much of this damage to the forests and grassland has in fact turned out to be irreparable. For this one cannot blame the first farmers, for they were engaged in an unprecedented operation and could not then know that they were to destroy so much in their agricultural revolution. The only law that these farmers knew was the old law of evolution, that they should fill the available living-space until stopped by the barriers of Nature or of other forms of life. As the power of these farmers grew, so the other animals were less and less able to erect any barriers against the man-tide.

The ultimate effect of the development of agriculture has been the creation of a single Man-dominated world, in which the only barriers to the growth of human communities are other human communities, and in which the limits to Man's expansion are the limits that spherical geometry places on the surface of a sphere.

Nevertheless there is still some wilderness left especially in the equatorial regions, and there are still some wild animals left, though probably in quantity only one thousandth of what existed a century ago. But it is now likely that unless Man effectively limits his expansion in the current generation, there will be no wilderness and no wild animals left anywhere, save in zoos and zoo-like parks, a century from now.

Man's use of the plough and the axe has, then, meant irreparable damage to the forests and soils and waters of many lands. But these forests and soils and waters have been part of Man's own environment, so in his development of agriculture he has often fatally damaged his own environment and thereby harmed himself. The agricultural carrying capacity of the Middle East, and of most of the Mediterranean basin, one of the cradles of civilisation, has been greatly reduced by the forestal, arable, and pastoral practices to which it has been subjected over thousands of years. The Fertile Crescent is no longer fertile. Algeria, Morocco and Tunisia, once Rome's main granary, are now comparatively desiccated and eroded, and are to-day compelled to import wheat to feed their present shrunken populations. When the axemen had finished with the forests they left a degenerate bushland called *maquis* and when the ploughmen had damaged their ploughlands they moved on, and the goats moved in on both types of land, guaranteeing that no forest would ever be able to return to heal the scars on the land. There is hardly a land bordering on this lovely inland sea in which human occupation has not meant the devastation and degradation of the soils, forests, and waters. The process was noted 2,500 years ago by Plato; "There are mountains in Attica which can now keep nothing but bees, but which were clothed, not so very long ago, with fine trees, producing timber suitable for roofing the largest buildings… The annual supply of rainfall was not lost, as it is at present, through being allowed to flow over a denuded surface to the sea, but was received by the country in all its abundance - stored in impervious potter's earth - and so was able to discharge the drainage of the heights into the hollows in the form of springs and rivers with an abundant volume… The shrines that survive to the present day on the sites of extinct water-supplies are evidence for the correctness of my present hypothesis."[8]

With the death of the soils, forests, and rivers has come the death of those very civilisations that did the damage. Dr. Walter C. Lowdermilk, the great emeritus soil conservationist, used these words to describe the man-made deserts of the Mediterranean lands: "the graveyard of civilisations."[9]

The day before writing these words my duties led me to visit Tebessa, a small Algerian town near the Tunisian border. As Theveste, this town was founded more than two thousand years ago. It lies on the edge of a plain and at the foot of a high range of hills. It faces north-west. To-day the plain is almost bare of trees and denuded of useful grasses, and is a semi-desert. Gullies which are almost always dry cut the plain every few kilometres. Miserable cabins known as *ghourbis* house the sparse rural population, whose livelihood consists in an annual gamble with the weather. Each year they sow wheat: once in five years the rain comes at the right time and they reap a respectable crop. At the time of my visit the rains had partly failed and the dwarfed wheat stood shrivelled and sunburnt only 20 cm high like the thin hair on a balding man's head. Scraggy sheep, goats and camels were searching for something to eat.

Then one enters the town, and is immediately struck by the poverty of the teeming Third World. The population of the town has increased threefold since the beginning of World War II, and its hunger and listlessness strike one with pain.

Yet two thousand years ago Theveste and its countryside were not like this. Even to-day the plain is studded with many remains of rich Roman villas, built magnificently of marble and limestone, and floored with colourfully glowing mosaics. Each villa seems to have had its olive oil presses, whereas when you leave Tebessa to-day you can pass two horizons before you see your first olive tree. The town of Theveste had its *thermae* or public baths, with hot and cold water baths. The baths needed great quantities of firewood for heating the water, so the surrounding hills now aridly covered with thistles and scree, must then have carried forests, probably of cedar and oak and pine. A riverbed passes through Tebessa. To-day it is dry, except for a few stinking green pools. It is called the Oued Zarour. In Roman times this stream must have been a fine river, for the Romans lined it with "large quays" and built seven bridges across it.[10]

The town was at its height under Septimius Severus, Rome's African emperor, in about 200 AD. His successor, the infamous Caracalla, built a fine quadrifrontal arch at the north gate, which still stands, mutely condemning in its contemptuous silence the shoddy French and garish Arab houses that to-day press around its limestone feet. Thus have withered in Tebessa power and magnificence.

Can it really be Man that has caused this disaster, that has strewn this deadly plague over Theveste? Could the real reason not be a general climatic change that has come over northern Africa? The question challenges every observer of the area. One of the most acute minds that considered it, just a century ago, was Lieutenant-Colonel R. L. Playfair, for many years British consul at Algiers, who was a noted traveller in Barbary. He has left this interesting answer to the question: "We subsequently journeyed for many days in this region (the Sahel coastal region of Tunisia); everywhere we found extensive traces of Roman occupation - vast Roman cities as well as isolated posts, proving beyond doubt that it was at one time capable of supporting a dense population. The entire Regency of Tunis (present-day Tunisia) must, during the Roman occupation, have contained little short of twenty million inhabitants, while now (i.e. 1877) the most favourable estimate places the population at not more than a million and a half.[11] Day after day in traversing these arid and treeless plains, intersected by water courses in which no water flows, the soil covered with sand and stones incapable of supporting vegetable life, we pondered over the causes which had turned a region once so fertile almost into a desert. The causes, indeed, are not difficult to find: they are written by the hand of nature on every hill we traversed, and confirmed by the daily actions of the inhabitants themselves. We know that at one time this country was covered with forests. I myself have travelled for days over plains where not a tree exists, and yet where ruins of Roman oil mills were frequently met with… Even in modern days the same destruction of forests has been continued… By the carelessness of (the Arabs) who never hesitate to set fire to a wood to improve the pasturage, or to cut down a tree when timber is required, but who never dream of planting another, or even of protecting those which spring up spontaneously from being destroyed by their flocks and herds.

In Bruce's notes, written in 1765, frequent allusion is made to forests through which he passed, where not a tree is now to be seen, and this is a work of destruction which must go on with accelerating rapidity year after year… In several places, where deep cuttings had been made by winter torrents, I distinctly observed layers of alluvion several feet below the surface, underlying strata of water-worn stones and barren sand"[12].

During the century which has elapsed since Playfair looked at North Africa, the damage has continued with unbroken momentum. Man the warrior, Man the grazier, and Man the ploughman has continued to make inroads on those forests that had survived into the nineteenth century. In Algeria in 1930 there were, on paper, 3,174,616 ha, of forest land,[13] or some 10.7% of the total area of the Tell,[14] but much of this forest land had, already by 1930, been degraded[15] to secondary maquis.[16] Now, in 1967, the figure for true forest land must be greatly inferior to three million hectares, for during the war of independence of 1954-1962 much of the finest forest was burnt deliberately by the French armies in an attempt to smoke out the guerrillas. Matters have been considerably improved since independence, and the free Algerian government has shown a laudable desire, and even an ability, to reduce the extent of the annual fires in the pine forests. Nevertheless much of the strict French-imposed law is a dead letter, and the grazing of goats and sheep in the best forest land goes ahead virtually unchecked. An air flight over the Tell, the richest part of Algeria, in the summer season shows that all that is left of the glorious forests that almost certainly covered the Tell two thousand years ago, forests of various species of oaks and conifers with high cedars on all the high mountains, is a series of isolated patches of trees, with human settlement pressing round their edges, and vehicles and men moving in the forest like fleas on the coat of a mangy dog.[17]

Another part of the world which I know fairly well is southern Africa. There, too, degradation of soils, and the disappearance of fountains, and the deforestation of the hills have followed the development of agriculture.

Up till a century and a half ago Man used the land mainly for hunting and for grazing, and his demands on the accumulated soil fertility were insignificant. Until large-scale ploughing began there is conclusive evidence to show that the land was well-covered by grasslands, savannah, and, round the southern and eastern coasts, by forests of high and densely-packed trees. Except in the desert of the Kalahari and the semi-desert of the Karoo, the land was fairly well-watered, with many springs and permanent rivers and streams that ran with clear water.

During the last 150 years much of the country has been dried out. It is notorious that the map is covered with place-names ending in "fontein" where to-day there is no water, and, as one writer said: "when you fall into a Free State river you pick yourself out and brush the sand out of your hair."[18]

During this period much of the country has become a dustbowl and the resultant soil erosion, though much more recent than that of northern Africa, is already much more serious. In the memory of living men, gullies have been born and have cut right down to bedrock. Some of these gullies are thirty metres deep. This erosion has been cutting back and upwards and to-day the central sponge of South Africa, the Drakensberg in and around Lesotho, is crumbling rapidly. This beautiful, 3,500 metre high mountain range feeds most of the river basins of the country. I have drunk, near the top of Mont-aux-Sources, out of pools that fall into the Vaal, the Orange and the Caledon, and eventually into the Atlantic, and walked 20 metres to another pool that falls into the Tugela and the Indian Ocean.

Before Man the ploughman tilled these plains, these rivers and their tributaries wandered clear as glass, through meadows and woodlands, through rich, stabilised soils, deep and with a crumby texture, in stark contrast with their present state. Fortunately we have contemporary evidence of the health of the soils and rivers of this area, for the very first literate visitors seem to have had a special interest in these things. They were the pastors Arbousset and Daumas of the French Reformed Church, and of the Paris Society of Evangelical Missions. (It is because they were French that Mont-aux-Sources has a French name). They described in minute detail the physical state of the various rivers which they crossed in the course of their travels. One small river that they forded was the Phuthiatsana or Little Caledon. Nowadays it is a seasonal river in which a muddy trickle flows down to the Caledon near the Lesotho capital Maseru. After heavy rains it becomes a raging avalanche of silty water. But a hundred and thirty years ago this is how it looked to Messrs. Arbousset and Daumas: "The Willow or Little Caledon river has two sources: the stronger is at ten leagues to the north-east of Thaba Bosiu; the weaker is at 5 or 6 leagues to the south-east of the capital town of the basotho.[19] The waters of the Little Caledon are good, clear, limpid and, in some places, deep. At the ford where we crossed it, it flows over a bed of very hard sandstone, the "ironstone" of the English."[20]

The same missionaries described the Malimong area of Lesotho, near Teyateyaneng, to-day a dry land as "fertile well-watered, and enjoying an excellent climate."[21]

Rivers of this purity and abundance are a sign of the basic health of the lands through which their courses run. Unfortunately, since those times, the picture has been radically altered. This Lesotho, which was so well-watered before the arrival of the Europeans, is now the scene of some of the most horrible soil erosion in the world. Crowded by the advance of the whites and by the iniquities of South Africa into this small country, this small nation has almost certainly already reduced the potential carrying capacity of the land by a half. No part of Lesotho is free of gully-erosion. Significantly this gully-erosion is at its worst round the old capital, Thaba Bosiu, for it was there that for over a century men and cattle were concentrated. Round Thaba Bosiu the area covered by gullies is greater than the area of the surviving soils, and sometimes all that is left of the original soil level is a small fertile black block, capping a red pillar of subsoil ten or even twenty metres high. Where, a century ago, there used to be fat pastures of redgrass (*Themeda triandra*) and weeping lovegrass (*Eragrostis curvula*) there are to-day stretches of sunbaked red clayey subsoil, out of which the gaunt repellent prickly pears *(Opuntia ficus-indica)* thrust their grey-green spiny arms that so well characterise the land's leprosy.

Probably the erosion in Lesotho is worse than that elsewhere in southern Africa, but, as we have seen, no corner of the sub-continent is unthreatened. Even in the blissfully lovely south-west, the winter rainfall area round Cape Town, new wounds on the mountains can be seen from afar. These are desiccated watercourses, cascades of whitish broken Table Mountain sandstone that have replaced the little brooks that were there when I was a boy and used to scramble over the mountains. These are the scars of repeated bush fires, often deliberately started.

Centuries ago, in that very region, a high-canopy forest used to exist in many of the *kloofs,* or mountain valleys, and in the mountains there was a unique flora. Only 20km south of Cape Town, at Hout Bay (wood bay), the forest was used by the first Dutch colonists for many years in the seventeenth century as a source of good timber for their ships. Here not one single tree of the original forest remains.

Two hundred and fifty km to the north, a forest of indigenous cedar-like conifers (*Widdringtonia capensis*) gave its name to the 2,500 metre high Cederberg. Of this forest only a few trees remain to-day.

Three hundred km to the east of Cape Town, at Grootvaders-bos, the evergreen rain forest used to begin, and from there it used to stretch in great belts right along the coast to near Mozambique. It was dominated by giant yellowwoods (*Podocarpus spp.*) and stinkwoods (*Ocotea bullata*), the hard and heavy ironwood, the rooiels, the sneezewood, the camdeboo stinkwood, the umzimbeet, and many other trees that live nowhere else in the world. To-day only scattered fragments of this forest remain, and they continue to shrink, as "scientific" forestry replaces these unique trees with the more commercially successful eucalypts and pines. These Australian and European immigrant forests may balance the budget of the forestry department, and may represent a very high degree of forestry skill, but there are two things that they will not be able to do: maintain the indigenous ecological totality, with its wildlife and its genuine South African character. Nor will they maintain the fountains and streams.

Formerly these forests, the forests of Knysna and Tsitsikamma, the forests of the Ciskei and the Transkei, of Griqualand, Natal, Pondoland and Tembuland, teemed with a fauna of great variety and interest, which has almost disappeared; with an avifauna which has largely survived; and with a flora which is still one of the glories of the world, and one of the delights of the world's botanists. Encroaching on these beauties one sees from the air the mean huts and luxurious villas of two unusually unhappy branches of the human race: the oppressed and the oppressors of modern South Africa. In the room left by the departed yellowwood giants, with their damp soils, their mosses and streams, are the dry lands and falling water-tables of modern commercialised farming, the skinny cattle of the African peasants, and their appropriate environment: the stunted bushes and sand-filled watercourses of a dying continent.

Dissimilar in so many ways, northern and southern Africa resemble each other in the degradation that Man has inflicted on the soils and waters. But this degradation is not limited to any country or continent. Here is a dramatic word-picture from the highlands of Ethiopia, the highest African lands north of the Kenya volcanoes: "As we dropped off the Embaras ridge we came upon a man committing the act of a maniac. At 11,600 feet (3,600 m.)

just below a small crag, on a slope where effort was needed to keep one's balance, he was ploughing. With phrenetic energy he was goading a pair of oxen to drag a plough through the tussock grass that had grown there for centuries. Another man with a hoe relentlessly dug out any tussocks that escaped the plough. The oxen would stagger a few steps and stop, panting, to be flogged again into reluctant action... Never in twenty-three years in Africa, in the course of which I have seen some pretty senseless acts, had I ever seen anything to equal this. The slope on which the plough was working was so steep that a man could not stand on the loose clods without pushing them downhill; stones and boulders dislodged by the plough rolled downhill on their own accord... The end-result of his labours was certain. In a few years the soil would have gone from that slope and it would support neither tussock grass nor crops. In progress before my eyes was the process by which the hills of Tigre had been ravaged and reduced from once fair and forested mountains to barren slopes of scree and scrub."[22]

In a neighbouring part of the world, Somalia, damage of a different kind is being inflicted on the land. In a report by a Swiss botanist, Peter Bally, a dearth of grazing is reported, so serious that the owners of goats and sheep have begun the practice of moving them by trucks to any area where rain has fallen. In such circumstances the grass and wildlife have little chance of survival. During the fourteen years, from 1943 to 1957, of Mr. Bally's regular visits to Somalia, he has been appalled to note the rapid degradation of soil and vegetation. Where, seventy years ago, travellers in British Somaliland (now northern Somalia) described the pleasant park-like country, inhabited by elephants, hartebeests, wild asses and rhinos, there is now "a grim wasteland without cover or water in which no elephant could possibly exist". This, comments ORYX, is the disastrous result of increased domestic herds, occupation by Man of the scarce watering places, and lack of cover and shade due to ruthless cutting down of trees and bushes... The Somali wild ass, now hunted from jeeps and landrovers, is on the verge of extinction, and Swayne's hartebeest, once exceedingly common, is gone.[23]

In Jordan, in nearby western Asia, an even worse picture

exists. Yet its enlightened ruler, King Hussein, unlike most of his neighbours, is trying to save what is left before all is destroyed. At his invitation an expedition went to Jordan in 1963 under the leadership of a British ornithologist, Guy Mountfort, to find out how the country's wildlife, vegetative cover, and ancient monuments might be protected.

Mountfort's report describes catastrophic damage to fauna and flora, much of it of recent date. Here are some of his remarks on the forests: "Closely allied to Jordan's losses of wildlife has been progressive and now accelerating loss of vegetation. The Middle East contains the largest areas of man-made desert in the world. In Jordan one sees the clearest evidence of the means by which this is brought about. Almost none of the country's once extensive original forest now remains. The process of denudation was gradual up to the outbreak of the First World War. It was then greatly aggravated by the Turkish army, which stripped Jordan almost bare of trees in order to fuel the locomotives of the Hejaz railway. No country has ever suffered such a determined onslaught on its trees. To-day large trees are completely absent from the greater part of the country. The steady drain on the smaller vegetation is continued by the Beduin who every day cut hundreds of acres of desert shrublets for their camp fires; and by the ravages of millions of hungry goats which swarm everywhere.[24] As the vegetation disappears, wind and water rapidly erode the topsoil, and the desert advances."[25]

A picture of deforestation in a high-rainfall area half-way round the world from Jordan, shows that soil degradation is no monopoly of any group of countries nor even of the drier lands. The picture comes from Hong Kong, a small British enclave in China. Nowadays Hong Kong is more or less deforested, and is, of course, densely populated with an industrious human population.

A scientific assessment of what Hong Kong was like a thousand years ago appeared recently: "Up to a thousand years ago tropical rain forest covered the Hong Kong region. Wildlife was prolific: elephants, tigers and leopards roamed the hillsides, and there were crocodiles and dugongs in the estuaries. Apart from a few aboriginal coastal traders, and scattered garrisons of the T'angs, the region was almost uninhabited. In the forests Yoa tribes are reputed to have been present. Although there is little evidence, it is probable that these hill tribes lived by clearing areas of the forest, planting a few crops of upland rice… (and burning fresh areas).

"The deforestation from 920 AD onwards has severely affected the vegetation and the soil, and possibly also the climate. To-day in the rural areas the mountain peaks and hillsides are covered with low scrub and grassland with a poor soil. (This has led to the growth of conifers, podsolisation and erosion gullies). Moreover the farmers, by grazing cattle on the hillsides and collecting firewood, successfully prevent the natural regeneration of hardwoods, while bush and grass fires, which they often start deliberately in order to dry out the brushwood and force the growth of green shoots for the cattle, further reduce the cover, and so does the spill from wildcat wolfram mines. Once the soil is exposed erosion quickly follows… The few mammals and birds that remain are being hunted and trapped either for pleasure or for the high prices they command as food or for medicinal purposes…"[26].

Not surprisingly this colony is beginning to suffer a serious water-shortage, and in 1965 water had to be imported from the People's Republic of China in tanker ships. An agreement was come to then, and still subsists, whereby Hong Kong buys a minimum of 15 million gallons of water each year from the Chinese authorities, at a cost of just over $(US) 0.17 a thousand gallons - a contract worth nearly $(US) 3,000,000 a year to China[27].

Of course, Hong Kong's water shortage is due not only to the deforestation from which it has suffered, but also to the huge population that for political and economical reasons now seeks a living on its hilly slopes. To ensure future water supplies for this population will cost vast sums, much of which might have been unnecessary if the forests had not been destroyed. Some of these water projects are of such interest that they deserve mention here. They include: street-flushing with seawater to save freshwater; desalination of seawater; the damming-off of a whole bay of the sea, Plover Cove, which will become a freshwater lake holding 135 million tons, or double the colony's present storage capacity; and the building of tunnels 35km long through the mountains so that all the drainage from distant hills may be brought to the city.

To round off the Hong Kong picture, it has become the practice of Hong Kong poachers to use dynamite to kill whole shoals of fish, and also to remove blocks of coral for use as a building material. [28] Another part of the world where a precious and lovely forest is in danger is Madagascar. This great island, 1,600km long was, when the Europeans first arrived, almost encircled by a forest-belt. In this forest lived trees quite unknown elsewhere. One of the most famous is the Traveller's tree, a tree with a tall columnar trunk, topped by a fan-like spread of leaves like those of the banana-tree. This tree has the curious quality of being able to catch and store many litres of rainwater and of being able to preserve it in a pure state. A thirsty traveller has only to pierce one of the stalks of the huge leaves with his knife for a supply of drinking water to gush out. Other Madagascar forest trees give excellent woods for construction and for furniture-making. This forest is a rain-forest, with all that this implies in terms of cool, humid air, of mossy banks of deep soils and of permanent clear streams.

The Malagasy and the French have, of course, "exploited" this forest, so that it is to-day much reduced in size. But enough of it remains for it to be one of the wonders of the world, harbouring a fauna strangely unlike that of any other country. Madagascar is like a lost world, lost in the vast southern ocean. It is from here that the tenrecs, aye-ayes and other lemurs come. It is true that something is being done to replant the forests of Madagascar, but when I was there in 1954 I was saddened to note that much of the replanted forest consisted of Australian eucalypts. The eucalypt, though a formidable tree and a fast turner of dollars, changes the landscape when it is introduced into a foreign land, and replaces the authentic character of that land with a semi-Australian ambiance. Needless to say that in Madagascar a eucalypt forest is quite useless for preserving the island's unique fauna. The eucalypt, too, is greedy for soil nutrients and water, and is often a primary cause of soil erosion, as it has the gift of suppressing most non-Australian undergrowth. Its capacity to desiccate the soil is astonishing, and in the scheme to drain the Pontine marshes in Italy a few eucalypts were able to rival the capacity of a mechanical wind pump; For these reasons eucalypts are trees which, in the drier parts of the world, should be planted only after the most careful consideration of all the ecological factors. They are trees which will never preserve resources of soil, water or wildlife. And so I felt that the Madagascar authorities were mistaken in replacing a few parts of their once-glorious forest with eucalypts, and in neglecting to replace others.

A different problem that arises with the clearing of indigenous forest is seen in countries like England. The problem there is the destruction of a climax vegetation of beauty and variety, and its replacement by a Man-dominated landscape. The English countryside used to be one great forest, varied by stretches of fenny marsh. There were oaks and beeches, hornbeams and sycamores, birches and larches, alders and yews: their very names carry with them a whiff of an English morning, a flash of green, the fluff of a catkin, a rustle of dry leaves, or a glint of sun on a spring-time bud. This forest has almost gone. In its place is a neatly-tailored, Man-dominated countryside, a commercially-clipped and cleared large garden in which wildlife lives in a vestigial manner and on sufferance, when it lives at all. Where there had been one great wood is now one great farm, with its pylons and its tractors, and its motor roads that have quadrated the wilderness and corralled off the wild things and prevented their necessary migrations and movements. The graph of the area under concrete moves irresistibly upwards, while the graph of the badger, the partridge, the trout in his stream, and the wild violet moves as irresistibly downwards. Is this the best that a great, nature-loving, rich people like the English can do with their own home-land? If so, the prospects for countries poorer in these qualities are indeed dark.

One of these countries is Botswana, till recently known as the Bechuanaland Protectorate. This vast land, some 568,000 km² in area, with only some 540,000 inhabitants, is one of the emptiest parts of the world. It is the home of some of the world's most valuable semi-desert grasses, and was the home until recently of vast numbers of wild animals. It is approximately divided into three parts: in the eastern border area live some 400,000 people of Bantu origin. This area is relatively well-watered, with a rainfall of about 25cm annually, and the people live by stock-farming and ploughing. In the vast central area, the area of the Kalahari Desert, live about 20,000 Bushmen, tiny pale-brown men who call themselves the San. They live by stone-age hunting methods, and they have perfected the art of finding small droplets of water either under moist sand or in wild melons. The third area, in the far north, a large river, the Okavango or Cubango, throws itself into a desert delta and loses itself in clear pools, reedbeds, the Kalahari sands, and a dry atmosphere. The pools are overshadowed by noble acacias, such as the Kameeldoring (*Acacia giraffae*) and the Mukusi or Rhodesian teak (*Baikiaea plurijuga*), though the latter has been all but exterminated in Botswana by greedy commercial exploiters. This delta was, until recently, the home of millions of wild animals. What has happened to all three areas is typical of what is happening to many of the arid areas, as the man-tide races out over hitherto empty lands.

In the delta area many hundreds of thousands of antelopes were exterminated by government order, according to an unproven hypothesis of some veterinarians that if they could be totally exterminated, the tsetse fly with its attendant diseases could be controlled and human and cattle populations could move in. Many hundreds of thousands of antelopes were killed at the same time by poaching and hunting, the distant government being unable to enforce its own game preservation laws. And vast numbers of crocodiles were and are being shot to supply skins to the fashion markets of London and Paris. (You shoot them at night with a powerful flashlight that reflects light off the crocodiles' eyes and gives you a target to aim at).

In the eastern farming area the government has dug many thousands of tube wells (boreholes) to enable the farmers to increase the size of their herds of cattle and goats. But the increased herds have damaged the pasturage which is exceptionally fragile because of the nearness of the desert.

In the vast central area the government is building motor roads.

Along these roads the population has fanned out, colonising with their cheap houses areas previously untouched, soils relatively poor and probably easily eroded.

To fly over this hitherto romantic and beautiful land is to see tentacles of ugliness, ignorance and destruction spreading out along Man's roadways in all three parts of Botswana, just as a melanoma cancer spreads along the body's lymphatic passages.

Similar destruction has been caused by the Soviet decision to plough up millions of hectares in the so-called "virgin-lands" of Kazakhstan in the USSR, a huge central Asian territory stolen since 1917 from its erstwhile Kazakh owners by Russian infiltrators. Any American soil conservation extension officer could have told the Prime Minister, Nikita Khrushchev, what the risk was, and what has in fact happened. A new and colossal dustbowl has been created. In a rainy season the "virgin lands" do in fact yield handsomely, since the ploughmen are still mining the accumulated soil fertility of the millennia. But the season of 1965-66 was dry in Kazakhstan, and as the (non- political) east wind blew gale-strength across central Asia, the skies of Odessa, Sofia and Vienna darkened with the red topsoils of the once virgin lands.

Human folly is unlimited, and some of the unwisest human beings are the ploughmen and graziers of the vast semi-arid areas of the world who are able with little hindrance to do what they like with their land. As a result, when one flies over such lands in the dry season, the whole planet seems shrouded in a haze. This haze is composed of the smaller dust-particles, mixed with smoke particles which come from the burning bushes and grasses. For six months each year this haze hangs over the whole African continent south of the Congo. It is the pall of death of a dying continent.

And so Man the farmer has degraded the soils and forests of the world, his own environment, the ground of his own being. The dangers are widely understood, but mainly by enlightened men in the richer countries. How is their knowledge of the dangers to be communicated?

Unlimited Massacre

This deforestation and this ploughing have already deprived

almost all wildlife of its habitat. In addition Man has never ceased to be a hunter, and he has hunted the wild things without mercy. As a result it is probable that only a thousandth part is left of the populations of the larger animals that existed only a century ago.

Much of the hunting has involved deliberate and bloodthirsty massacres by Man of the wild animals. These massacres have probably caused more suffering to living things than any other process in the whole history of the world.

Sometimes Man's motive has been self-defence; sometimes it has been economic need and hunger, but often these massacres have been caused by Man's perverted obsession with bloodshed and death, by his love of watching animals die, and die in pain.

In an attenuated form this lust to torture and kill animals is seen even in a nation that prides itself on its gentleness and its love of animals. In England and Scotland anglers go after a "sporting" fish. And a fish is held to be "sporting" if it violently resists the steel hook and the nylon line, if it fights a tug-of-war with an angler fifty times its own size, and if it takes a satisfactorily long time a-dying. Similarly, on the Zambesi the only fish which interests anglers is the tiger-fish, because it struggles ferociously on the hook. The fish is a mass of bones, so the anglers do not eat it but throw it away as garbage.

Anglers have satisfied themselves, despite these struggles of the fish on the hook, and despite the flight of fish from predator-fish, that fish do not feel pain. The day before writing this I went on a fishing expedition on a glorious summer morning from a small Algerian port. Three lines, each baited with small pieces of shrimp, were let down to a depth of about eight metres through the clear blue water to the rocky bottom, which was hazily and refractively visible. Within minutes of the first line being let down a fisherman announced that he had caught a *cochon de mer* (hogfish). He began to pull the line in, and, down near the bottom weaving backwards and forwards, there was the hogfish manoeuvring, twisting, turning upside-down, as it tried to free itself from the hook. But the hook was too sharp, and the nylon line too strong, and soon a second fisherman had a landing-net underneath him. Out he came, some

2kg in weight, shaped like a gibbous moon, beautifully coloured, something like his cousin the beautiful angel-fish of the coral reefs. The hook was through the prognathous jaws, which were well-equipped with strong teeth. He had an expressive eye which dilated and contracted as we watched it. It was a "sporting" fish, and as its captor bent to cut the hook out of its jaws it snapped at him in a last attempt to defend itself. Then the fish was placed under one of the boat's benches to die a slow death. The hogfish took nearly a half hour to die. Even though it was out of the sea it seemed able, to some extent, to be able to breathe, since it gulped down air in regular paroxysms. A quarter of an hour after it was caught it flapped and twisted its body, and at one moment it danced on its tail under the bench on the hot deck. Then it lay still, and I watched its eye dilating and contracting faster than before. The breathing became feebler, and towards the end it uttered a cry, a cry that was quite comprehensible across the hundreds of millions of years that separated us. This cry earned it a kick from its Muslim captor who remarked "Le cochon de mer est très méchant, il est comme le cochon de terre."[29] He then explained that he had caught so many that he had no interest in eating them.

A few minutes later the fish died.

Man's love of the hunt and of the kill is not surprising, for it was, as we have seen, by becoming a killer ape that Man emerged into his humanity. But the fact that killing is human does not make it moral, and I have gone into some detail here to remind readers how ugly it is. The love of killing is very likely inherited genetically, for children, if anything, are more inclined to cruelty than are grown-ups. Small children enjoy pulling insects to pieces, to enjoy watching their wrigglings. They are usually unable to leave alone a fledgling bird or small frog that has had the ill-luck to be caught. On some pretext or other the unhappy small thing has to be imprisoned or played with until it dies.

Cruelty has thus reinforced the effects of farming in reducing the populations of wild animals. There is still another factor that has caused the deaths of many hundreds of thousands of wild things: the economic value of their skins and ivory. Of recent years the numbers of dik-dik, an East African pygmy antelope, that have been killed annually has run into hundreds of thousands because of the value of their skins. In America and Africa crocodiles face extinction because their skins are used in the richer countries for shoes and bags. Ivory hunters still exist who live by killing, for the sake of its huge teeth, one of the noblest animals that has ever lived. Then there are the rhino hunters. Unfortunately the Chinese believe that a rhino's horn is an aphrodisiac, and in China powdered rhino horn commands a high price. And so the last of the Sumatran rhinos face extinction, and in India and even in Africa rhinos are one of the favourite targets of the poachers. In Africa the cheetahs and the leopards face extinction because coats made of their fur are fashionable. In Rhodesia, for example, where tens of thousands of cheetahs used to roam, only *500-800* are left, according to official figures issued by the Wild Life Department, despite the best protection that the government can give them. One finds it difficult to see how a woman who puts on a coat made in this way is different from Ilse Koch, the notorious wardress of Belsen, who used to make her lampshades of the skins of murdered Jews. In some ways her crime is worse, for the extinction of the human race through such cruelty is not conceivable, yet the extinction of the cheetahs and leopards through such cruelty is highly probable.

Perhaps the most discouraging aspect of this trade in animals and their skins, teeth, and horns is that, as the numbers of the animals shrink, so the simple laws of economics send the prices up, so that it becomes ever more profitable to be a poacher. Whatever the motives, what is certain is that the killing of wild animals that has occurred over the last five to six centuries is unprecedented, and that we are now living through the very last stage of it. Either we continue on the path which we are now treading, or we make a radical change, so that something of the kingdom of the animals may be saved from extinction. In either case the chapter of unlimited massacre is now closing. Many valuable and beautiful animals have already become extinct. Here is a very partial list: there is no space for mention to be made of more than just a few. In some cases an approximate date has been added for their disappearance.[30] The

MOA *(Dinornis marimus)* of New Zealand, the 4-metre high giant bird whose remains are still sometimes found. It was flightless, and when the Maoris landed in the fourteenth century AD they managed to exterminate it; the LESSER MOA *(Megalapteryx didinus)* of New Zealand, 1773; the GREAT ELEPHANT BIRD *(Aepyornis)* of Madagascar. This bird was even larger than the Moa, and probably gave rise to the fable of the roc in the story of Sinbad the Sailor.

Its eggs are sometimes still found. This bird may have been exterminated by the Malagasy on their arrival from Melanesia, or perhaps by their predecessors, the Bantu Vazimba; the GREAT AUK, 1844, which was exterminated solely by Man's greed; the MAURITIUS BLUE PIGEON, 1830; the DODO, 1681, and its cousin, the SOLITAIRE, 1746; twenty-nine species of PARROTS, PARAKEETS, and MACAWS; the STEPHEN ISLAND WREN, 1894, a tiny, short-winged New Zealand wren, probably destroyed by man-introduced rats; and, perhaps the most striking extinction of all, the North American PASSENGER PIGEON. In less than 50 years its numbers were reduced from hundreds of millions to nil by ruthless shooting, the last wild bird dying in 1899.

Here are the names of a few of the better-known mammals that have gone: the QOAHA (Quagga) half wild ass and half zebra, that used to roam the South African plains in herds of millions, and that was totally exterminated in just two generations of greedy shooting; the URUS, or Aurochs, the wild bull of the Hercynian forest; the IRISH ELK; the TASMANIAN DEVIL; and perhaps more species of marsupial than still survive, for the record of greedy destruction by the white Australians is perhaps the worst of all, - worse even than the current extermination of wildlife going on in Latin America.

These are some of the better-known mammals and birds that have vanished because Man their cousin killed them. There are many thousands of less well known species that have likewise disappeared for ever. In addition, there is another list, the list of those species that are on the threshold of extinction. In a most valuable compilation the International Union for Conservation of Nature and Natural Resources (IUCN) has partially listed the mammals and birds that in its opinion are "rare and in some danger of extinction."[31] This RED DATA BOOK was published in 1966 in two volumes in a loose-leaf format, and purchasers are entitled to receive future sheets adding to or correcting the original lists up to December 1970. Some sheets are of pink paper: these are the sheets used for the species which are in the greatest danger. To read these two volumes with any care demands a considerable effort of will, for one is constantly harrowed by feelings of disgust at the manner in which the majority of six hundred species of mammals and birds are being driven relentlessly into extinction. Hunting has, of course, done much to destroy these animals but more important factors in the process have been the destruction of their habitat, usually forest, and the introduction of pigs, cats, goats, rats and dogs, Man's fellow-travellers.

One is left with a feeling of certitude that the majority of these species, and many other species and sub-species too, cannot be saved unless the present destruction of forest and wilderness is stopped. And with human populations booming as they are, what hope is there of stopping this relentless tide? Many governments encourage their citizens to go out and colonise the forest. Others try to stop them but find that their edicts are not obeyed. And so our generation may expect to lose many species of parrots and macaws, lemurs, egrets, eagles and pheasants, of rhinos, great apes, tigers and leopards. And in their place, unstoppably, Man with his dirt and his mangy domestic animals, creeping in, will destroy forests, soils and water resources. The following are a few of the species which are listed in the RED DATA BOOK as facing extinction:

1. THYLACINE or TASMANIAN WOLF (*Thylacinus cynocephalus*). The largest Australian carnivore, the thylacine used to be common on the mainland of Australia and in Tasmania, but is now extinct on the mainland, and very nearly extinct in Tasmania. Its numbers are unknown. From 1888 to 1909 the government paid a bounty of £1 for every thylacine killed: now that it is nearly extinct a huge reserve of 600,000 hectares has been set aside for it, and there is a specially heavy penalty for killing it under any circumstances.

There are thirty-five other species of marsupials on this danger list. Even the kangaroo is now in danger: during the drought of 1962-66 the population of red kangaroos may have declined by as much as 75%, and during the last ten years there has been virtually unrestricted shooting of them in Queensland and New South Wales. An expedition across Australia from south to north recently saw no more than a dozen live kangaroos, but more than 100 carcasses of animals that had been shot near the roads.[32]

2. BROAD-NOSED GENTLE LEMUR *(Hapalemur sismus)*. This Madagascar lemur is one of thirty-eight species and sub-species of primate that are on the danger list. It is said to be "very rare… and has neither been observed nor captured for many years". Like the other lemurs which are nearly all disappearing fast, its disappearance is believed to be mainly due to "reduction of habitat", i.e. the felling of the indigenous forest.

3. Another lemur that is listed is the FORK-MARKED MOUSE LEMUR *(Phaner furcifer)* and the reasons given for its decline are even more explicit: "Destruction of forest accounts for its decline… Plantations are now extending over the whole of (Madagascar), the destruction of forests by burning and rooting up trees is being pushed ahead in order to provide grazing for huge herds of cattle. So the tree-dwelling prosimians are fast disappearing because their environment is being lost to them".

4. ORANG-UTAN *(Pongo pygmaeus)*. It seems that there may be only 8,000 left in the wild, with perhaps 280 in the world's zoos. This animal is so famous and interesting that a great trade in young ones for the world's zoos has flourished recently, despite isolated attempts to repress it. "It seems… that orang-utans have declined drastically in the past hundred years". The reason for the decline is the usual one: destruction of forest, but an interesting and unusual reason is added: "The biggest menace to orang conservation is the Indonesian army… they hunt orangs in Sumatra with automatic weapons and sell the babies to smugglers."

5. MINDANOA GYMNURE *(Podogymnura truei)*, mentioned here because of the solemn note struck in one of the comments: "… it can be stated safely that (excluding rats) virtually any form of wildlife surviving to-day in the Philippines is threatened…"

6. MOUNTAIN GORILLA *(Gorilla gorilla beringei)*. In some ways this great ape is our closest relative in the wilds. He, like many other animals, is threatened principally by the reduction of the forest. Quite apart from the extraordinary biological and zoological interest felt in this animal, its very name is of historical and etymological interest, for it first occurs in the Greek account of Hanno's voyage, in the 5th or 6th century BC from Egypt to West Africa. The historian reported that gorilla was the name in an African language of a "wild or hairy man" (actually a female) captured by the explorers.

7. MEXICAN GRIZZLY BEAR *(Ursus nelsoni)*. Once thought extinct, some 30-40 of these great bears appear to survive in the Sierra del Nido of Mexico. But, "unless some rapid and decisive action is taken by the government to protect these majestic animals, there will soon be no more".

8. POLAR BEAR *(Thalarctos maritimus)*. Weighing up to three quarters of a ton, measuring up to three metres in length, with its well-known whitish coat, this best-loved of the bears is menaced by civilised men who are ruthlessly hunting it on motorised snow scooters and by Eskimo hunters who desire its meat and its fur. [33] As a result "the polar bear's range has shown signs of significant contraction since the 1930's at least". There may now be as few as 10,000 left in the whole arctic. Fortunately the Soviet government has banned all shooting of these bears in the Soviet arctic, and has created a reserve for them on Wrangel Island, the most important denning area.

9. SOUTHERN SEA OTTER *(Enhydra lutris mereis)*. This beautiful American sea otter was once thought to be extinct, but it fortunately now seems to be recovering in numbers, and is strictly protected by Californian and American Federal laws. Yet, "there is little hope of re-establishing sea otters in much of their former range along the Pacific coasts of the US and Canada unless oil pollution of the seas can be effectively controlled. If soiled, the soft fur loses its insulating properties and as a result the animals may die from chill and exposure". It is noted for the mother's habit of holding her young in her arms to sleep as she swims on her back.

10. There follows one of the most distressing lists; that of the great cats which are endangered. Nothing in Nature surpasses the grace and beauty of these superb animals. Because of their formidable strength and courage they have deeply impressed Man's consciousness from the beginning. They need no description, and I shall merely list the full list of those in the RED DATA BOOK, with the best estimate of the numbers left alive; SPANISH LYNX; "several hundred"; FLORIDA COUGAR; "less than one hundred"; ASIATIC LION: 285; AMUR TIGER; "does not exceed 100"; CASPIAN TIGER; "between 50 and 80"; JAVAN TIGER; differing estimates varying from 9-25; SUMATRAN TIGER; "status seriously deteriorated"; CHINESE TIGER; "uncontrolled hunting probably accounts for the decline"; BALI TIGER: "three or four at the most"; BARBARY LEOPARD; "about 100"; ASIATIC CHEETAH "may be less than 100 in Iran" (but also possibly in the USSR and Afghanistan).

Apart from the above-listed felidae there are others such as the lion which is extinct in North Africa and Europe, and whose numbers are low even in East Africa and South Africa. The prospects for the Bengal tiger in an Indian continent which is continually filling up with people cannot be good either. How, even in the parks can any of these, perhaps Man's oldest enemies, hope to survive? What could be more incompatible with the spread of twentieth century technology than the sight of a great cat, lazily stretched on some high crag or tree, licking itself, then yawning, as it waits for its prey, perhaps some antelope - or with increasing probability, one of Man's domesticated animals - to come within range? Certainly incompatible, and perhaps even superior: if anyone is sure that twentieth-century Man, sunning his flabby frame on some crowded beach, is necessarily a superior form of life let him come up with some proof, for to a truly unbiased observer the proposition is anything but self-evident.

Let us look further down the list of endangered species.

There is the

11. ATLANTIC WALRUS *(Odobenus rosmarus rosmarus)*. This great seal, almost ox-like in size, well-known because of its ivory

tusks which grow up to 60 cm in length, can attain a length of 5 metres, and can weigh up to 1.5 tons. "The herds in the Barents, Kara and White Seas were once of considerable size, but are now reported to be close to extinction". Fortunately there are perhaps 25,000 left in the world, so the walrus does not face immediate extinction. Nevertheless many are killed, and what is needed is an accurate count on which might be based a safe limit for the annual kill.

12. MEDITERRANEAN MONK SEAL *(Monachus monachus)*. Used to be common all over the Mediterranean, but now perhaps only 500 are left.

13. STELLER'S SEA-COW *(Hydrodamalis stelleri)*. This colossal sirenian, reaching a length of 8 metres, was thought to have become extinct in 1768, after relentless butchering by European navigators. But, most excitingly the Russian whaling vessel 'Buran' recently encountered, at a range of only 80-100 metres, a group of large unidentified sea animals, each 6-8 metres in length, near Cape Navarin, the cape jutting out south-east from the eastern extremity of Russian Asia. These were probably Steller's Sea-cows. If they were it is perhaps the most dramatic return, after two centuries, of a species from apparent extinction.

14. One of its cousin sirenians, the FLORIDA MANATEE *(Trichechus manatus latirostris)* had been virtually exterminated in Florida Bay, and one of the reasons given is that there has been "ruthless hunting of it for food by local people who specialised in killing the baby ones because they are tender". The manatee gave rise to the legend of the mermaid and looks like following the legend into swift oblivion.

15. The WHALES. Perhaps the most tragic story of all the massacres concerns the whales, huge, warm-blooded mammals, some of which are larger than any animal that has ever lived, that is to say larger than the largest dinosaurs. The blue whale has a length of up to 30 metres, a girth of up to 13 metres, and weighs up to 160 tons.

Like their cousins the dolphins, they have a language and a system of echolocation, and seem to be highly intelligent and affectionate towards each other.

Before Man began to hunt them methodically two to three centuries ago they ranged round the world in all the oceans, and in the oceans they were the unchallenged kings.

Unfortunately their carcasses were found to have high commercial value. They are at present used as a source for whale-oil, out of which margarine is made, and meat, which is eaten principally by pets in Europe and people in Japan. I have eaten a whale steak: it is like beef though somewhat coarser. Because of their commercial value they have been hunted remorselessly, and with increasing efficiency, and the effects of this hunting on their numbers has been appalling. Since World War II there has been an International Whaling Commission, but on this commission the voice of commerce and greed has always out-shouted the voice of science and prudence, and no effective measures have been taken to protect the stocks of the world's whales. The most unhappy story concerns the largest whale, the blue whale. In the nineteen thirties over 30,000 blue whales used to be caught in a single season: but in 1964 only 100 could be found and caught, and the world total was thought to be between 650 and 1950.

The other whales have suffered somewhat less than the blue whale, but it is touch and go whether any whales will be alive in a generation's time.

The improvidence of the operation takes one's breath away. At its height the industry used to bring back from the Antarctic 250,000 tons of edible oils and another 250,000 tons of by-products such as meat each year. To achieve such production nearly twenty fleets were fitted out, each with a factory ship and a large number of small catcher ships. Air-planes and helicopters have also been used. Now, with the virtual disappearance of the stocks, all this investment is worth little.

There is no hope for the blue whale unless it receives total protection. On paper this was granted at the July 1966 meeting of the International Whaling Commission, on a proposal by the South African delegate, Dr. B. de Jager.[34] But it remains to be seen whether this protection can be imposed in the oceans. On the assumption that it can be imposed, Leviathan will have been given a respite from what Herman Melville called "so remorseless a havoc". But even if Man holds his killer hand at this late moment, is it certain that the blue whale can make a come-back? Are enough left in the vast empty oceans for male to be able to meet female sufficiently often for mating to take place? If it is, as I fear, too late, the twentieth century will have committed one more crime for which many succeeding centuries will execrate it.[35]

The probable end of the blue whale is occurring in front of the eyes of millions of informed men of the twentieth century, with scarce a protest to be heard. The sequence is full of foreboding for Man himself, for this unquenchable greed, this rejection of the idea of conservation of stocks, is likely to be seen as each of the great natural resources reaches its end.

As world hunger presses on us in the seventies, for instance, it is quite likely that there will be a fishing free-for-all round the world, as each nation intensifies its fishing to get as much as it can for itself, and to prevent other nations from enjoying the last netful.

So much for the whales, the information for which did not come out of the RED DATA BOOK. To complete the list of some endangered mammals, let us look again at the RED DATA BOOK.

All the rhinoceroses are endangered, and I give the RED DATA BOOK figures for them as I did the figures for the great cats:

The GREAT INDIAN RHINOCEROS: 740. The government has made a great effort to preserve them, and there has been some improvement over recent years; JAVAN RHINOCEROS: about 40; SUMATRAN RHINOCEROS: 100-170; SOUTHERN SQUARE-LIPPED RHINOCEROS (the "white" rhino): about 1000; NORTHERN SQUARE-LIPPED RHINOCEROS: estimates vary from a few hundreds to 2000; BLACK RHINOCEROS: 11,000-13,500. A valiant fight to save the Southern square-lipped rhinoceroses has been partly successful, and a fight is beginning to increase the dwindling numbers of the Black rhinoceros. The main hope for this animal lies in translocation, moving specimens back to areas from which they have disappeared, thus multiplying areas where they survive. But it is clear that, outside reserves, this great armoured quadruped is doomed by the pressure of farmers and graziers.

The above list of endangered mammalian species is only a small proportion of the species listed as being in danger: about one twentieth. Space does not allow a fuller excerpt, and I have done little more than select some of the more striking and well-known of the listed species.

I have followed the same principle in going through the second volume, the list of endangered birds:

1. SHORT-TAILED ALBATROSS *(Diomedea albatrus)*. Confined to Toroshima Island, Bonin group, near Japan. "One small population of 47 survives, a remnant of over one million alive in the last century".

2. CHINESE EGRET *(Egretta eulophotes)*. Possibly extinct, "brought to the verge of extinction by plume hunters towards the close of the 19th century".

3. JAPANESE WHITE STORK *(Ciconia ciconia boyciana)*. "Certainly very rare, localised and endangered". "In Japan the relict population is now estimated to number no more than 15 birds… during the 1963 breeding season 5 nests were built but no hatchings resulted; the 1964 season was no better and the failures are undoubtedly due to egg infertility.

4. HAWAIIAN GOOSE or NENE *(Branta sandviciencis)*. In the late 19th century there were estimated to be about 2,000 of these lovely geese in the Hawaiian Islands. Then predation by humans reduced the numbers to about 50. Emergency action was taken, and birds were captured and kept at Slimbridge, England, and in the United States and bred there. Since the captive stocks increased, about 150 birds have been released in the wild in the Hawaiian Islands, and there are now about 285 birds alive in the wild. The Nene has now been made the official bird of the Hawaiian state, and its future seems assured. So far this rescue has been a dramatic success, with a noble bird snatched at the last moment from extinction by the action of a few individuals, among whom the name of Peter Scott, artist, glider, yachtsman and conservationist cannot ever be forgotten.

5. CALIFORNIAN CONDOR *(Gymnogyps californiensis)*. In 1960 60-65 individuals were left. In 1954 only about 40 of which

one third were not of breeding age. "Pesticides also constitute a threat".

6. SPANISH IMPERIAL EAGLE *(Aquila heliaca adalberti)*. "About 100 birds."

7. AFRICAN LAMMERGEYER *(Gypaetus barbatus meridionalis)*. "Rare and decreasing… Reasons for decline: shooting and poisoning…" This is perhaps the noblest of all birds of prey in southern Africa. From my own observation the only breeding pairs left in southern Africa are in the high mountains of Lesotho and probably less than 50 pairs are left, if as many. Often when some farmer shoots one it is reported in the press approvingly, and the report is usually illustrated with a picture of the intrepid hunter.

8. SOUTHERN BALD EAGLE (*Haliaeetus leucocephalus leucocephalus*). This is the national bird of the United States, but its political importance has done little to protect it for it "is becoming rare and generally decreasing… it is evident that there is some reduction in the fertility of pairs, resulting from the use of insecticides in agriculture". Estimated numbers in 1962: 3807 birds.

9. MONKEY-EATING EAGLE *(Pithecophaga jeffreyi)*. "Probably less than 100 of these interesting Philippine eagles are left; it seems also to have become locally popular to own a mounted specimen in the home, and this local demand constitutes the most serious threat to the survival of the species".

10. Seventeen species of PHEASANTS and TRAGOPANS, those most brilliant of the game-birds, are on the list. For their decline the most usual reasons given are "human predation and destruction of habitat".

11. WHOOPING CRANE *(Grus americana)*. This large North American crane has been dragged back from the brink by determined, dramatic, and extraordinarily expensive efforts on the part of bird-lovers. Nevertheless, in 1964-65 only 50 birds existed, of which 7 were in captivity. "Undoubtedly threatened". Apart from the whooping crane, six other species of crane are on the danger list.

12. ST. VINCENT PARROT *(Amazona guildingii)*. "Rare and

decreasing… " "This species is protected by law but a great deal of shooting is said to continue, and the killed birds are used in stews… it is believed that none has as yet been reared in captivity, but suspected that this may be due to the fact that most captured birds kept or sold as pets are usually slightly wounded".

Apart from the St. Vincent parrot, twenty-one other species and sub-species of parrot and parakeet are listed as being endangered.

13. KAUAI OO *(Moho braccatus)*. "Very rare, said to be nearly extinct… this is the last survivor of the four species of Hawaiian OO, whose yellow feathers were used for human adornment".

14. HAWAIIAN NUKUPUU *(Hemignathus wilsoni)*. "Very rare and restricted in range… Reasons for decline: destruction of forest habitat… valleys filled (in 1860) with magnificent forest trees are now devoid of native vegetation…

There is another list, larger than these lists. It is the list of nearly all the surviving wild animals, of those which, though not yet on the IUCN danger lists, are nevertheless threatened by the Man-tide. Their living-space has been greatly reduced, and they spend a good deal of their time in trying to avoid Man, his farms, his vehicles, and his domesticated animals. It is true that there do exist large parks, in Africa principally, where at present some of the remaining wild animals can find asylum. But no one who knows how serious poaching is in these parks, and no one who considers for a moment the probable political upheavals of the last third of this century, and the increasing hunger of the swelling human populations, can feel easy for a moment that the dykes around these parks will really hold for long.

It is true too that there exist schemes for game-farming. Some conservationists have come to believe that the salvation of the wild animals lies in game-farming. Under such schemes. Man would cull from these herds enough to keep their populations constant. To a certain extent the idea is valuable, and many parks are already being compelled to cull and often earn revenue by selling the meat. But to cull wild animals is not really to farm them and there does not seem to be much substance in the idea that wild animals really could be farmed. Firstly, Man's goats and sheep and camels and cattle have shown qualities of docility and profitability that are unlikely to be equalled by tamed elephants, giraffes, rhinos or elands. And, secondly, even if game -farming were to succeed, how would Nature survive? Man would merely have extended the boundaries of his world-farm. The mere fact that such farming would increase the varieties of domestic animal would not make the African savannah any less of a farm, and we would be compelled to envisage the succeeding stage which presumably would be the battery-rearing of antelopes, and the de-horning of rhinos to make them more easily marketable. It seems that there is no half-way house, and no decent solution short of Man's strengthening and enlarging the system of parks and thus voluntarily abdicating his universal domination over all of nature, and thus handing over a generous portion of the world's surface to wilderness and to wildlife.

Let us look summarily at this other list the list of the wild animals that are not necessarily on the IUCN list, and let us look at the conditions in which wild animals are living in some of the key areas round the world. Jordan is one such area. We have seen how King Hussein invited an expedition under the leadership of Guy Mountfort to examine the resources of Jordan, and we have looked at some of their findings on the denudation of the country. The expedition also reported on the losses of fauna that had occurred there through hunting and the destruction of habitat. Here are some extracts: "Jordan's losses of wildlife, particularly among the larger animals, have been disastrous. The asiatic lion, the chief joy of the Ummayad hunters in biblical times had disappeared early in the fifteenth century.[36] The big losses began to be noticed around 1900, when the last roe deer, addax antelope and crocodile were recorded. The wild ass was killed off by 1920 and the fallow deer by 1922. The Syrian bear was exterminated in the 1930s. The last ostrich was seen near Jebel Tubaiq in 1932, and Jordan's last oryx was probably shot before 1950. The cheetah may now have been lost as there have been no reports since a female was shot in 1962 and her cub taken. A few ibex survive in steadily decreasing numbers in the more inaccessible mountains, but unless given effective protection they will not be there for long. Wolves are also beginning to die out…" The report describes how plentiful the two species of gazelle have been until recently, but that there has now occurred a catastrophic decline in their numbers. "The chief cause of the catastrophic decline in Jordan is the raiding parties from the neighbouring oil states, who, having killed off their own game, now cross the largely unguarded desert frontiers to continue their motorised slaughter. The Jordanian Beduin cannot be blamed, as very few of them have cars… The other major factor… is that, although admirable laws have been devised to regulate hunting in Jordan, they are not enforced. We heard far too many stories of 'rich men from Amman and Army officers' shooting exhausted animals from cars. Gazelles have also been machine-gunned by fighter aircraft in several countries of the Middle East."[37]

Fortunately the latest news from Jordan gives much room for hope. A hunting club, the Royal Jordanian Hunting Club, and a newer and widely representative body, the Royal Society for the Conservation of Nature, have come into existence, and are cooperating for the saving of what is left, and perhaps for the reconstitution of Jordan's wildlife in a national park. Thus, perhaps, are being built the foundations of a new attitude in Jordan towards Nature.[38]

But there is never, in this field, any ground for complacency, and sometimes animals which have been effectively protected lose their protection. Perhaps through that protection their numbers increase. Or perhaps human activities round their park change, and produce a clash of interests between animals and men. This happened in late 1963 in the Northwest Territories of Canada in the case of the Barren-ground Grizzly bear. With the Kodiak bear this is the largest bear of all. "The Council of the Northwest Territories… removed the protection of the grizzly bear by an amendment to their Game Ordinance permitting anyone with a general hunting licence to shoot Barren-ground and Mountain grizzlies on sight, except in three game reserves, with no restrictions as to season, number, sex, age or location. This was the result of representations by trappers that the bears threatened their camps and their families. The Canadian Wildlife Service regard it as 'a retrogressive step'. The Council says that the number of bears killed will be closely watched, and if too many are shot action will be taken, but as the amendment removes the provision that all bears killed must be reported to game officers, it is not clear how they will know… Estimates of the slow-breeding Barren-ground grizzly population suggest that there are well below 1000 individuals."[39]

Sometimes, in his killings, Man seeks to act humanely. But often he does not care. The people of Kerala in India are unique in at least two ways: they are the only electorate in history ever to have put a Communist government into power by democratic means. And they are the only people who have been reported as using insecticides to kill wild elephants. The latter activity at least seems to be extremely effective: "In six months the chief conservator of forests in Kerala… came across the carcasses of thirty eight elephants, mostly the victims of poisoning by pesticides, some of festered gunshot wounds. With the destruction of their habitat, the elephants feed on cultivated plantations which are sprayed with pesticides to keep them away. Banana clusters similarly sprayed had been left along elephant walks; the elephants were dead at the nearest water-hole to which they had rushed to drink. In Mysore pesticides are accounting for tigers and panthers, and the jungle cats 'seem to have been wiped out from non-sanctuary areas' according to ANIMAL-CITIZEN."[40]

In India, as elsewhere, governments are unable or unwilling to act to enforce their own game preservation laws. The trouble is, of course, that men everywhere in the world are still hunters under their skin, and that they believe that they have an inherent right to kill any animal that they wish to kill. And governments everywhere are slow to act against men's deeply held beliefs. Therefore, right round the world if you want to find a poacher, just look for the nearest animal protection area.

Sometimes poaching has dragged an animal down to the brink of extinction. In Zambia, for instance the Black Lechwe is being poached to extinction. These rare antelopes are now found only in one place in the world: the Kafue flats west of Lusaka. In 1934 there were 150,000: but to-day there are perhaps 4,000.

Similarly the existence of the Red Lechwe is threatened in the same country. In 1934 there were 250,000 but to-day there are only 24,000.[41] These animals enjoy on paper, absolute protection, but unfortunately the Zambian government, although it cares for the Lechwes, and although it is the richest free African government, is quite unable to stop poaching both by guns and by wire snares. If poachers can flout the law only 250km from an enlightened and rich capital, what hope in the long run does any animal have in Africa?

Dark and depressing though the picture is in North America, Asia, Africa, Europe and the oceans, perhaps it is even darker in Latin America. Despite a relatively sparse human population, and despite the formidable barriers to the Man-tide in the high cordilleras and the tropical forests of the Amazon, men are daily and with little hindrance harrying the wild animals to extinction. This sombre fact appears in a report on the wildlife of Latin America made by Ambassador Philip. K. Crowe.[42] Ambassador Crowe is an unusual man: when ill health brought a distinguished diplomatic career to an end he took up the cause of wildlife conservation round the world. Over the last two to three years he has visited countries covering the major part of the world's surface to report on the state of conservation and to encourage conservationists. Here are a few excerpts from his Latin American report: "There is no protection for any animal in the jungle territory of Peru, except for one fish and for crocodiles under one metre in length... The vicuña is in very bad shape. Despite strict laws against killing them and selling the skins, the Indians of the high cordilleras, tempted by prices as high as $100 for a single pelt, continue to poach these little animals... The position may well be that no government can to-day enforce game laws among the hungry Indians of the high Andes.

Another resident of the high Cordilleras is the chinchilla, a squirrel-like little animal with a coat... that may well bring about its extinction. A wild chinchilla wrap in New York, if available at all, may sell for $ 50,000. Except in captivity the Peruvian chinchilla, known as the Royal chinchilla, may now be extinct".

Ambassador Crowe gives distressing details of the gap that exists in Latin America between conservation of wildlife as it exists on paper, and as it exists in practice. "The Cutervo National Park (in Peru) was founded m 1961, but it exists only on paper… Chile has more game reserves than any other country in South America, but the nineteen parks and twenty-six forest reserves have little significance, for in most of them, people are living, and people always mean poaching and fires… As a result Chile's wildlife is declining. The little indigenous Chilean deer is scarce; the Chilean condor is shot and becoming rare. The puma is under heavy pressure from hunters: at one hacienda in the south forty were killed in a single month…

"Argentina has the largest system of national parks in South America and has every right to be proud of them. However, 41 million acres (2 million hectares) of reserves are policed by only 50 wardens and the entire budget for their maintenance is only $100,000 annually… Since most of the land of Argentina is privately owned and such game laws as there are stop at the gates of the estancias, the choice of conserving or destroying wildlife is largely a private matter…

"Most Uruguayans (and for that matter most Latin Americans) shoot everything which moves…

"The future of conservation in South America depends primarily on education… Such game laws as exist have virtually no significance because they are seldom if ever enforced".

Such are some of the appalling judgments of the Crowe report on Latin America, an area in which political turbulence is increasing, and in which the increase of the human populations is unequalled. The best that can be hoped for in Latin America is that some Noah will keep at least a pair of each of its marvellously varied animals alive until the deluge of human populations, ignorance and cruelty has subsided.[(43)]

The first massive animals were reptiles, and as the IUCN lists do not yet include reptiles little has been said about them in this chapter. Perhaps it is good to bring our list to an end with a mention of the larger tortoises and turtles. One of the best- known is facing extinction: it is the Green turtle *(Chelonia mydas)*. This immense reptile which could have taken an honoured place in the age of the extinct dinosaurs, and very likely did, used not so long ago to breed in great numbers on many of the world's beaches, including those of the Hong Kong islands. Unfortunately for them, the fisher folk regard them as a symbol, of longevity, and their eggs are also "much prized for medicinal purposes especially by mothers as they are reputed to be efficacious in the, prevention of diarrhoea in young children... In 1962 and 1963 only one Green turtle was known to have returned to Hong Kong, and during this period two others were killed in Hong Kong waters."[44]

Across the Indian Ocean things are going just as badly for *Chelonia mydas* in islands that, from time immemorial, it has regarded as its own particular home; the Seychelles. "The Green turtle population of the western Indian Ocean has reached a dangerously low level, thanks largely to excessive killing... the species needs complete protection for a number of years with some form of hatching control, on certain islands, and an accurate check made on its status... a protein-hungry population eats as many as it can get... (The law for their protection) is enforced by the police on Mahé, the main island, but enforcement is impossible on the outlying islands."[45]

Another race of tortoises which has been harried to a danger-point on the road to extinction is the Giant tortoise of the Galapagos Islands, celebrated since Charles Darwin's visit there in the Beagle. These animals are being exterminated by hunting and by the destruction of the islands' vegetation by goats and drought. Fortunately help is on the way: a research station has been set up in the islands (called the Charles Darwin Research Station) and this station "has as its most urgent duty the protection of the remaining Giant tortoises."[46] Unfortunately this will be no easy task, as the human population of the islands with its attendant goats is well dug-in.

These facts, quoted above, are merely a few of the stories in the unlimited global massacre of the animals by Man. Many thousands of species have already become extinct, and many hundreds of species are on the danger-lists, some with their surviving populations to be counted in a few dozens. The decision whether to continue with this massacre or to halt it lies on this and the succeeding generation.

The question has more urgency than any merely intra-human problem. Human problems may look larger, but we know that (short of total nuclear destruction) all human rivalries are in the end settled. Human greed and hatred are not permanent, if only because old forms of rivalry die out, even if they are replaced by new forms. In many human problems the solution lies in our capacity to procrastinate, to delay the solution, to use the *solvitur ambulando* approach. Unfortunately, such methods are not suitable for the protection and the rescue of the world's wildlife. With all honour due to those who are active in this cause, the imagination of those in power has hardly been touched yet. And such is the current force and speed of the Man-tide that procrastination means defeat for conservation, and an end, in the lifetime of many now living, to wild animals on our Earth.

Man's development of agriculture, then, has led to the destruction of much of the fertility of the globe on which all life, including human life, ultimately depends. It has also led to the unlimited massacre of the wild animals. Perhaps this massacre may hurt Man as much as his destruction of the soils and forests. For just as no man is an island, so no species is an island. "All Life is One," said the ancient Buddhists; and their wisdom comes very close to the latest findings of science. "There is no difference in 'perfection' from the bacterium to Man - they are different branches of one single Life, each adapted to their own Life."[47] said Jacques Monod, the French molecular biologist and Nobel Prize winner, one of the pioneers of modern science.[48]

Can a single branch attack and destroy all the other branches without harming the whole tree, including itself? Surely not, yet this is what we are doing: this is what we have nearly completed doing.

The truth is that we and all living things are indeed all cousins of each other, and that animals are just as perfect as Man. Children understand this instinctively and rejoice in the sight and touch of an animal, and enjoy stories about animals. It is also understood by anyone who has looked lovingly at the soft feathery curve of a swallow's throat. It is understood by one who has cruised under the sea among the corals and rocks, followed curiously by his cousins the fish. It is understood by anyone who has placed his five-fingered hand next to that of a frog, or who has compared the bright eyes of the animals with the matt, often bloodshot aspect of the human eye.

Perhaps, once again, the hope is that "A little child shall lead them". In England children have shown themselves readier than the older generation to support appeals such as that of the World Wildlife Fund, a fund that has done so much for the mobilising of public opinion. If these children are able to prove constant and steadfast in their support of this cause, the greatest of all, and if they can carry their determination right through to adult life, then our cousins the animals do have some hope of survival. If not, there will be no hope of avoiding, probably within the lifetime of many who are now alive, a final irreparable and self-mutilating act of fratricide.

REFERENCES

(1)   Forests come before the peoples, and deserts come after them.

(2)   Recent exterminations are well-documented from North America and Europe. It is thought that the first men crossed into North America across the landbridge that then lay where the straits of Behring now run about 11,000 years ago. It is known that they became redoubtable mammoth-hunters before that woolly, spiral-tusked elephant died out, probably as a result of over-hunting. During the Pleistocene, between   about 15,000 and 6,000 years ago the mastodon, the giant sloth and the camel became extinct in North America. According to Paul S. Martin of the University of Arizona, they may have been overhunted and exterminated by the same well-armed hunting bands that hunted the mammoth, also about 11,000 years ago. (See *Scientific American,* December 1966, page 58).

(3)   "The Origins of New World Civilisation", *Scientific American,* November 1964.

(3a)   "Preliminary analysis of plant and animals remains has revealed that during their 10 centuries of residence the villagers ate nothing but wild foods. The bulk of their meat came from wild cattle, wild ass and gazelle;

they also fed on fallow-deer, boar, wolf and hare. They oven-roasted and also ground wild forms of barley and wheat and gathered wild lentil and vetch. Curiously enough, in spite of the river location of the village, the inhabitants apparently did not eat fish... the number of families living in the village at any one time may have totalled 200." *Scientific American,* May 1966, page 53.

(4)   The excavations here have been carried out by a French archaeological team. The oldest level appears to date back to earlier than 7,000 BC. In this level the houses had floors of beaten earth, and the fireplaces were surrounded by animal bones, flint arrowheads and other arms and tools. The oldest inhabitants, according to these finds, lived by gathering and by hunting, and did not know agriculture, and "the population of Munhata lived... in the absence of all domestic animals." *Le Monde* 17 August, 1966 (my translation).

(5)   *New York Herald-Tribune.* Paris, 23 June, 1966.

(6)   *The Epic of Gilgamesh.* Penguin Books, London.

(7)   *I Chronicles,* 2: i-xviii.

(8)   From his dialogue *critias,* quoted by G. Gardin in *Population, Evolution and Birth Control* (page 59); W.H.Freeman and Co.

(9)   From the introduction to "Written in the Syrian Desert" in *American Forests,* the magazine of the American Forestry Association, August 1941.

(10) *Tebessa, Antique Théveste,* by Sérée de Roche; Service des Antiquités, Algiers July 1952; page 12.

(11) The population is about 5 million at present.

(12) *Travels in the Footsteps of Bruce in Algeria and Tunis,* by Lt. Col. R. L. Playfair, London, 1877; pp. 154-155.

(13) *Notes Sur Les Forêts de l'Algérie,* by H. Marc; Larose, Paris, 1930, p. 513 (Collection du Centenaire de l'Algérie).

(14) Tell: the relatively fertile coastal strip of Algeria.

(15) "The existing forests have been degraded over immense areas, and are now only able to fulfil their rôle imperfectly" - Ibid. p.310.

(16) Low, unlovely thicket, "the result of Man's activity on the 'primeval' evergreen forest." from *Flowers of the Mediterranean,* by Polunin and Huxley, Chatto and Windus, London, 1965 (see their definition of *maquis).*

(17) "Algeria, a Mediterranean region, has been deforested by Man's hand, as is proved by historical documents, the customs of the 'indigenous peoples, as well as by agricultural methods used before, and even after the conquest (1830)." - *Notes Sur Les Forêts de l'Algerie,* by H. Marc; Larose, Paris, 1930, page 513.

(18) from *A Fool on the Veldt*, by Leonard Fleming.

(19) A league =3 miles =5km

(20) *Relation d'un Voyage d'Exploration en 1836 par MM. Arbousset et Daumas*, Paris, 1836, page 8 (my translation).

(21) Ibid, page 108.

(22) An incident in the Semien mountains of Ethiopia, reported by Leslie Brown in "Ethiopian Episode", *Oryx*, December 1965, page 199.

(23) "Creating new Deserts in Somalia", a note in *Oryx*, August 1964, VII: 5.

(24) One acre = 0.4 hectare.

(25) "Disappearing Wildlife and Growing Deserts in Jordan" in *Oryx*, August, 1964; VII: 5.

(26) "Plans for conserving the Wildlife of Hong Kong", by P. M. Marshall and J. G. Phillips, *Oryx*, August, 1965. VIII: 2.

(27) 1000 gallons of water (English) = 4.544 metric tons.

(28) *Oryx*, August 1965, VIII: 2.

(29) (The hogfish is very vicious: it is like the land pig). This remark, made in all seriousness, echoed the French satirical verse: Cet animal est très méchant: si on l'attaque il se défend. (This animal is very vicious; if you attack it it fights back).

(30) The dates come from the *Red Data Book*, of which more later.

(31) *Red Data Book;* Vol. I; Mammalia; Vol. II; Aves, published by the Survival Service Commission of the International Union for Conservation of Nature and Natural Resources, 1110 *Morges*, Switzerland, 1966.

(32) "Why Kangaroos are not seen", a note in Oryx April 1967 IX: 1, page 4.

(33) *Observer*, London; 14th May, 1967.

(34) *Southern Africa*, 25th July, 1966.

(35) The information about whales has been gleaned from: "The plight of the Whales", by J.A. Culland, Oryx, August 1965: VII: 2; and from the *April 1966* issue of *Geographical Magazine*. Those interested should also read "The Last of the Great Whales", by Scott McVay, in *Scientific American*, August 1966; page 21.

(36) The Ummayad dynasty flourished in the 7th century AD.

(37) *Oryx*, August 1964; "Disappearing Wildlife and growing Deserts in Jordan".

(38) "New Hope for Wildlife in Jordan", by Maisie Fitter, *Oryx*, April 1967; IX: 1.

(39) *Oryx*, August 1964; VII: 5.

(40) quoted in Oryx, December 1964; VII: 6.

(41) "Radio Newsreel"; BBC World Service; 22 August 1966; and *Oryx*, April

1967; IX: 1, page 6.

(42) *Oryx,* April 1965; VII: 1.

(43) As already noted, Ambassador Crowe's report is in Oryx. April 1965: VII: 1.

(44) "Plans for Conserving the Wildlife of Hong Kong", by P. M. Marshall and J.G. Phillips: Oryx, August 1965; VIII: 2.

(45) "Green Turtles in the Seychelles", *Oryx.* April 1965: VIII: 1.

(46) "The Giant Tortoises of the Galapagos Islands", by D. W. Snow, Oryx, December 1964; VII: 6.

(47) *Le Monde,* 9 December 1965: The whole passage runs:

"Le critère de l'évolution c'est la multiplication. C'est une erreur de croire que l'évolution doit être liée a une notion de perfectionnisme. Cette idée de progrès est une conception subjective, mais elle n'a aucun sens objectif. Il n'existe aucune différence de 'perfection' de la bactérie à l'homme – ce sont les différentes branches d'une même vie, toutes adaptées à leur propre vie."

(48) Compare Samuel Taylor Coleridge's: "Nature has her proper interest, & he will know what it is, who believes and feels, that every Thing has a life of its own, & that we are all *one Life.* " ---- quoted in *The Observer,* p.17, 21 August 1966.

4 Man develops Political Power

"The problem of the twentieth century is the problem of the colour line."

W.E.Burghardt du Bois [1]

IN EARLIER chapters we have seen how the humanisation of Man and the development of agriculture could be considered as "super-events" in history. Political power, the subject of this chapter, grew out of a third "super- event": the development of the state. The state was born out of simple towns and villages, and small confederations. State rulers soon made demands on individuals which had never been made before and with the product of these demands maximised their power. This power was used, no longer merely against wild animals, but against other similar human groups.

In this chapter we shall examine some basic characteristics of power and politics, and how the present-day world is divided between power-groups in struggles as bitter as those between different species in the evolutionary development of life. With the development of the state, the law of inter-group relations became the law of the jungle: kill or be killed; seize or lose living-space. In this way did the ancient law of evolution --- that one form of life fills its niche until halted by the frontiers of the niches of other forms of life --- become in our times the law of inter-state relations. In this struggle size has been a characteristic that has favoured survival, and so, over the centuries the size of states has constantly tended to grow. The process must conclude with the establishment of a world state.

Rulers of the state have used many instruments to aggrandise their power: superstition and religion, habit, rewards, and power. Of all these instruments only the last-named has been indispensable:

power, the power to compel obedience, the power to neutralise, eliminate and even to kill disrupters. Politics has become in its essence an exercise in power.

There have been many theories about power and about what drives men to reach for it. In the Greco-Roman world and in the Renaissance it was believed that men wished for power for the sake of glory and fame. To the marxists men seem to wish for power for the sake of economic advantage.

I suspect that the court of President Kennedy would have replied: "for the fun that it gives". I offer a definition here somewhat different, that men seek power in order to preempt the character of the world in which their grandchildren will have to live; so that the world of their grandchildren will be constructed in a manner, and according to a scale of values familiar to themselves. If this definition is of merit, the question of how many grandchildren they have is of paramount importance.[2]

If such is the nature of the drive for power, what is the nature of power itself? What is the nature of power in society? I offer a definition: the power attained by Man is the degree by which the direction taken by the group on which he acts diverges from the direction which it would have taken if he had not acted upon it. Let this divergence be x°: a man's power in history can be expressed as

$$x° \; yz$$

where y = the number of people in the group

and z = the power of that group as a fraction of the totality of power in the world.

A public figure aims to get his hand on the tiller of the ship of state, the state to which he belongs. Having grasped part of the tiller he seeks to press the vessel towards the point on the horizon towards which he believes that the ship ought to sail. A public figure steers by the stars, and also by the direction previously taken by the ship. As Abraham Lincoln said: "If we could first know where we are and whither we are tending, we could better judge what to do and how to do it."[3] Of course, no one man, not the most powerful, the most eminent, or the most dictatorial, can ever steer the ship all alone: there are always other hands on the tiller. Eloquence and power have always gone along together, and the successful leader is he who knows how to persuade the majority of those other guiding hands that his direction is the correct direction.

Many leaders are moved by a desire for posthumous fame. This desire has often puzzled people: How can such fame mean anything to a man, they ask. On my definition of power above it is quite understandable, for posthumous fame means that the dead leader's system of values is acceptable after his death, and it means that it will be more likely that his grandchildren will live in a world of which he would have approved.

What wins posthumous fame? It is usually won by an acknowledgement by those that came after that the dead leader analysed correctly the direction that affairs would take, and led his group successfully in the direction which, according to his scale of values, it ought to have taken.

The word "ought" is, of course, a question-begging word unless one has previously defined one's scale of moral values. So far as this book is concerned the definition will be found in the last chapter. The rights and wrongs of the direction to be taken by a ship of state can only be justified if they are ultimately seen to harmonise with the rights and wrongs of the direction taken by the human race as a whole. For the purposes of this book it may be taken that an attempt will be made to see right and wrong in an ultra-long time-scale. The scale is, in fact, so vast that the ship of state must be compared to a galley far out on an unknown sea. Most of the men on it are slaves, chained to their oars, knowing that the chains will not be broken until their death. A few have managed to avoid the chains. They have formed a small group at the stern. Of this group a few leaders have managed to preserve their grip on the tiller. Whether the ship is of the fleet named "autocracy" or "democracy" or "dictatorship" the actual picture differs little and most of these galleys are controlled by a small group of men, usually fewer than ten in number.

Inside this small group a debate springs up: to which point on the horizon should the ship sail? The voyage is into the future, towards that final landfall to which a million human years have pointed. As knowledge of the past accumulates, there comes a greater possibility of knowing the approximate course ahead. But in our time there exist the most complete differences of opinion as to what that course ought to be. Some counsel a radical change of course, and some even counsel a return backwards. Some are actuated unselfishly, others selfishly, while yet others are actuated by an inherent love of opposition: by stasis, as the quarrelsome Greeks in their small classical city-states used to call it. After a trial of strength, sometimes involving deaths, a decision is reached and, for a while, an agreed decision is taken and maintained.

The picture is similar for the steering of the human race. Those that acquire power, as defined in the first pages of this chapter, seek to steer the vessel of humanity in the direction which harmonises with their beliefs about the true nature of Man and the world. If we saw quarrelling at the tiller of the small ships of state, this quarrelling is as nothing to the disagreements that rage over the direction that the world ought to take. These disagreements are nowadays expressed so loudly that it is difficult even to understand what the various counsellors and leaders are trying to say. Does this mean that there must be no sailing?

I think not. In the foreword I suggested the image of humanity and life lost in a forest, and I suggested that it might be possible to find a short-term objective on which all might unite. To transfer this image to the background of the oceans which we now have before us, it is possible that there exists, somewhere near the ship of humanity, a calling-in station on an island. This island may not be on the course that ultimately will be seen to be correct. Nevertheless it is a beautiful island, and might provide things necessary for the much longer voyage. It might also offer a breathing-space, and a look-out from which the longer course into the future could be espied. It would seem sensible to steer towards this island. A decision to steer towards it involves an acceptance that, until we have reached and passed many horizons we shall not know the final landfall, and cannot therefore agree on it to-day. Yet we should decide to steer towards it because it is intermediate, provisional, knowable, reasonable and certain.

Even this intermediate landfall will be difficult enough to reach, for it represents nothing less than the working towards a creative relationship between the various forms of life, including Man, and the Earth. And such a relationship is far from us, for our political life is cruel and is becoming crueller; our wars are vast and are becoming vaster; and our social life is evil and is becoming more evil.

In future chapters we shall examine this pessimistic thesis more closely: in this chapter we shall examine only the dark political prospects.

The world's political life is based on the fact that there are three principal groupings by means of which the human race is now divided, three groupings each of which is large enough and deeply enough divided to carry within itself the risks of a third world war.

The first is the grouping which places all those peoples of European biological origin on one side, and all the rest of humanity on the other. This if often called the race division of humanity.

The second is the grouping in which all members of a nation consider themselves on one side of the division and all others on the other. Naturally nations form alliances, but the nationalist grouping is the hard core of the matter.

The third is the class grouping of humanity, by which I mean the placing of the rich nations on one side and of the poorer nations on the other. This is somewhat similar to the Marxist analysis, which would place the "proletarian" peoples and classes from all nations on one side, and the "bourgeoisie" and "imperialists" on the other.

I believe that each of these divisions could produce a third world war. But if history should, in the next decade, drive an overwhelming majority of "Europeans" into the same *kraal* (4) as the richer peoples, and an overwhelming majority of the "non-Europeans" into the same kraal as the poorer peoples, and if their nationalist feelings could be inflamed against those in the other kraal, and if the pressure of world population were to raise world temperatures significantly, and if world hunger, should escalate into a mega-famine, then the world would be in greater danger than it has ever been in in previous history. For behind all our human differences there is now a cloud, at present very distant, but which nevertheless rumbles with unimaginably destructive thunders and lightening.

Various opinions are held as to which of these, groupings is the most important. To me the most important is unquestionably the division of the world into those people who activated the European expansion of the last five centuries, and those peoples who suffered its impact; between those people who gained from this expansion territorially, politically, economically and psychologically, and those peoples who lost; between the "Europeans" as defined biologically and (with a few exceptions) the "non-Europeans".

I believe that the expansion, and now the contraction, of the power of the Europeans is by far the most important fact of human history since the fall of the western Roman Empire, and that its effects will continue to influence human history for centuries. To me, present-day public affairs are quite incomprehensible unless one allows due weight to this immensely important factor. To me, the other two ways of grouping the human race are largely mere facets of this principal grouping. If the flow, and now the ebb of this European tide is seen as the central fact of our times, then many things that are otherwise confusing fall into place and are understandable.

At its height, this European tide produced the nearest thing to world domination that has ever been seen. It is often forgotten how nearly complete was the control that the Europeans gained. In 1400 they occupied a moderate-sized peninsula jutting out westward from the Eurasian landmass; by 1919 they had conquered the inhabited world, except for Japan and a few small countries such as Liberia and Persia. During these five centuries the Russians (white-skinned people speaking an Indo-European language) spread eastwards across the steppes, conquering, exterminating, and annexing.[5] During the same five centuries, Iberians and Anglo-Saxons (whites like the Russians) crossed the Atlantic, and found a New World. In this New World they spread westwards, conquering, exterminating and annexing. During the eighteenth and nineteenth centuries the Europeans conquered and ruled Asia except for China and Japan:[6]

in China they imposed a semi-colonialism, but in Japan they failed: as a result, Japan is the great exception to the congruence between the rich world and the biologically European world.

In Australia and in New Zealand, in the eighteenth and nineteenth centuries, the English conquered, exterminated and annexed. The degree of extermination varied from the practice in New Zealand, where the settlers and the Maoris reached a sort of modus vivendi, to the practice in Tasmania, where the settlers killed off the whole aboriginal population in a genocidal series of hunts in which men, women and children were deliberately exterminated. In ways like this, English settlers were able to add 7. 5 million km² to their living- space.

In Africa during the nineteenth century the Europeans divided up their colonies and spheres of influence on the drawing-boards of the conference-halls and chancelleries of Europe, and by 1919 they had established their sovereignty over every square metre of the continent outside Ethiopia and Liberia.

The sheer size of the outward flow of the emigration of the Europeans was quite unprecedented in the world's history. Earlier migrations were counted by the thousand; but this numbered many millions. A notable pioneer of demography has estimated that "it is likely that at least 65 million persons moved overseas in those years (1821-1932)" and that 7 millions of Russian Europeans passed into Asiatic Russia in addition.[7] This migration took place at the height of the European demographic expansion, and in the empty and emptied lands the settlers multiplied at speed, their birthrate probably reaching, at the zenith of the curves, 50 per thousand.

This migration, especially if the enslavement of millions of Africans is seen as part of it, was one of the cruellest chapters in human history. Yet the medal has another side: this migration is the foundation on which the modern age has been built. The geographical expansion of Europe triggered the intellectual expansion that caused, and was also caused by, the industrial and scientific explosions. At all events, whether its effects have been constructive or destructive, its importance is indubitable.

Unfortunately there is a problem in semantics here. It is not possible, without explanations, to describe those who powered the expansion of Europe as "Europeans" without arousing criticism , for many citizens of the two super-powers which were built on the expansion of Europe, the Soviet Union and the United States of America, would reject the name "European" .

And, similarly, there is no convenient word to describe those who suffered by the expansion of Europe. These peoples are often referred to as the "Third World". This vogue phrase, which originated in the early nineteen fifties in France to describe those peoples who did not belong to the two worlds of Communists and non-Communists, a division which, in those years, was felt to be the most important grouping of the human race. Such a view might have been reasonable at that time, but now, with the rapidly growing congruence between the Soviet and the American ways of life, and with closer Russo-American political co-operation probably also on the way, it is clearly no longer a valid analysis.

Yet, if the expression "Third World" is not acceptable, what expression would be preferable? "Ex-colonial World"? Yes, but it is awkward to pronounce. "Freed World"? Yes, but there is no more personal freedom in the "Freed World" than there is in the "Free World", if as much. Would the "Poor World" or "Developing World" do? Yes, but these expressions ignore the origin of the grouping which, as we have seen, was between those who powered the expansion of Europe and those against whom it was directed. Would "Southern World" do? Yes, but the geographical exceptions are too many: there are rich peoples in Latin America , in Australasia, and rich minorities in southern Africa.

"Non-European World"? But the Japanese are not Europeans. Proletarian World"? But one cannot lump all classes, nations and tribes in Africa and Asia into a vast proletariat without doing violence to meaning. It seems, after all, that it will be necessary to keep the expression "Third World". At least it is short, even if it is fairly meaningless. It has been generally accepted, even if it is no longer clear which are the First and the Second Worlds.

For the purposes of the present study, therefore, the word "European" will be taken to mean all those peoples of Indo-

European languages, who, living in Europe, or leaving it during the past five centuries, settled in other continents. And the expression "Third World" will apply to those peoples who suffered the impact of the expansion of the Europeans.

As with the tides of the sea, so with human tides. No sooner had the European tide reached its high watermark in 1919 than it began to recede. The peace settlement introduced the principle of self-determination. Armed with this principle the dominated peoples of the Third World began to wrench their destinies out of the hands of their European conquerors. This process reached flood proportions after the Second World War, in the nineteen-fifties and -sixties, and as a result the Europeans no longer control the Asian and African continents.

The imaginative Communists, inspired by Lenin's work on imperialism, foresaw this ebb-tide more clearly than did the colonial powers, and tried to profit by it. Lenin had realised the inadequacy of the marxist class-hypothesis to explain let alone to refashion, the Third World and so he grafted on to it his own hypothesis of "imperialism the last stage of capitalism". There is a great deal of truth in this hypothesis, especially if the rise of "imperialism" is equated with the expansion of Europe. The problem for marxist thought here is that if imperialism is equated with the expansion of Europe, then the Russians must be seen as imperialists. After all, the fact that Russian administrators rule at Tashkent and Alma Ata today is due to Tsarist conquest, not to any intellectual conversion of the Turkic peoples of Central Asia spontaneously, to Communism.

The Chinese have not been slow to notice how strong is the European racial link between, say, the Americans and the Russians.

Lenin's work on imperialism acknowledged, as I see it, the importance of the expansion of Europe to any deep analysis of the present age. I believe that, as I have said, the European expansion is at the heart of this modern age. It explains much of the uniquely important scientific character of the age. And it explains many political phenomena that are otherwise puzzling. It throws light on the anti-imperialist struggle, and on the opposition to colonialism and neo-colonialism. Neo-colonialism is a reality, for it is certain that, as the European colonial powers withdrew their direct political control of the African and Asian continents, they tried to maintain economic control through discreet commercial links.

The European hypothesis also throws a good deal of light on the concept of race. The concept of race is a new concept. It was unknown in the Greco Roman world. It was, indeed, unknown anywhere until Europe began to expand. The very word "race" is of unknown origins, and is first recorded as having appeared in Italy in the 14th century.[8] The date is appropriate, since the concept of race is closely associated with the expansion of Europe, and Europeans have been, and still are, racists in a manner unknown to men of other origins. It is of interest to note that when the pale-skinned Indo-European conquerors swept south into India thousands of years ago, they found a dark-skinned population, the Dravidians. The caste system which they imposed on the conquered bears similarities with the apartheid system which has been imposed on the peoples of South Africa, and the very word for the caste system in Sanskrit is "varna", the word which also means "colour".

During the last five centuries, as the Europeans swept out from Europe across the world, they preserved a certain unity despite their intra-European wars at home. Two factors symbolised the unity of the world-conquerors: the Christian religion and their European racial and biological similarities. As the power of their religion waned, so in the nineteenth century did the racial factor gain in importance. It became the uniform that distinguished those who powered the expansion of Europe from those who suffered from it.

Racism is immensely strong, and is, in the twentieth century, the most important sequela of the expansion of Europe, the most important of the many lines that divide the human race, more important than the other two principal dividing lines already mentioned; those of class and nation. For this reason perhaps the best insight into our post-colonial age was that of W. E. Burghardt Du Bois with whose most striking quotation this chapter begins.

Racism has many sources of strength. It satisfies certain widely-felt psychological needs. In an age of weakened family and tribal solidarity it supplies a sense of community and cohesion. Although modern communications tend to weaken racism by increasing our knowledge and understanding of other peoples, in the short run they can also exacerbate racism just because people who had previously had little contact have now been suddenly forced into uncomfortably close contact. Furthermore, in the present unified commercial world the exploiter, for historical and sociological reasons, has often as not been a European, and the exploited has been the man of the Third World. Here racism is often used as a unifying uniform to strengthen the solidarity of the exploited and also of the exploiter.

Racism answers, too, to a sociological need. Men, at birth, have certain behaviour-traits built in to their being. Among these are what might be called a "pole of attraction" and a "pole of repulsion": the need to love and the need to hate. Society is built on these poles. It is built by arranging that the poles of attraction of its members shall be directed towards other members and towards objects approved of by that society, while the poles of repulsion shall be directed at non-members and at objects disapproved of. Men seem to need to exercise both poles: they need to love and to be loved to hate and be hated. Tribal life used to exercise both poles admirably, but the modern regulated life of the industrialised city deprives people of this necessary side to their emotional lives. There is often no one to love or hate profoundly. The juvenile gang thrives on this deprivation and keeps both poles well exercised. But adults, too, have this need and in the absence of a genuine tribal enemy many have made for themselves an *ersatz* enemy. The white man treats the coloured man as if he were a tribal enemy, and, later, he receives the same treatment from the coloured man.

Finally, racism has been able to thrive on the fact that each culture produces its own distinctive type of ugliness. Between different cultures there is not much variation in the actual quantity of ugliness and nastiness, but this nastiness is manifested in different cultures by different sorts of individual and in different ways. The racist sees with the keenest of eyes the nastiness produced by the culture which he dislikes yet he tends not to see the nastiness produced by "his own people", and he hates what he sees.

The most serious form of racism is the racism that is directed against black people. People of African descent encounter it in most parts of the world, even in Asia and Latin America, but it is at its worst in the Anglo-Saxon countries. There is unfortunately no quick solution to anti-African racism, for it is due to two objective factors, in addition to the subjective factors already touched upon: first that the Africans were in fact the last-comers to the technologically unified world, and hence are still the least acculturated to it. And, second, that their biological inheritance makes their appearance distinctive: physically they are distinguishable from the other branches of the human race to a greater degree than these branches are from each other. To far too many millions of Europeans and Asians a black skin is the uniform of poverty. Nothing can overcome this idea except the winning of real self-respect by the African peoples of the world. Other peoples in our times have won their own respect and that of others by demonstrating great fighting ability in a war, and it is likely that until Africans have fought bravely against some of their enemies, anti-African racism will continue to poison human relations.

Many anti-African racists hold the view that the distinctive African biological characteristics are more *animal-like* than are those of the Europeans and Asians. This myth was amusingly and conclusively exploded by Dr. M. D. W. Jeffreys of the University of Johannesburg. He pointed out that whites share more physical traits with animals than do the Africans. The most important of these traits is the tendency to hairiness. Many Africans are quite hairless, except for the head and the pubic hair. Some do not even grow beards. Yet most Europeans have a considerable amount of body hair, and I once saw a Hungarian count in a swimming bath who resembled nothing so much as a large water-spaniel. Also the *kind* of hair supports this thesis. No animal has the African's peppercorn-type hair, and when the Basotho first saw European missionaries they called out to each other that "people with white skins and baboons' hair had arrived". Lastly, the thick lips of the Africans are less animal-like than are the thin lips which the European shares with the chimpanzees and other primates. The exception is the flatter nose of the Africans, which is closer to that of the primates than is the more prominent nose of the other branches of the human race.

There are two areas where anti-African racism is producing crises. One is in the United States of America, where although slavery and discriminatory laws have been abolished, the Afro-Americans are still painfully rejected by the dominant white society. The ordinary white American simply does not see Afro-Americans as being fully American in the same sense as are the descendants of, say, Irish and German immigrants. Here again, the "European hypothesis" throws light. The Germans and Irish and all the other white-skinned immigrants and their descendants have been fully integrated in American society precisely because they were of the peoples who powered the expansion of Europe. The Africans (and smaller groups such as the Amer-indians from Mexico) have not been integrated in American society, precisely because they were of the peoples against whom the expansion of Europe took place. On the "European hypothesis" this division, between the Europeans and the Third World is the major division in the world. The Afro-Americans seen in the light of this hypothesis, are men of the Third World captured and forcibly transplanted into the physical, but not yet the social, area of the world of the Europeans.

The other area where anti-African racism has produced a crisis is, of course, in southern Africa. "From the Zambesi to Simon's Bay" a white nation of European stock has taken root in the same territory as a potential African nation. In order not to be absorbed or dominated by this African nation the white nation has assumed total power to dispose of the good things of life, land, money, jobs, education and prestige, and to dominate the African nation. The white nation has refused assimilation and comradeship to the African nation and the inhibition of life for the African nation has been made the condition for the affirmation of life for the white nation.

As a result of this domination, mutual dislike has now grown between the two nations to the extent that it is unlikely that the two will ever be content to share one territory between them, and it is unlikely that because of this the power will be wielded in the future either by a government of African character or by a government of European character. In either case the future will be decided by force, by a politico-military clash. There is a growing chance of partition, and the longer that it takes the Africans to liberate themselves, the greater will be this chance. What is no longer possible is to expect that there will be established in southern Africa a "multi-racial" or "multi-national" government in which an African nation will lie down in peace with a European nation, and in which society and the state will be shared by these two nations.

Here, too, the "European hypothesis" casts light. The retreat of the tide of European world-domination has left this large tidal pool at the foot of the African continent. Will this pool, the pool of total European control, continue to exist there? Will it shrink and remain, or will it, like the similar pool that existed in Algeria before 1962, disappear? The answer will lie in the extent to which the dominant whites maintain their politico-military power in the south, and the extent to which the Africans, in Africa as a whole and in the south, can break this monopoly. It will also lie in the extent to which the developed world is willing to tolerate a state whose constitution is based on the thesis that Africans are unfitted to participate in its government.

The "European hypothesis" casts light on many areas of struggle in the present-day world. Why is the Communist movement of the world split into so-called revisionists (the Russians) and so-called dogmatists (the Chinese) and why is the split so bitter? Is it really because of differing interpretations of the marxist gospels? Or is it, on the "European hypothesis", because the Russians were a people who profited, and profited mightily and to the extent of half a continent, from the expansion of Europe, while the Chinese were one of the principal losers? The bitterness with which they face each other across the Pamirs and the Amur is the bitterness with which men of the Third World face the men who gained a world at their expense.

Why are the Americans fighting so hard in Vietnam? Why are the Vietcong resisting so hard? And which side will win? The Americans say that they are fighting to stop Communism from expanding into South Vietnam. But, on the "European hypothesis", they are fighting to keep in power in Saigon a government that is willing to accept the place in the world allotted to it by the Americans (on this thesis, Europeans) and to keep out of power a government that would reject this place... It is probable that the Americans will lose, for South Vietnam is too far away from the tide-line, too far from the line to which the European tide has already retreated and is still retreating. It is possible that the Americans may win a purely military victory, in the sense that the British won a military victory against the Boers in South Africa in 1902. But an American military victory in Vietnam will not be the end of the story. Eventually any Vietnam government will have to come to terms with Asia as a whole and with China in particular, and in my view the Third World will win in Vietnam, as the Boers won the peace against the British in South Africa.

The above are a few of the considerations which make it reasonable, in my view, to hold that the basic division in the world to-day stems from the expansion, and now the contraction of Europe. Within the framework of this basic division the various states are competing, jostling, warring for increased living-space and power and prestige. There are two other groupings which are important enough to unleash a world war. These other two divisions are the nationalist and the Class grouping. The nation-state took its rise almost contemporaneously with the expansion of the Europeans. That is to say that before a colonising power sent out its Magellans and its Drakes, it first achieved national unity at home. The lateness of the Italian and German colonising efforts were due largely to the lateness of the birth of the Italian and German national states. Nationalism had and has a strongly positive side: it binds together peoples who need unity, and revivifies their historical roots. But however positive nationalism can be, it has its most dangerous side. Two world wars have been begun because of nationalism, the second largely because of German nationalism artificially stimulated by Hitler. And now, twenty-five years later, American nationalism is in danger of beginning the third world war in Vietnam. Fortunately in the developed world nationalism is rapidly losing its power, and in the Third World its wane cannot be long delayed, though for the moment it is important for all the new nations in Africa and Asia to build nationalism to a certain extent: in a community where everyone belongs to a trade union nobody can afford not to belong to a trade union.

The class division of the human race is the third grouping of importance. We owe the word "class" in its political context to the marxists, and classically the marxists would divide all nations into proletarians and bourgeois, and would say that all the proletarians of the world belonged together, just as all the bourgeois belonged together. But many crises have shown that this analysis is shallow: during the Algerian war the French "proletarians" fought with their "bourgeois" against the Algerians, proletarians and bourgeois. There is however a more refined marxist analysis which would divide the world into "proletarian nations" and "bourgeois nations". On this analysis the proletarian nations, under the leadership perhaps of China, would bring pressures and force, perhaps even large-scale war to bear on the bourgeois nations. They would attempt to isolate them, form a world alliance against them, and harry them with guerrilla fighting in the equatorial forests, to win equality from them and to set up a Communist world.

Lin Piao, the Chinese minister of Defence, has likened this world-struggle against the bourgeois states with the national struggle of the Chinese Communists against the Kuomintang, and has called on the proletarian nations to put a cordon sanitaire round the bourgeois states, and to isolate them, in the way the Chinese Communists holding the countryside, isolated the Kuomintang-held cities. And, in the remote forests of Bolivia, Che Guevara has attempted to repeat the success that he and Castro achieved in Cuba in the Sierra Maestra.

Whether this vision of the future will be justified or not... and my judgement is that it will not, largely because in the final count I believe that 20th century technology will outweigh nineteenth century Marxism... there is no doubt that the class division of mankind is a reality. It is a reality if one does not try to read too much into it, or to base a philosophy on it, but simply accept that there is an immense gap between the rich world and the poor world, and that this gap may well be growing larger rather than smaller. It is a hideous truth that in a world which has become economically and scientifically one, many hundreds of millions of people eat too much and many hundreds of millions do not eat nearly enough. If each of us that eat enough or too much were to keep our consciences as sharply focussed as they ought to be, we should not be able to get a mouthful down in comfort. In this anomaly lies a major danger of chaos, revolution and war.

Here, too, the "European hypothesis" is helpful. With one exception, Japan, all the rich nations are of European origin, a fact that should not be surprising, since Europe's expansion powered and was powered by the development of industry and science. This exception, Japan, is not really an exception, for on the earlier definition of the Third World, Japan is not a member of it. Japan, though biologically non-European, was not one of the countries that suffered at the hands of the European colonialists. For a century Japan welcomed the first Europeans who, as in other countries, were the Christian missionaries. Then, with incredible foresight, noting that the danger of European conquest was growing, the Japanese expelled all Christians, i.e. Europeans, in 1639 and forbade them to visit Japan, a prohibition that lasted 210 years, until Japan was strong enough and able to join in the world as an equal.[9]

The size of the gap between the rich and the poor nations is often expressed in money terms. It shows that the richest nations have a *per capita* income about 100 times as large as that of the poorest. Yet this is clearly an exaggeration. Many of the poor nations are rural, and it is notoriously difficult to attach a money value to the transactions of peasants. Perhaps more truthful figures, yet no less telling, are the figures that show the expectation of life in the rich countries, compared with that in the poorer countries. We note here that in Sweden the expectation of life is 73 years, while in the Upper Volta it is 32 years.[10]

Many statements are made that the size of the gap is growing. Often these statements are made by politicians of the Third World, many of whom are professional political mendicants, and such statements therefore tend to be dismissed. To compare the standard of living of a Papuan against that of a Kuwaiti or of a Mississippian is probably, in the final analysis, impossible. Too little is known of the various folkways and the various satisfactions and of their relation to money for a real comparison to be possible. Nevertheless, each year, more and more skill is applied to the accurate assessment of per capita incomes, and each year the comparisons become more meaningful. It is on some of the most recent assessments that Mr. Raul Prebisch, secretary-general of the United Nations Conference on Trade and Development (UNCTAD), speaking at a meeting of that conference at Geneva on 31 August 1966, said that, during the first half of the UN Development Decade the rate of economic growth of the under-developed world had reached an overall mean of 4%, less than the lowest estimates which had been a 5% rate. He also showed how the contributions from the developed world were shrinking. In principle it had been hoped that they would give 1% of their gross national product to aid the development of the Third World. Yet, whereas they had given 0.83% in 1961, by 1965 this percentage had fallen to 0.69%.[11]

At the same gathering the acting president, Mr. Jose Pinero, said that the per capita income of the Third World had risen by only $(US) 2.00 a year in the four years 1960-1964, whereas the equivalent increase in the richer nations was $(US) 60.00 for the same period.[12]

If the size of this gap represents a danger to the world, what can be done to reduce it or remove it? The accepted philosophy is that aid and investment from the richer countries will bridge the gap. Countries such as the Ivory Coast and Madagascar, Taiwan and Hong Kong, Jordan and Libya, certainly lend weight to this thesis. Yet this accepted philosophy is far from being the whole story. A noted dissenter from it is the People's Republic of China, the most populous nation in the world, perhaps destined to assume the world leadership of the Third World. Despite earlier reliance on Russian aid, the Chinese leaders to-day state proudly that a poor country can raise itself out of abject poverty by its own efforts alone.

There is a good deal of truth in this Chinese thesis. The Japanese experience lends weight to it. Japan raised herself out of the feudal age, after the Meiji Restoration of 1868, by her own boot-strings. The Japanese received no penny of aid or investment during those early hard years. Yet, in forty years, Japan had caught up the occident in military power, and defeated Russia in the war of 1904-1905. And now, a century after the Restoration, Japan has caught up and in many ways surpassed the great European nations in economic and technological progress. The Japanese have raised themselves out of weakness by the exercise of will and intelligence. If, during those developing years, the developed European nations had rushed to help the Japanese, with aid and investment and technical cooperation, would it have been so easy for the Japanese to have developed the immense act of will that in fact raised them up? It is, to say the least of it, an open question.

There is, of course, a major difference between the Chinese and the Japanese processes of modernisation: the Japanese took over European capitalism, whereas the Chinese have taken over European Marxism as the framework for development. It will be most interesting to see whether the Chinese will do better than the Japanese. They have, after all, the immense advantage that results from a century of hindsight, and they are doubtless learning from Japan's mistakes.

It is not here suggested that Japan is a typical case. Japan was certainly as advanced as Europe before the European expansion, perhaps more advanced. In 1565 Miyako, the capital, was probably the world's greatest city with its population of 800,000. Nevertheless it is likely that, if Christianity had not been suppressed and the Europeans expelled, Japan, too, would have fallen to the near-irresistible drive that came from Europe. The success of Japanese policies, over four centuries, is due to a more accurate assessment of the European expansion than was made anywhere else in Africa, the Americas or Asia.

It is likely that the gap will eventually be closed, but not rapidly, much as the similar gap between the living standards of the European and American working classes on the one hand, and

97

the upper classes on the other, was reduced. It was reduced by a multi-pronged attack on poverty, low wages, bad education, by the use of trade-union power and by the religious appeal to conscience. It has taken the working class of Britain well over a century to remove the most glaring inequalities between their condition and the condition of the rich, and on the world scale we shall be doing well to remove greater inequalities in an inherently more difficult and complex situation in three centuries. Will the world's poor have the patience to wait as long as this? Or will they take up more drastic weapons to force the tide of European power backwards and to extort either that the poor must be enriched, or that the rich must be robbed of their wealth?

The answer to this question lies in the future interplay of individual leadership and of social and political currents, an interplay which also includes a large measure of luck and is therefore fundamentally not foreseeable. Much will however depend on the future performance of the Europeans. To what extent will the European tide retreat? To what extent will the future image of the human race be a European image? To what extent will the Europeans maintain their present leadership? And to what extent will the inheritance of European biological and cultural traits be correlated with power, wealth and prestige?

We saw earlier that the power-struggle is really a struggle to preempt the future with the aim that the world of one's grandchildren should be constructed according to a scale of values of which one approves. Certainly most Europeans desire that the preponderantly European character of the world would be preserved.

In fifty years the human race has lost much of the exclusively European character that it used to have. But has the change been adequate? Only a long-range look-back in history can suggest the answer. If there had been a United Nations General Assembly in the year 1400, its character would not have been particularly European. There would, on the other hand, have been gorgeous delegations from the Inca, Mayan, Aztec, Indian, Chinese, Japanese, Polynesian, and Arabian peoples; Siberian tribes, Mongols, Turks, as well as European and African delegations (dressed at that time in *genuine* African attire!) The European delegations would have done well to have rivalled in numbers and splendour those from India alone.

Five hundred years later, the expansion of Europe had changed the public *persona* of the human race. In 1919 when the League of Nations was established and the Peace of Versailles signed, the tide of European world-domination reached perhaps its high water mark. With few exceptions those great international gatherings were gatherings of Europeans. Dressed in European dress, they spoke through an assembly created on European pattern to a world created by Europeans in which Africa and Asia appeared on sufferance.

Twenty-seven years later, when the United Nations held its first General Assembly in 1946, the balance was already much juster, and, as Asia and Africa freed themselves from colonial status, the balance became juster still over the next fifteen years. In about 1960-1963 the United Nations reached its peak of power. It is no coincidence that these years corresponded with those years when Africa was not over-represented in the General Assembly. But as the tide of African independence continued to flow, more and more of the postulant members were micro-states, and Africa became grossly over-represented. To-day the pattern of power inside the world body bears only a tenuous relationship with the pattern of real economic, political and military power in the world outside. Gambia, for example, has inside the UN a vote equal to that of the United States with thousands of times the power of Gambia, As a result, the power of the United Nations has sunk to a low point, and meaningful diplomacy now goes on outside, rather than inside its framework.

If meaningful diplomacy now takes place outside its framework, it is also true that the real political struggle, the struggle over the world's finances, armaments, trade, space and frontier readjustments, goes on outside. This struggle is still overwhelmingly dominated by the Europeans, the Haves. The major struggle during the next hundred years will inevitably be: to what extent will the exclusive club of the Haves open its doors to Asia and Africa? Everything points to the changes being slow, yet everything also points to the changes being ineluctable, if for no other reason than that in this democratic age the Europeans number scarce a third of the human race.

To what extent will the slow backward movement of the Europeans be territorial? The question is anxiously considered in countries like Australia, for if the European tide were to ebb too far it might sweep them away with it, like some piece of stranded driftwood sucked back to sea by some unusually strong backwash, deep enough to have floated it off its temporary stranding-place.

And if important changes are ineluctable, in what way will they occur? Most political changes in history have occurred as a result of war and violence. Yet, in theory, war is now outlawed; and disputes are supposed to be submitted to the Security Council. Yet, as we have seen, the Security Council is increasingly impotent.

There is, nevertheless, a fairly strong tradition of peaceful change, a tradition that seems to be growing as it creates its own precedents, though even here such change is often made under the threat of more violent change. Sweden and Norway, one kingdom until 1905, decided by mutual consent to become two kingdoms, and sixty years have proved the rightness of the decision. In 1962 the Netherlands gave up the Western New Guinea to become, subject to a plebiscite to be held in 1969, part of Indonesia. This settlement was as a result of peaceful negotiations under the aegis of the United Nations. And Singapore quietly seceded from the Federation of Malaysia in 1965.

Despite this tradition of peaceful change, there have been a far greater number of examples in this most brutal century, of changes effected by unprecedented violence. One thinks first, of course, of the destruction of the Jewish communities of Western and Central Europe by the Nazis. But our century can show other massacres which are less well-known yet nearly as indefensible.

Six hundred thousand to a million Armenians, quite unable to defend themselves, were suddenly massacred by the Turks in Turkey in 1915.[13] In suppressing the Madagascar rising of 1947 the French are said to have killed between 20,000 and 100,000

Malagasy.[14] In a few seconds, at Hiroshima and Nagasaki, some 150,000 Japanese civilians were snuffed out by the two operational American atomic bombs. Near the end of the Second World War British and American bomber planes killed some 135,000 defenceless German civilians in Dresden which was at the time an open city, and which was crammed with helpless refugees from further east.[15] Perhaps 500,000 Communists and sympathisers were killed in Indonesian massacres in 1965-1966.

In less directly murderous ways, but none the less cruel, in 1943 the Soviet government exiled, and thus destroyed, killing the majority, seven of the smaller peoples belonging to the Soviet Union: the Chechens, the Ingushes, the Karachai, the Balkar, the Kalmyks (a tribe of harmless Buddhist nomads), the Crimean Tartars, and the Volga Germans. Of these peoples the Volga Germans and the Chechens and Ingushes had been previously given the security of being granted the status of constituent republic or Autonomous Region of the Soviet Union. This paper status did not help them when they were rounded up by the Red Army and herded into cattle-trucks and sent to the far ends of the Union. Often the men went east, while the women and children went west.

Tough Russian policies of enforcing change on Central Asia continue, and the government is continuing to settle millions of Russians and Ukrainians (white Europeans) in the lands that rightly belong to the Uzbeks, Tadjiks and Kazakhs, so that in Central Asia the Europeans already amount to 40% of the population, and in Kazakhstan they already outnumber the Kazakhs.[16] Apt to learn some of the more unpleasant behaviour of their Soviet teachers, the Chinese, it is reported, are following a policy of obliterating the Tibetan people, not by direct massacre but by a process of pouring in millions of Han Chinese settlers, so that the distinctive cultural and sociological character of Tibet shall be ploughed under, and their nationality stifled in their own country.

In 1926, in the Soviet Union, by a deliberate act of the government, a million Ukrainian peasants were starved to death so that collectivised farming might be imposed, a form of farming that has not proved a success. And, after the Second World War, by a unilateral decision of the Soviet government, no fewer than ten million Germans, most of them quite innocent of any crimes, were expelled from Prussia, Brandenburg, Silesia, and other lands that had been German for many centuries.

The above are just a few of the brutalities perpetrated by the twentieth century, the century in the course of which knowledge and science have reached their zenith. What is relevant to the present study is that the worst of these brutalities were committed by the Germans, one of the most cultured and educated peoples of all. The Europeans pride themselves on being the leaders of world-culture, yet no excesses, no cruelties, no aggression, and no massacres in the whole of world history have approached those perpetrated by the Europeans. Here again we see the sinister correlation: the greater the power and the knowledge, the greater the cruelty.

And when one thinks of the two super-powers, the United States and the Soviet Union, calmly aiming their doomsday weapons at each other and calculating the expected deaths in hundreds of millions, then the correlation becomes even clearer.

Does all this mean that humanity has reached the stage when all should be unconditional pacifists? By no means. In our times there have been several just wars. One thinks of the Irish rebellion against the English, when they rose and cut the Gordian knot that had constricted them for centuries; one thinks of the Algerian revolution against French colonial domination; and one thinks of the right claimed by the oppressed African people of South Africa, at some time in the future to take up arms against their oppressors. In each of these situations all peaceful and constitutional methods had been tried by the oppressed, without any success. In each of these situations I have little doubt that future ages will look back in approval at the taking up of arms.

It seems, then, that the problem of change is still only partly soluble by peaceful methods, and that humanity still will have to have recourse to limited wars where the international bodies are unable to modify the *status quo* adequately or in time for institutions to reflect the realities of life.

Limited wars tend to be guerrilla wars, and the twentieth

century is replete with examples of justified and successful guerrilla wars. This is not to say that guerrilla war is a legitimate weapon in every crisis. In particular, to foment guerrilla war in Latin America can only hold back the conquest of poverty there, and can serve but one purpose: the purpose of the anti-American world conspiracy. Mexico's experience over the last twenty years, during which the maize crop has been doubled through the use of hybrid corn, and during which there has been an immense economic expansion, raising per capita income, is surely an indication that real economic progress is possible, even in Latin America, through normal and peaceful ways.

On the other hand, there are areas in which guerrilla war may be the only way, and some of these areas may be felt to be somewhat surprising. There is a good case to be made for the use of guns by the Afro-Americans in the United States in, self-defence and to earn the apprehensive respect of white Americans. Up till the present it is the whites who have presumed to use force and to kill in their clashes with the Afro-Americans, whether such force was legal and justified or not. The use of guns by the Afro-Americans might paradoxically bring nearer the day when their white fellow-citizens understand that it is not enough merely to legislate civil rights, and that the black Americans can have no peace, and can allow them no peace, until all the hearts and doors in America are open to all Americans.

It may shock many white Americans to think of guerrilla war being a legitimate method of struggle in the modern world. Most such risings have admittedly been planned by America's enemies, the Communists. And in their eagerness to defeat the Communists everywhere a whole department of so-called "counter-insurgency" has been set up inside the Pentagon. It would be well for this department, and for the United States government as a whole to remember that if they do set out to smother insurgency everywhere, they will be attempting to prevent changes in the life of the peoples being reflected in institutional changes. And they will have cast themselves in the disagreeable role of being the Hapsburgs of the twentieth century, a strange role for a people which proudly won its own independence at the point of the musket...

One might have thought that the failure of the Americans to impose their will in Vietnam, the failure of the world's mightiest military power to crush one of the world's smaller peoples into submission, would have shown the weakness of mere military strength against a well-matched combination of political and military and nationalist strength. But unfortunately at the date of writing this, May 1967, there is no indication that the Americans have learnt the lesson. And there is every indication that they continue to confuse the two concepts of "very powerful" and "all-powerful", and that under the guise of being "the world's policeman" they are prepared to oppose every outbreak of anti-American military power, right round the globe, with unlimited American military assistance. Such an attitude has won certain political dividends, such as the withdrawal of the Russian missiles from Cuba, and, perhaps, the collapse of the Indonesian Communists. But it is a game that two can play at, and the day may come when the Russians are able to walk nearer the brink than are the Americans.

Fortunately it is a game that, till now, only two can play at, and the rest of us can devote ourselves to creeping into our burrows and writing our wills.

If only the Americans had more confidence in the attractiveness of what they say they are fighting for: free-enterprise and democracy. The whole movement of the world shows that most men everywhere want these things and the prosperity that they have brought to Europe and America, in the intellectual field the seduction of Marxism is a thing of the past. As that is so, would it not be wiser to be calm and let these great ideas make their own way in the world. Here again, surely the Japanese have a lesson for the world. Since 1945 they have settled down to a life without an army and almost without a foreign policy, a foreign policy so modest that they themselves term it a "low-posture" foreign policy. They have turned to serving the world and themselves in the commercial field. Twenty-one years later their influence is far higher in the world than it would have been if they had spent their substance in maintaining a fleet and armies "west of Suez". They have shown the traditional virtues of modesty and industry, and they have done it by adopting the American virtues of democracy and free-enterprise. Japan's success stands out like a brilliant beacon in an orient dark with the failures of the Communists. To the north the Japanese see the Russian Communists rapidly becoming western liberals. The Chinese Communists in the west display the writings of Maoism in Mao's last years; and to the south they see the wreckage of the Indonesian Communist party, the biggest in the world that had not managed to seize power.

There's every reason, in this and the following century, to feel confidence in the strength of the liberal system. Unlike the autocracies and dictatorships it embodies the principle of feedback, the two-way flow of energy and information that is the basic principle of life and, now, of cybernetics. Just as the helmsman (cybernetes) keeps his eye on the horizon and his hand on the tiller, just as he uses data collected by the former to correct the movements of the latter, so does the modern democratic leader govern with his ear to the ground, gathering every available murmur of popular reaction to his government. Freedom of speech guarantees, in a democracy, a high level of feedback. And, in commerce, the same principle permits the customer, in the market, to prevail over the producer and the middleman.

From its foundation in 1917 state Communism has denied the principle of feedback. In the October revolution Lenin's Bolsheviks seized power from Kerensky' s democrats in order to impose Communism on the Russian state and the whole society of the Russian Empire. The confidence of the Bolsheviks, acquired no doubt from having read excerpts from DAS KAPITAL, or from at least having placed it prominently on their bookshelves, resembled the confidence gained from books of similar obscurity by Muslims and Protestants. With this confidence they imagined that if only they could capture the state they could use the state power to communise all life by a unidirectional flow of power. The absence of feedback encouraged the Bolsheviks to establish the most intimidating dictatorship of the century, and under Stalin it is notorious that the only free speech in the Soviet Union was in the vast concentration camps, camps that held, at their height, perhaps 20-25 million detainees and that significantly reduced the population. True figures were not published until well after the Second World War when the deaths caused by Stalin could be masked behind the deaths caused by Hitler.

What is inspiring now inside the Soviet Union is to see that the Lenin idea for the remaking of society has been quietly abandoned, and that the principle of feedback in both politics and commerce is making its appearance. With greater freedom it will be interesting to note what will happen when the immense achievements of pre-revolutionary Russian free-enterprise receive their due honour [17].

When public debate is once again unrestricted in the Soviet Union, books such as Lenin's will stimulate the inevitable question: if this is what we Russians could achieve under capitalism eighty years ago, and if we are now returning to a greater measure of private enterprise and freer government, was the Revolution of 1917 with its immeasurable suffering really necessary? If to-day we are given to understand that we went too far in collectivising and centralising agriculture, and that to-day we are freeing farmers from unnecessary controls, did a million peasants die in the Ukraine for nothing? When that day comes books like these will shake Russia. And such is the contrariness of human nature that it may well be the Russians who will demonstrate to an astonished Third World how precious is the right of an individual to found and operate business privately and freely.

All this is not to say that, for the rest of time, capitalism will be with us. It has obvious faults, even though governments have everywhere compelled it to put aside its more shocking harshnesses. For our time, however, it is surely still better and gentler than its only competitor, and twice as efficient.

One of the ways in which social control can be wisely extended to business is through the growth of businesses in size. Like the state, which, as we have seen, tends over the ages to grow in size, so business also tends to grow in size until it is essential for government (under the control of the voter) and business (under the control of the consumer) to interpenetrate each other.

And if through this interpenetration capitalism can be still further civilised, the human race may be yet enriched for many generations by its "colossal productive forces". Nevertheless, capitalism, like its competitors, remains the law of the jungle, that old evolutionary law that says that life fills the living-space available, and that the fittest survives and that the unsuitable and weak go to the wall. As in the case of states, this law, over the ages, has produced a tendency for human organisations to grow in size. This tendency must, in the end, result in a world state, a development that is urgently necessary if peace is to be assured and if there is to be any early reduction in human inequality. Perhaps the growth in size which is due to the old law of the jungle may be the means of one day repealing the law of the jungle.

The growth of human populations makes this repeal a matter of urgency. If it is not soon repealed, the collision of group with group, and of Man as a whole with nature, must leave our lovely planet an evil-smelling slagheap, a desert, and perhaps a smoking and radio-active ruin.

REFERENCES

(1)   From *The Souls of Black folk, 1903.*

(2)   cf. Chapter 5.

(3)   Quoted by Eugene M. Zuckert, in "The Service Secretary, *Foreign Affairs,* April 1966, p.476.

(4)   South African: for a cattle enclosure. The term used in East Africa is the Arabic word *zeriba.*

(5)   "The Muscovite conquest of Siberia (got under way) after the capture of Kazan (in 1552)… It then went rapidly ahead, proceeding from the north. The only opponents were the primitive tribes armed with nothing more than bows and arrows. In 1558 Ivan (the Terrible) made a large grant of land along the Kama River to the Stroganov family *of* merchant-adventurers and colonisers. This settlement was soon developed into a vast commercial enterprise, which exploited to the full the natural resources of the region and also of the trans-Ural areas - iron-ore deposits, copper, tin, lead and sulphur. *Muscovite penetration has been well compared to the operation of the last India Company* in *combination with the Spanish conquest of Peru and Mexico."* - from *The Making of Modern Russia,* by Lionel Kochan, Penguin Books, A 529; page 58 (My emphasis).

(6) The feelings aroused in some Asians by the European expansion are shown in a 1955 edition of the Koran (translated by Maulawi Sher'Ali, Rabwah, West Pakistan). At the end there are given certain explanations of Arabic words. One of the words is "jinn". Five definitions are given and the first is the usual one of "evil spirits… agents of Satan." The third reads as follows: "the inhabitants of northern hilly tracts of Europe, of white and red colour, whom other peoples looked upon as beings separate from other human beings and who lived detached from the civilised peoples of Asia but who were destined to make great material progress in the latter days and to lead a great revolt against religion".

(7) Sir Alexander Carr-Saunders: *World Population.* Oxford 1936, pp, 50, 56.

(8) *The Oxford Dictionary of English Etymology.* ed. C. T. Onions, 1966.

(9) The Dutch, who were permitted to stay on at Deshima near Nagasaki and to trade during all the years when Japan was closed to the outside world, persuaded the Japanese to make an exception in their case by a stratagem that contains some theological humour. Being Protestants, and the expelled Christians being Catholics, the Dutch told the Japanese that they were not Christians like the others. Permission was granted to them on condition they trampled and spat once a year on the cross, which they did quite happily. Profits were good.

(10) UN Demographic Year book for 1963.

(11) *Le Monde,* 2 September 1966.

(12) *Le Monde,* 1 September 1966.

(13) At least 600,000 died and another 600,000, including many kidnapped women, were lost. "The forgotten Final Solution", *The Observer,* 25 April 1965.

(14) Since writing the above, I have seen, in *Le Monde* of 4 April. 1967, a letter from the distinguished ex-governor and professor Hubert Deschamps. He says that in his book, *Histoire de Madagascar* 1960, he wrote that the total death-roll of the rising was 11,342, of which only 4,126 were killed by the French, and that this figure, based on a careful investigation, has never been contradicted with good evidence. In the face of this I think that the widely-believed figure quoted in the text above may be allowed to sleep.

(15) According to David Irving's *The Destruction of Dresden,* New York, 1964, "135,000 died on 13 and 14 February 1945", and the view is expressed in the book that "the raids were not justified".

(16) From "China in Central Asia", by Sir Olaf Caroe; *The Round Table* No. 224, October 1966, page 381.

(17) Amusingly, one of the most eloquent and best documented accounts of the achievements of Russian capitalism was written by Lenin himself, partly in exile. It is called *The Development of Capitalism in Russia* (2nd,

revised, edition, 1908). Lenin's purpose in writing it was, admittedly, to prove to the Narodniks that capitalism had really arrived, and therefore that Russia was ready for the "next stage". In the course of his argument, Lenin shows, with a forest of statistics, how dramatic and sudden had been the development of production caused by the capitalist developments of the fourth quarter of the nineteenth century, the age of the building of the Russian railways. Space is wanting to do more than quote the railways statistics themselves, but they give an index of the speed at which development was taking place in all fields, agricultural as well as industrial. Lenin records that "from 1865 to 1875, the average annual increase in the length of the railway system was 1,500 km, and from 1893 to 1897 about 2,500km The amount of railway freight carried was as follows: 1868: 7 million tons; 1873: 18 million; 1881: 41 million; 1893: 78 million; 1896: 99 million; 1904: 178 million, representing an increase of 2500 in 36 years… No less dramatic was the growth of passenger traffic; 1868: 10.4 million passengers; 1873: 22.7; 1881: 34.4; 1893: 49.4; 1896: 65.5; 1904: 123.6 million". - see pp. 552 et seq. of the English reprint of the 1908 edition. Lenin was not surprised by the vitality of capitalism. After all, Marx and Engels themselves had spoken about this vitality in the *Communist Manifesto* of 1848: "The bourgeoisie has… accomplished wonders far surpassing Egyptian pyramids, Roman aqueducts, and Gothic cathedrals… the bourgeoisie, during its rule of scarce one hundred years, has created more massive and more colossal productive forces than have all preceding generations together". - see pp. 44, 47 of 1965 edition, Moscow.

5 The Scientific Age

"Be fruitful, and multiply and replenish the earth and subdue it: and have dominion over the fish of the sea, and over the fowl of the air, and over every living thing that moveth upon the earth." [1]

Three earlier developments, each important enough to deserve the appellation "super-event" increased Man's power to such a degree as to change the quality of his life. The first was the weapon: with its killing power a higher ape dominated the other animals and became Man. The second was agriculture: on its food surpluses Man built his first cities. And the third was the state: on its power he built the structure of his politics and his wars.

There is a fourth super-event, equalling the earlier three in importance and in its capacity to change the quality of Man's life. That is the development of the scientific method and its application to every branch of activity.

As with the earlier super-events, no precise date can be set down for the birth of the scientific age. Yet, with some precision, it may be set down at 250-300 years ago. The tide of science, having sent a wavelet ahead some 2,500 years ago to the beaches of Greek Ionia, began to flow in earnest in about 1650-1700 AD, when Europe's best minds formally rid themselves of the idea of the infallibility of the ancient authors. Soon the ideas of science were being applied to the industrial and economic fields, and here they caused the dramatic expansion that has been called "the industrial revolution". This expansion first became important in the eighteenth century in England.

Three centuries later the ideas of science have been accepted in all provinces of knowledge; and in the industrial age, with its market, its timetables and its ideology is now a reality for about one third of the human race, and is now spreading to the other two-thirds.

The scientific method is a new rigorous method of discovering and recording truth. It respects only such hypotheses as will stand up to experiment. It cares nothing for the unproved beliefs of former ages, nor for the subjective distortions of individuals or nations. It has already radically altered the conditions of life for a third of the human race. Here are just a few of the effects of the scientific age: In three centuries Man has discovered and mapped the world's land surface, and has greatly altered it. He has changed the composition of the atmosphere, and is beginning to discover and map the contents of the oceans. He has spun a spherical network of communications round the planet, a network which already touches every human community, however isolated. He has sent communications filaments to the Moon and past Mars and Venus. Soon human travellers will follow these probes. He has cut death-rates, no unmixed blessing as we shall see; and he has even revived the dead. He has split the atomic nucleus, and converted mass into energy. He has built vast fleets of passenger, freight and military aircraft: in thirty years the atmosphere has replaced the sea and land as the most important field of international transportation. He has built electrical brains that are comparable in some respects with human brains and that operate much faster.

These achievements are only a few of the many new developments that have given Man godlike powers, powers far beyond the imagination of the fathers and the grandfathers of this generation. Naturally, the effects on human life have been remarkable, and it is likely that the quality of life has changed more in the last three hundred years in the developed countries than it had changed in the previous three hundred thousand.

In no field has the change been more impressive than in the field of medicine. We are approaching a near-total victory over disease. Plagues whose very names have terrified men for thousands of years: plague, cholera, syphilis, tuberculosis, malaria and leprosy, have lost much of their power, and the secret of cancer is being prised open by determined research in many countries. As a result, the death-rates have been rapidly reduced. The birth-rates however, save in the richer countries, have not been similarly reduced, and as a result the world's population is ballooning faster than ever before. Such is the fecundity of our age that the terrible modern wars which have carried millions of dead down Time's never-ending stream have had almost no restraining effect on the increase. The effects of these two world wars may be looked for in vain in all except the most detailed graphs of the population. The following graph shows an almost unbroken rise for all the continents. The curve is upward, and it is becoming exponential.

Fig. 3.

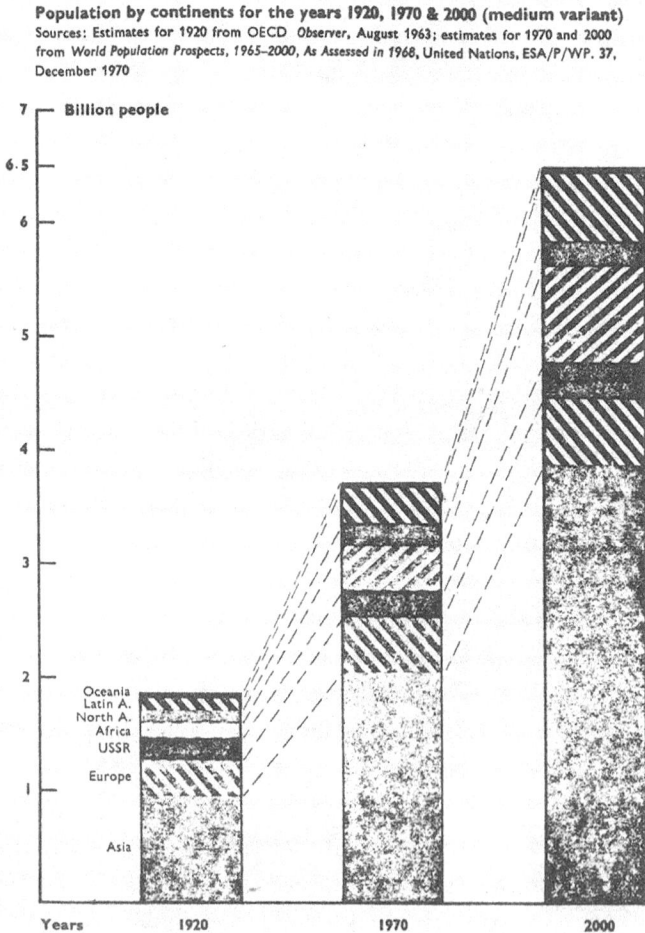

Population by continents for the years 1920, 1970 & 2000 (medium variant)
Sources: Estimates for 1920 from OECD *Observer*, August 1963; estimates for 1970 and 2000 from *World Population Prospects, 1965–2000, As Assessed in 1968*, United Nations, ESA/P/WP. 37, December 1970

The special character of the Asian population stands out from this graph, and as the decades roll on, the fate of the whole human race seems to be becoming ever more dependent on the fate of its Asian branch. (See Figure 3.)

Hitherto there has been much guesswork in the estimating of the human populations, but the counts are being performed with ever-increasing accuracy, and the techniques of collecting accurate vital statistics are spreading to the newer countries. The United Nations Organisation, in its Demographic Yearbook, has collected a great array of facts, and there are, in addition, various public or semi-public bodies round the world which have made it their job to collect and publish such information. One of these is the Population Reference Bureau, of 1755 Massachusetts Avenue, Washington, to whom the accompanying table is due: (See World Population Data Sheet which is printed as an appendix to this book)

According to the above, the population of the world stood at 3,479 millions in mid-1968. As we saw in Chapter 2, the population of stone-age hunters, over the whole world, has been estimated to have been five millions some eight thousand years ago. Agriculture enabled an immense multiplication to take place, so that, at the time of Christ, there may have been 500 millions. For the Roman Empire alone Gibbon's estimate was 12.0 millions in the time of Claudius (50 AD). With the decline and fall of the Roman Empire it is likely that the population did not rise much above 500 millions during the next 1400 years, and the best estimates are that there may have been 500 millions in about 1600 AD. Thereafter, with the expansion of Europe, and with the scientific and industrial revolutions, there followed a rapid multiplication. By the end of the nineteenth century the total passed the billion mark. By 1930 it had passed the 2 billion mark. In 1959 it passed the 3 billion mark, and is due to pas s the 4 billion mark in the mid 1970s, That is to say that it took Man a million years to reach the first billion whereas at the present rate of increase each remaining decade of this century will see the total rise by more than a billion. And unless a catastrophe occurs, according to the United Nations figures, the population will have exceeded 7 billions by the end of the century, for there is little that can be done and that the human race is prepared to do, to slow this increase in the 33 years that are left.[2]

The crowding of the world is already almost intolerable. Most Africans, and I speak from my own point of view as an African - find the countries of Western Europe oppressively small and over-populated. Few who have enjoyed the delight of the wide horizons can ever settle comfortably in the cribbed hutches of Europe. Wide horizons have their own contribution to make to creativity, and it is significant that two of the super-powers, the United States and the Soviet Union, are still relatively empty lands, lands in which each citizen has the knowledge that, if he should need it, absolute solitude is still available.

If the crowding is almost intolerable in Europe, it is already intolerable in the great cities of the Third World. In these cities there exists a vast and undifferentiated proletariat which exhibits a huge birth-rate. To this natural increase is added a tide of immigration from the countryside, as a wretched peasantry spills its surplus into the pool of the wretched unemployed proletariat of the cities.

Calcutta now holds six million people. It is already unable to accommodate them, and not only do millions live in filth and squalor, but hundreds of thousands sleep in the streets, for they have no homes or beds. Yet the curve of Calcutta's increase shows no signs of flattening. According to one observer, the city will probably contain 12-16 million in the 1970's, and his extrapolations for the population of this single giant city in the year 2000 AD range from a lower figure of 35.6 millions to an upper figure of 66 millions.[3]

One of the world's most alarming demographic situations exists in Peru, a country without an apparently alarming overall density of population.[4] The estimate for mid-1965 was 11.7 millions, but it has a population growth rate of 2.8% (one of the world's highest), and at present rates the population will triple by the year 2000 AD. Sixty per cent of Peru's labour force is employed in agriculture, though there is less than 0.2. ha. (0.5 acre) of arable land per head. Food consumption is of the order of only 2000 calories a day. Less than half the population is literate, and one third of the population cannot speak Spanish, the official language. Life expectancy has increased from 34 years to 57 years since 1940, and the population of Lima, the capital, has increased three-fold since 1940, yet 60% of the population of the capital have no electricity supply; only 11% of the population has adequate housing; and 66% of the roads are unpaved.[5]

How in the light of such figures, can a largely illiterate and underfed population of parents give birth to anything but a largely illiterate and underfed generation of children? As one looks into the future no light is visible. At this time there are ten cities in Latin America with more than a million inhabitants: there are expected to be 26 by 1980.[6] And similar increases of populations living in urban squalor are occurring throughout the Third World.

Those who suffer the fate of having to live in such cities, and those who control their destinies, undergo the tortures of Tantalus and suffer the pangs of thirst just out of the reach of water. For coexisting with the appalling underemployment that is the trademark of the Third World, is the need for huge infrastructural works for roads, drains, water-supplies, electricity, sewage and hospitals. The two missing factors are skills and capital. It is safe to say that to a rapidly increasing extent the main preoccupation of the world's rulers will henceforth be the making of a place - in the fullest sense - for the billions now fated to be born during this century.

It follows from the above that the highest priority in the poorer lands is an effective contraception policy. Such a policy is necessary for the prosperity of the world as a whole. And, as the Japanese have demonstrated, it is also necessary for the prosperity of the country in question. It is no coincidence that the astonishing economic progress of the Japanese since 1945 has occurred at the same time as the unique success of their contraception and abortion policy. Perhaps this Japanese success is even more relevant for the Third World than has been Europe's more gradual success in the same field. There is no more authoritative witness to this Japanese success than Mr. Chikao Honda, chairman of Japan's Population Problems. Research Council. He has written: "Hard-pressed by the rapid increase in the population, Japan has had to deal with it by her own efforts. And she did it with a noticeable success. An epoch was made in the nation's birth-control movement in 1948 when the Japanese Diet passed the Eugenic Protection Law to permit induced abortion and sterilization. Since then the number of induced abortions increased year after year until 1955 when a total of 1,170,000 cases were officially recorded. This was about five times as many as the figure for 1949. Birth-control, the practice of contraception in particular, was now widely recognised by both the government and private organisations… Despite the post-war baby boom in Japan, the birth-rate has steadily declined, due to a planned parenthood movement. According to official statistics, the birth-rate in 1959 registered 17.55 per thousand - nearly half the birth-rate in 1947, the year it hit the post- war peak."[7]

Will the Third World follow Japan's example? Perhaps the best hope lies in the expanding frontier of contraceptive knowledge, that some totally undemanding and foolproof technique which is safe and cheap will be discovered.

Will China, in particular, follow Japan's example? It might be that China's rulers still see political advantage in a rapidly expanding population. In this case the outlook for China and the world is serious. The question is important, since China is at the same time the most populous and the most dissatisfied of the nations. The few answers that come out of China to this question are contradictory.

No reliable figures exist for China's population. The best current estimate was 710 millions for mid-1965. Its vital statistics are quite unknown, though Chinese sources claim an annual growth rate of 2%, which would give an annual *increase* of 14 millions. An optimistic answer to the question appears in the view expressed by Dr. Kan Majima, a Japanese pioneer of contraception. He said: "From this last visit to China (a visit during which he met Chou En-Lai, the prime minister) I bring back the certitude that the leaders in Peking are much less preoccupied with invading the world with famished millions than with braking the increase in the birth-rate, in order to prepare, in future, a logical and human relationship between the number of mouths to be fed and the available food. Much has been said about the Chinese demographic peril. Everything to-day points to the fact that the Chinese government knows this peril better than others."[8]

Unfortunately, there is little supporting evidence for Dr. Majima's certitude, and it is known that for some time China's rulers have made a habit of speaking moderately to Japanese visitors. Other reports are far more pessimistic. One followed the visit to China of a French women's delegation in 1966. The visit was interestingly recorded by one of the delegates named Ménie Grégoire. In Shanghai the delegation visited the main maternity hospital, and put some questions to the matron, who said that contraceptive advice was given to women, but only for reasons of health, and not for any population limitation policy. "We do not wish to reduce the birth-rate", she said, "Our annual rate of increase is 2% and is perfectly reasonable... China is rich. She can feed her children. We are only cultivating to-day the ninth part of our area. Our main need to-day is manpower."[9]

The matron's views are, of course, nonsense. The eight-ninths of China that are not cultivated are marginal lands with low potential yields, and so the babies that she encourages. to come into the world will have an even harder task than their parents - and heaven knows that the lot of the Chinese peasant is and always has been a hard lot - to draw sustenance from the crowded soils of China. To what end her attitude? It can only be political: that the voice of a billion Chinese will be more audible than is the voice of the present 710 millions in the counsels of mankind.

Nevertheless it is not from the communists that has come the most obstinate opposition to contraception. As all know, the Roman Catholic Church has an unequalled record of blind opposition to any artificial limitation of births. Repeatedly, international conferences have failed to make progress towards the control of births because of the need to placate this vast interest-group. For example, "Dr. Abraham Stone, one of the leaders of the American planned parenthood movement, was invited by the government of India (in 1951) through the World Health Organisation (WHO) to investigate the possibilities of reducing fertility in Indian villages. Since the Catholic countries in WHO threatened to resign if he advocated birth-control by contraceptives, he had to agree to propose limiting births only by the rhythm method."[10]

Even in Japan the Catholics tried to prevent the occurrence of the family planning miracle, for when the government, with the backing of the Supreme Commander Allied Powers, introduced the legislation mentioned above, the Catholic Women's Club of Tokyo-Yokohama protested.[11] Fortunately the intended sabotage was unsuccessful.

At the time of writing in April 1967 the official Roman Catholic position is still defined in the encyclical "Casti connubii" dated 31 December 1930. In this encyclical Pope Pius XI had laid down solemnly: "The Catholic Church... raises her voice... any use whatsoever of matrimony exercised in such a way that the act is deliberately frustrated in its natural power to generate life is an offence against the law of God and of nature, and those who indulge in such are branded with the guilt of grave sin."[12]

It is true that this church is in the process of re-considering its attitude, and that there is a commission of 50 experts which in early 1966 was charged with re-defining this attitude. Since then, leaks from the Vatican indicate that though the commission has recommended a considerable liberalisation, the conservative opposition has successfully mobilised itself against any change, and that no change is likely in the foreseeable future. The Pope himself said unmistakably that the Roman Catholic Church could not act quickly in the matter. Passions on the subject tend to run high, and the Pope is probably weighing whether the losses of church members who are more and more leaving the church in order to practice contraception are more serious than the probable withdrawal of the conservative wing which might well follow a decision to liberalise.

The population crisis is due to birth rates that are too high and death-rates that are too low. And so, not only should it stimulate a rethinking on the subject of contraception and abortion: it should stimulate a rethinking on the subjects of suicide and euthanasia. None of these great questions can be decided if the overall direction of human progress is not defined, and I shall give my definition later. In this definition I state that an optimum human population should be aimed at, and that there are probably already more people in the world than this optimum figure. It follows that there should be a more favourable attitude to euthanasia and suicide than has existed in the past, and that they should be freed from the atmosphere of false mystery and hysteria which now surrounds them.

There is surely a basic right to suicide. If a man has reached the point where he wishes to resign from the human race, why should he be prevented? Why should his friends not ease his path, if they feel that the decision has been calmly and rationally made, for this path is difficult enough in all conscience? Other ages have admired suicide: for the defeated Republican Roman and the disgraced Japanese officer suicide was *de rigueur,* and the ages to which they belonged were not the least honourable of history.

Euthanasia is more difficult to justify because it appears to contravene the age-old prohibition of murder. Yet there are obviously times and places when euthanasia is justified. How can the prolongation of life in a hopelessly-ill patient be justified if the patient wants to die? How can the keeping alive of helpless defective children be justified? There are at least two sides to this most difficult question, but to me the clinching argument is that in a world of unlimited suffering and limited medical care it is in any case necessary to ration the medical care and to choose which lives shall be saved. In addition many thousands of doctors would admit if they were to confess frankly that they had many times acted to shorten suffering by shortening life. And so, in practice, euthanasia has always been with us.

A frank statement that euthanasia will be with us to an increasing extent in the future appears in a lecture given by Mr. Bourgeois-Pichat, director of the French National Institute of Demographic Studies (INED). Speaking at the first European demographic conference held at Strasbourg on 30 August 1966, he showed how Man's rapidly increasing control of death would lead inevitably to the need to choose who should live long. "Tomorrow's death", he said, "will thus be a social phenomenon for which we must now invent the laws."[13]

Such laws are now being invented in England. The main stimulus has been the invention of new methods of treating gross failure of the kidneys. The lives of such sufferers can now be saved by kidney transplants and also by artificial kidney machines which remove wastes from the blood by haemodialysis. Unfortunately, the cost of such treatment is prohibitive if all are to receive it, even for a community as rich as the British. In Britain there are about 2000 new occurrences of kidney failure each year. To treat 2000 would cost between £7 and £16 million in capital equipment alone, a cost beyond the community's resources. So, some will live while others are to be left to die. The trouble is that no one has yet worked out the criteria for judging that one human life is more valuable than another. Is a philosopher in his nineties more or less valuable than a new-born infant? Is a lovely young woman more or less valuable than a 55-year old mathematician? The doctors have shrunk from the responsibility of deciding, and in Nottingham they have persuaded some responsible citizens to form a secret panel for considering such cases. And so these life-and-death decisions will be made by an unknown panel in secret according to criteria unknown to the patient and to the public. Such an arrangement is unlikely to be acceptable in the long run.

This English dilemma is likely to reappear in other countries and in England with increasing frequency and to present our age with one of its thorniest moral problems. Thus, once again, does the technological age pose ineluctably the problem of the very nature of Man and of life. As techniques improve for the use of biological spare parts, for the use of new methods of fertilisation, and for the lengthening of life's span, this central question will present itself ever less avoidably.

Just how immense are the possibilities of lengthening life was suggested in a lecture given in London in 1966 by a professor of physiology. He told a young audience that some of them might live to be 180 years old, and that ages of 200 years were not impossible to imagine.

Men have prayed for victory over death for thousands of years. But it is one of the wishes that is fraught with danger, as Swift saw. In his VOYAGE TO LAPUTA he described how a small proportion of the Laputans had been granted immortality – but without youth.[14] They were called *struldbrugs*, and lived in all the discomforts of extreme senescence. They spent most of their time praying for death to release them.

In a senescent world an assured exit becomes a prime social necessity, for if you annihilate death you leave no room for youth and beauty.

Yet suicide and euthanasia are no answer to a rapidly filling world. What is necessary is for the excessive births to be prevented. At the moment there are about 130 million births a year, and about 65 million deaths. If we were to act rationally we would act now to prevent 65 million births from happening. That is the measure of the eugenic challenge our age faces. If we continue to fail to meet the challenge the prospects are dark indeed. As Eugene Black, who was president of the World Bank from 1949 to 1963, said: "I must be blunt. Population growth threatens to nullify all our efforts to raise living standards in many of the poorer countries. We are coming to a situation in which the optimist will be the man who thinks the present living standards can be maintained. The pessimist will not look even for that. Unless population growth can be restrained, we may have to abandon for this generation our hopes of economic progress in the crowded lands of Asia and the Middle East."[15]

One wonders why Mr. Black limits his pessimism to Asia and the Middle East, since the population growth figures and the indexes for poverty are worse in Africa and Latin America than they are in many parts of Asia, And one wonders why, if standards may sink in this generation, what long-term favourable factors exist for being more optimistic about the following generation.

Recent statistics confirm his pessimism. In a report published by the Food and Agriculture Organisation of the United Nations (FAO) occurs this passage: "The developing countries made impressive gains in food production… over the last ten years, but the production increase was in the main wiped out by the rapid growth of population". Speaking of food, the report recommends that "since the world is now in effect a single trading area, consultation and coordination must ultimately be on a global basis."[16]

If the problem of hunger is left unsolved too long, the means that will have to be adopted to deal with it may be as unpleasant as they will be drastic. It may be necessary and possible to impose universal rationing, so that the shortages may be equally shared by the peasant of Bengal and the Wall Street stockbroker. Even more unpleasant, personal freedom is unlikely to survive the strains of world hunger. The case has been well put by Dr. Walter C. Lowdermilk: "My former experiences with famines in over-populated areas of China present a terrifying picture of what many less developed or backward countries face as populations double without a proportionate increase in food production. There is nothing more terrifying than food riots, and there is no more terrible way to reduce population than by starvation… I have found that hungry people do not keep their treaties, neither will they keep the peace, nor will they stay within their own boundaries. Hunger and poverty are the enemies of liberty and breed totalitarianism and communism. There is no substitute for food."[17]

Hunger and overpopulation must lead to the loss of liberty. This proposition can be seen in concrete terms if one considers the mountain pastures of Lesotho, an area I know fairly well. In these mountains there is only one economic activity: the pasturing of flocks. So long as the population of men and animals remains sparse there are few ways of life more idyllically free, as all will admit who have heard the scrannel notes of the *Lesiba,* the herdboys' strange feather-flute under a blue sky. But when the mountain-pastures fill up the herdboys begin to fight. And over the years their herds begin to destroy the pastures and the soils begin to wash away. This is happening at present. There are only two cures: one is to reduce the population of men and animals to what can safely be carried using the old-fashioned methods. And the other is to impose new methods. But to impose new methods will require a tough government, backed by a large police force, with the threat of prison in the background. In either case the earlier pastoral freedom is inevitably destroyed, and destroyed by overpopulation.

It is self-evident that there is a type of amenity that is destroyed if more than a certain number of people try to use it. Some of the great churches of Europe are now nothing but centres of tourism. Take the case of the cloisters of New College at Oxford. They were built in 1379 by William of Wykeham, the founder, to give the fellows and students a place of beauty for their silent meditations. To-day their silence has gone. Outside there is the roar and stench of traffic a few feet from the ambulatory, and inside are the noisy tourists. Increased access has destroyed the purpose for which this marvellous building was built. It might just as well be demolished now and replaced by buildings that would at least serve a purpose: perhaps a garage or a department store.

There is a similarity between financial devaluation and this rapid increase in the human populations. Financial devaluation leads to inflation, or a situation in which too much money is chasing too few goods and services. Human devaluation is a situation in which too many people are chasing too few goods and services. In one case there is a reduction in the value of money, and in the other there is a reduction in the value of people. This human devaluation is leading to a downgrading of the value of the individual.

Here are a few examples: There is the callousness with which people contemplate the world-wide increase in violent crime, the disregard for the 150,000 deaths that occur annually on the highways. There is the vast unemployment and hunger in the Third World which worries few of those who do not suffer directly. There is the calm acceptance that nuclear war may cause the deaths of hundreds of millions. And there is the fashionable violence of the young radicals. Thirty years ago to be radical was to be pacifist, but to-day young radicals are competing on a "more violent than thou" basis. The old idea that, one human life was infinitely valuable, is no longer very fashionable. A century ago most human beings lived in houses, but to-day hundreds of millions are stacked like battery-hens in huge blocks of apartments, mechanically filed away after work, as it were in giant human filing cabinets, undoubtedly the normal human dwelling of the future. One sees the effect of this human devaluation over the centuries at Timgad, Algeria, where the magnificent marble remains of Hadrian's square city contrast sharply with the mean grey cubes, built in unfaced concrete by the French for low-income Algerians. There is only one rational reaction and that is that in every country all possible be done to apply the brakes, and that thereafter, much hard thinking be done to determine what, In fact, is the optimum population for each country and for the world.

The need for a hard application of the brakes is visible in a country like Algeria where the baby boom is neutralising the laudable efforts of the authorities to improve the people's educational standards. The authorities have recently awoken to the fact that, although 21% of the budget is already being devoted to education, the birth-rate is so high that *half the population will still be* illiterate in 2000 AD, and that the absolute number of illiterates will be greater in that year than they are now. Growing illiteracy is not peculiar to Algeria: Unesco estimates that the number of adult illiterates rose from 700 millions in 1950 to 740 millions in 1963.

The Algerian Minister of Education, Dr. Ahmed Taleb, courageously opened public discussion of contraception in Algeria, a subject till then taboo, by saying through the press "For Algeria economic emancipation can only come through family planning".

In considering the optimum for Algeria it might be objected that there is little danger of over-population, since it is one of the emptier countries. It is true that the density is only about 5 to the km², since its area is 2.3 million km² and its population is about 12 million. There is little weight in this objection. Algeria is composed of two very different kinds of country: there is the "long and narrow tract of the African coast", the Tell and the High Plateaux, where settled human life is possible. Nearly all the population lives here. The other part to the south, is Algeria's share of the vast Sahara. It is almost empty. And if one does not count the Sahara, Algeria is already densely enough populated, and Dr. Taleb' s warning is valid.

Another objection to a braking of the Algerian population might be that with modern technology it will soon be able to "reclaim" the Sahara. There exist many schemes for doing this. Some involve the releasing of sea water into the shallow salt lakes called *shotts*, some of which are below sea level. Others involve the pumping up to the surface of the *bahr taht el erd*, the "sea below the earth", or *nappe saharienne*, perhaps the largest known underwater deposit of fresh water. Others involve the planting of huge areas of trees.

All these schemes aim at the immigration into the desert of human colonists. Is such an immigration really desirable? Has this vast wilderness no intrinsic value? Many travellers have visited those silent sunlit plains, have walked on the sand-dunes that are man-free and always clinically clean, have breathed the unpolluted air, have felt the sun and the solitude, and have returned refreshed and re-created. They are fiercely hostile to any plan to hand this beautiful land over to human domination, noise and pollution. They believe that the solitude is of unique value.

Surely the need to be alone at times, or to know that if needs be one can be alone, is a prime need. Jesus and John the Baptist were only two of many who have retired to the wilderness to prepare for their life's work. If the wildernesses are all to be filled up with settlements, and if the populations continue to grow, there will be a growth of mass-claustrophobia, a feeling of desperation at being closed into the world, too close to one's fellow-men, with no opportunity of a respite. If this is so then the Sahara should be seen as the hermitage of the world. And if it is, then Algeria ceases to seem an underpopulated country.[18]

Another illustration of the danger of applying crude population density rates to countries when thinking of the optimum population is Madagascar, where some 6 million people live in an area of 595,790 km², giving an overall density of some 10 to the km². This compares with the density in Europe of 88 to the km². On the face of it, therefore, Madagascar is an underpopulated country. Yet what would be gained in assuming that the optimum for Madagascar was the present European level? The great island is not the habitat of Man alone: it is also the habitat of a unique flora and fauna. Many of the world's most interesting and beautiful fish, mammals, insects, birds, flowers and trees are to be found in and near Madagascar. Most of these forms of life are already endangered, and would disappear entirely if the population were to increase significantly. At present the population is increasing at the appalling rate of 3% per annum. At this rate the population will equal the present density of Europe in only 75 years. Such a population could only feed itself if it were to convert every fertile corner of the huge, 1600km -long island into a farm. Present grazing and ploughing methods are appallingly bad, and have caused huge gullies in the drier western areas and much sheet erosion in the eastern areas. If there were a continued rise in the population, the farming methods would have to be greatly improved if the whole island were not to become a desert, with its topsoil lying in the Indian Ocean. Now if the island were to be converted into one huge farm, where would the lemurs, the aye-ayes and the tenrecs go? What would happen to the forest? Tall and moisture-creating, it is already seriously diminished, having been thoughtlessly exploited by Malagasy farmers and French capitalists. And for what benefits would such great losses have been incurred? How would it profit the world if the Malagasy population should increase from 6 millions to 50 millions? Here again, one cannot consider the optimum population without facing again the problem of the very nature of Man and of life. How does one balance the value of human settlements against the wilderness, and against the desert?

To sum up, it is probable that both in Algeria and in Madagascar it would be better for there to be no increase, and that the quality of life in those two apparently empty countries cannot fail to suffer if increase takes place. Looking round the world, one could make a similar case against an increase in the population of most of the so-called empty lands. When they are considered as constituent parts of the planetary whole it becomes clear that the human population is already too big, even in these "empty lands" for any imaginable benefit or purpose.

Be this as it may, it is almost certainly too early to begin to look for an actual decrease of the human populations anywhere, such is the present surge in the birth-rates. The most that can be realistically hoped for is that many governments will rapidly build dykes against the tide of babies that is at present flooding into the world, following the example of Japan, and that much creative thinking will be done to determine what is the optimum.

This key question, what is the optimum, cannot be answered to-day for several reasons. First, we do not know with sufficient accuracy the reserves of useful substances contained in the world. Second, we do not yet know the ideal standard of living, and therefore cannot judge its requirements in terms of raw materials. Third, we do not know the extent to which our children and grandchildren will be able to synthesise substances, to tailor atoms and molecules to suit their needs. Fourth, we do not yet know the ideal balance between Man and the other animals, and between Man and his total environment.

What is, however, quite certain is that there are already far too many people, even in the so-called empty lands, for any imaginable benefit or purpose, either on their own account or on the account of the rest of the human race, or on the account of non-human life. It is also certain that the wilderness, the forest and the desert have great value, both for human and for non-human life, and that the areas occupied by them are already far too small. It therefore follows that, unless some qualitative benefit can be conclusively proved to accrue from further human increases that the optimum must lie considerably below present world populations. Thus, even before it is possible to determine the optimum the obvious first step is to begin to apply the brake in every way possible.

There are so many ways in which the brakes might be applied. Countries like Britain and France, that give allowances to parents for each child born, might make it fiscally expensive to have more than a minimum family.[19] Instead of such a rational move, both countries have recently increased all child allowances, thus in effect paying parents to aggravate the problem in these overcrowded lands.

A fierce attack might be concentrated on enemy strongholds such as the Papal Curia that stand in the way of birth limitation, and Catholic parents be encouraged to boycott their church pending a new encyclical to repeal *Casti connubii.*

All international aid to countries with birth-rates over 20 per thousand to be firmly tied to contraceptive conditions. Already the legal power to do this appears in the new American Food for Freedom public law.

Financial aid to be stepped up by the great foundations to all units doing hopeful and creative research into the "perfect contraceptive". I salute the Ford Foundation for their extraordinary and valuable aid in this direction, and trust that their example will be followed by other foundations, and that their very success may encourage them to press on and even increase their own valuable contribution. The "perfect contraceptive" is probably the only factor that can save us from the catastrophe of reaching the seventh billion by the turn of the century. The perfect contraceptive would be cheap, easy to apply, effective for very long periods, and approved by the major religions.

Pressures might be mounted in all lands for the legislation of abortion on demand, as was so successfully done in Japan. Enthusiasts might begin now by helping all women married or unmarried, who need it to have cheap and safe and discreet operations. Governments are very sensitive to changes in public opinion, and if they saw that the proponents of abortion were fearless and were growing in numbers, they would yield to these pressures fairly easily. A special responsibility rests on the advanced countries.[19]

At the same time as the practical work towards the applying of the brakes everywhere goes ahead, so must creative thinking be applied to determining the optimum. To do so will be extraordinarily difficult, for there are several factors that must be previously determined before a rational optimum can be determined.

The first, of course, is to have some idea of the purpose of life, and in particular of the purpose and direction of human life. It is my view that we are not within generations of attaining an idea of the final purpose. But it is the aim of this book to supply an interim purpose that is rational and that is likely to command the assent of a great majority of men. This purpose is the establishment of a creative balance and harmony between groups of men, and between mankind as a whole and the world, especially its biosphere and all non-human life. Man is here, in effect, to love the world.

Other factors which must be determined are such as these: what is the *minimum* human population, which would be able, with the highest level of technological knowledge now available, to achieve all existing and foreseeable tasks which face us, and to maintain a level of culture in a world-wide community?

How important is silence? How important is it that men should have the privilege of escaping from other men and living in primeval forest among non-human life? How important is it to maintain the virgin nature of the undersea world, and that it should not be converted into a farm? What is the level of pollution that nature can absorb, and to what population level would this pollution level relate? What are the true reserves of the fossil fuels? Of the phosphates? And of the other exhaustible minerals that our generation is mining so fast? What reserves should we leave for future generations, and what substitutes are there for them? How much time is left to life on this planet?

These are the extraordinarily difficult questions to which we ought to be applying our minds. For, as we shall see in a later chapter, it is already clear that our existing practices are wrong on nearly all the counts.

The first question was, what is the *minimum* population, not what is the *maximum* for Man, as we have seen, is but one species among three million species, and it is already clear that human populations are already more than any rationally justifiable maximum. Somewhere then, between three billions and one individual there must be an optimum, for one human being would not suffice to keep the race going. One is below the minimum, and three billion is above the maximum. Somewhere between these two figures there must lie a population level which is best for allowing the good life to men and animals and the world's biosphere. What would be this minimum? What can the existing 3,346 millions do that 2,000 millions could not do? Or 1,000 millions, or even 300 millions? With modern technology and communications three hundred millions could easily maintain a world-wide intellectual community, as richly productive, perhaps very much more productive than the present; could expand more effectively the frontiers of knowledge, and in general be more creative than the present three billions, obsessed with the insoluble population problem or just with being unemployed, living far too close to neighbours who make an appalling noise, or deformed by the need to compete in the horrible urban "rat-race". Even at present the proportion of the human race that creates anything is a tiny minority, perhaps not exceeding one million in the whole world. Remember that, in a world with only 300 million human beings in it, there would be enough space for each man to have a large garden with unlimited water for it; there would be enough spring water for each family to be able to drink their own; there would be enough accessible solitude for all to be able to enjoy silent meditation at any time, for everyone to be able to bathe (naked if he wished) in pure waters, in an uncontaminated sea or in unchlorinated swimming bath or in unsewerised rivers and lakes. The world would be empty enough for there to be, once again, mysterious lands that could be explored, empty enough for a rich variety of wildlife to return and to live without fear of Man.

If such a vision is unacceptable, if there are those who are not troubled by the prospect of seven billion human beings by the year 2000 - thirty-three swiftly-passing years from now - I think that they owe an explanation of what these vast crowds of people will be able to do for themselves and for the world, that 300 millions of highly educated and technologically advanced people, living in dignity and with peace and quiet, could not do.

REFERENCES

(1) *Genesis,* 1: xxviii.
(2) The United Nations "continued trends" projection, published in 1964, showed the 2000 AD population as 7,410 millions.
(3) *India's Urban Future,* by K.Davis; UOP., Bombay.
(4) 9 per km in July 1961.
(5) *Church World Service Reports,* New York; Feb. 1966.

(6) UN estimate, quoted by E.F.Schumacher, UK Coal Board, in a memorandum 28 May 1964.

(7) In *Our Crowded Planet,* editor Fairfield Osborn; G. Allen & Unwin.

(8) *Jeune Afrique,* 31 January 1965; my translation. The journey to China was described as "recent", a word in vogue with editors who wish to conceal the fact that their material is somewhat dated.

(9) "La Nouvelle Femme Chinoise " by Ménie Grégoire, in *Le Monde.* 21 June 1966, page 4.

(10) William Petersen, in *Population Review,* 1: 21-32, 1957; quoted in *Population, Evolution and Birth Control* by Garrett Hardin, P.276; W.H.Freeman & Co. 1964.

(11) Ibid. p 303.

(12) Ibid. pp. 256-257: see section 56 of the Encyclical.

(13) *Le Monde,* 1 September 1966.

(14) *Gullivers Travels;* part 3: A voyage to Laputa, by Jonathan Swift.

(15) in *Our Crowded Planet,* ed. F. Osborn, G.Allen & Unwin 1963.

(16) FAO, Rome, October or November 1965.

(17) "The Promise of Agriculture in the less developed Lands" chapter in *Our Crowded Planet,* edited by Fairfield Osborn, G.Allen & Unwin London, 1963.

(18) Cf. IX. 20.

(19) The view that Britain is already far beyond the optimum is spreading fast. At the 1966 meeting of the British Association for the Advancement of Science at Nottingham, the president, Sir Joseph Hutchinson, who is professor of agriculture at Cambridge, gave as his view that 40 millions might be the optimum for Britain. (22 September 1966) commented: "How to achieve this desirable result however, is a problem on which he could give little help, and indeed it seems insoluble. For already we are 14 million over the limit, and if the experts are to be believed by the end of the century we shall have increased by another 20 million".

Similarly for America Mr. P. K. Whelpton, speaking at the congress on Population and World Resources in Relation to the Family, at Cheltenham in August 1948 said: "It seems to me that even in countries like the USA the population is above the economic optimum; that is, we have more people even there than is desirable from the standpoint of the natural resources which we possess... if we could choose between a stationary population of, say, 100 million and 150 million or 200 million we should without question be better off with the former" (quoted in *Population, Evolution and Birth Control,* page 62; edited by Garret Hardin, W. H. Freeman and Co. , 1964).

World Population: See the current data in the World Population Data Chart for 1973 in the supplement at the end of this volume beginning on p.240.

6 Taking Stock Globally

MAN STANDS to-day on a pinnacle of power over Nature. We have seen how his power over the forests and the soils and the animals has been misused. We shall see now how he is squandering the rich deposits of metals and fuels with little heed for the future. Man's thriftlessness is partly due to ignorance of the potential: we do not for instance, yet have adequate knowledge of how much coal lies in accessible seams, how much oil, nor how much of the valuable metals, and so on. We do not know how to use fresh water to the best advantage. And, not knowing, we seem to act as if not caring.

Yet so much research is being done that our knowledge of these things is rapidly expanding. To an increasing extent such research must be international and world-wide: hence some most useful exercises that have recently been planned or carried out. Among others there is the International Geophysical year, the International Biological Programme and the International Hydrological Decade which began at the beginning of 1965.

In respect of non-renewable resources, the metals, fossil fuels, and so forth, the time has come when a general global statement of the planet's inventory should be widely known, and in respect of renewable resources for a series of global budgets to be drawn up and popularised.

The present state of research does not allow, in most fields, a very great deal of accuracy, but it does allow us to make a start, and this is being done.

In respect of the renewable resources, budgets are being drawn up. All over the world the processes of movement and life in the world are being noted and numbered. These processes involve a constant movement. There is a constant flow into the pool of life of many hundreds of substances, and as constant an outflow. There is an input and an output of many substances and of energy, of atmospheric oxygen and carbon dioxide, of sea-water and of fresh water, of soils; of foodstuffs; and, finally, of living creatures including Man. If the total environment is to be handed down to our descendants relatively unharmed, then the input and output of these substances must as soon as possible be brought into creative balance. Some of to-day's gravest problems arise from the fact that some of these budgets are in considerable imbalance.

Only global budgets, in which are shown the inputs and outputs of the various substances which are used in the processes of life, can indicate accurately what is being done to our planet and what ought to be done.

An illustration of the need and utility of global budgets can be seen in the science of forestry. There are two ways of working a forest. One may "mine" it, taking trees without any thought for the future. Or one may so work it that new trees are constantly coming on, to replace those that are taken in such a way that those that are taken are limited by the increment of those that are growing. The latter system is called "sustained yield" forestry, and it is the only forestry that is worthy of the name.

But "sustained yield" forestry is not possible until one has accurately estimated the input and output of all substances whose incoming and outgoing make the totality of the processes of life. This accurate estimate will be the global budget.

Forestry on a sustained yield basis is a true symbiosis between Man and tree. Each side gives the other something. But exploitative forestry, or tree-mining, is a form of parasitism, in which the parasite damages or destroys its host, sometimes destroying itself in the process.

Man's relationship with the world's resources resembles exploitative forestry. But the time has come when Man's relationship with the world must be placed on a sustained yield basis. Man must enter, for the first time, into a true symbiosis with the world. The global budget is the means by which he may inform himself for this momentous act.

So much damage has been done already that it is difficult, in our age, to think that it might be possible to restore the balance where it has been undone. But if anything ever is to be done to restore this balance we must begin to-day to make up the accounts. Only when a fairly accurate budget is known will our successors be able to work towards a creative balance. The words "creative balance" mean a balance that effects the accumulated capital in a direction agreeable to a creative long-term aim. This long-term aim must be the harmonising of the interests of the planet as a whole with the interests of all of its life, human as well as non-human.

In aiming at this symbiosis I suggest that the watchword be: Harmony and Diversity. Harmony implies that no form of life must grow in such a way as to damage or inhibit other forms of life; and Diversity calls for an end to the extinction of species.

Global budgeting could eventually apply to all activities, economic as well as biological. It would apply not only to the world's resources, but to life, and to Man himself. (Chapter 5 consisted largely of a consideration of the human global budget). The principle of the global budget is that the incomings and outgoings must be placed in creative balance - seen in the time-scale of at least a century. The alternative is to acquiesce while to-day destroys tomorrow.

Let me repeat: we are not yet in a position to draw up a global budget. But we are in a position to sketch out some parts of it, and to foreshadow what the great whole will look like when it is finally drawn up.

There follow a few examples of budgets that are important both from the point of view of understanding the damage that is presently being done and from the point of view of determining the future path. The heat budget is one of the most important from both points of view.

1. The Heat Budget.

The heat budget is the balance between the input of energy into the world, mostly from the sun, and the output of energy radiated out into space from the world. A combination of factors, mainly in the atmosphere, produce the result that although there are in space deadly radiation and extremes of heat and cold unfavourable to life, yet, on the surface itself, the temperature range is moderate; and the dangerous radiation does not get through the surface.

In the past the relatively insignificant scale of Man's activities has meant that he could not affect the heat balance for better or worse. Now, however, this state of affairs has changed, and Man's activities do significantly affect this balance. Since such changes may involve chain reactions and snow-ball effects, and since large changes might be fatal to life, it is urgently necessary to know the quantities involved.

Accurate figures are not yet available, but soon they may be, for one of the purposes for which the American satellite Nimbus II was put into orbit at the end of April 1966 was to "measure the total solar radiation received by the Earth and reflected or radiated back into space. For the first time an accurate 'heat budget' for the Earth will be available. This will be extremely important for calculating the climate future."[1]

Even though the figures are not known accurately, they are known approximately, and they are of interest. "The sun's radiation consists mainly of short-wavelength rays. Because these shortwave rays pass easily through transparent substances, only about 15% is absorbed directly by the air and stored (in the air) as heat by the water-vapour and carbon-dioxide content; 40% is reflected back into space by dust and clouds, though this amount varies with weather conditions. The solar energy (that reaches the ground) is therefore about 45% of the original output. Of this, 10% is reflected back into the air; only the remaining 35% actually heats the upper surface of the land and sea."[2]

How important this atmospheric insulation is, is shown by the fact that on the surface of the Moon, which enjoys no such protection, the temperature sometimes rises to 120°C.

But the atmosphere does not merely hold back the violent heats of the solar radiation: it prevents the Earth from losing its warmth at night to the unimaginable colds of space. This it does through the "greenhouse effect". We saw that the solar heat arrives as short-wave energy. But the re-radiation sent back by the surface of the

Earth is long-wave energy. Such radiation is largely stopped by the atmosphere, although it is transparent to the shorter waves. Thus the atmosphere acts as an insulating blanket, and is heated largely by the energy re-radiation from the warmed surface of the Earth. The glass in the roof of a greenhouse acts In a similar fashion, hence the name of the effect.

The moderate heats and colds of the world's climate are probably in a precarious balance. For instance, no one knows why the ice-ages happened, but whatever the cause might have been it is clear that the present-day balance between energy absorbed from space minus that reflected and radiated out is different from the balance established in the last ice-age thirteen thousand years ago. Thirteen thousand years geologically speaking, is just yesterday, and it is quite probable that, even without Man's recent activities, this balance would now have been in a process of change or oscillation: it is also quite possible that the existing ice-caps and glaciers are in the process of melting. Either process would involve the world in immense upsets. If the continental ice caps were to return, agriculture might become impossible in Europe and North America. And if all the world's ice were to melt 20 x 10 tons of fresh water, now locked up in the icecaps of Antarctica and Greenland alone, would be liberated into the oceans - enough water to raise the level of all the seas by 57 metres (185 feet). At the height of the ice ages the seas were 180 metres (600 feet) lower than at present.

It is indeed probable that Man's smokes and exhaust gases even perhaps the vapour trails of aircraft, are already affecting this precarious balance. Whether such activities are encouraging or discouraging the formation of ice is not yet certain, as the science of glaciology is too young for positive answers to be given.

As we have already seen, the atmosphere is more than an insulator: it is also a filter, and protects us from those of the Sun's rays that are harmful. The electro-magnetic spectrum, at the ultra-violet end, is harmful to life, and it is fortunate that there is in the atmosphere a protective screen which allows rays with a wave-length of more than 2,900 angstroms to pass through, but which stops rays with a wave-length of 2,100 - 2,900 angstroms. These latter are the dangerous ultra-violet rays. This protective screen is a layer of ozone which encircles the globe at a height of about 30,000 metres. The effectiveness of this ozone layer "is proved by comparison of the spectra obtained from rockets. For example, a V2 fired in New Mexico in 1946 showed a spectrum below the ozone layer, hardly richer in ultra-violet rays than one near the ground. Above the ozone layer, however, it showed a spectrum with ultra-violet rays from 3,900 - 2,200 angstrom units... If it gained in thickness, it would absorb not only the harmful ultra-violet rays but also those which bring the important Vitamin D to our bodies."[3]

Unfortunately various forms of pollution, especially those produced by giant space rockets are able to destroy this ozone layer. This is how it could happen: "On the side of the Earth which faces away from the Sun there are layers, at heights of about 30-70 kilometres, of almost pure oxygen. As this side turns towards the Sun, the oxygen is partially turned into ozone. Unfortunately, this ozone layer is not concentrated. There is so little of it, in fact, that the hydrogen now being released by space rockets could destroy it to an important degree. It is estimated that one Soviet rocket of the type Voskhod releases several dozen tons of hydrogen into the atmosphere, and that the American rocket, Saturn V will release into the atmosphere 2,000 tons of exhaust gases of which 200 tons will be hydrogen. It is believed that if 10,000 tons of hydrogen were released into the upper atmosphere there would result such immense rents in the ozone clouds that whole continents would receive deadly doses of ultra-violet rays. Such a quantity of hydrogen has, of course, not yet been released, but the margin of safety is not large. A group of American scientists asked by their Department of Defense to examine the question, has reported that "there is a strong possibility that accelerated American and Russian space programmes will cause grave disturbances in the upper atmosphere."[4]

The race to the Moon by the two space powers has been criticised on several grounds, but no criticism, in my view, is more telling than this one: that by duplicating the launches of these rockets they are doubling the quantities of pollutants released into the upper atmosphere, and possibly endangering the precarious balance of ozone, with unpredictable and potentially dangerous results for all life.

The condition of the atmosphere is, in fact, so important for our future that a decision to maintain it so far as possible uncontaminated ought to be, but clearly is not, a decision that is given the highest priority. Here again we see Man's lack of foresight, or perhaps his inability to control the course of civilisation, now careering downhill like a lorry whose brakes have failed.

2. The Atmospheric Pollution Budget.

At the beginning of this book we saw the atmosphere, whether one looks through it at distant Mountains, or whether one looks down on it from space, is coloured a brilliant azure blue. Unfortunately it is menaced by Man, and to an increasing extent.

A budget for the substances entering and coming out from the atmosphere is intimately connected with the heat budget but is not quite same. In the heat budget the air was considered merely as an insulator and as a filter: in the air budget the atmosphere is seen as the ocean in which terrestrial life moves and has its being, and which it breathes.

The weight of the atmosphere is fairly easy to estimate. We know that at sea-level the atmosphere exerts a pressure equal to that of 10.33 metres of water. We know the areas of our globe. A simple calculation tells us that the atmosphere weighs about 5.2×10^{15} tons or 5,200 million million tons. All this mass of air, with the exception of about 52,000 tons, is found below a height of 300 kilometres, and nearly all of this 52,000 tons is found between the heights of 300 and 900 kilometres. A bathtub contains about 50 grammes of air, and if one puts one's hand outside a car travelling faster than 100 kilometres an hour, the sheer weight of the air is impressively felt.

Air is a subtle blend: it consists of

Nitrogen   78%

Oxygen	21%,
Argon	1%
Carbon Dioxide	0.03%

and traces of Xenon, Neon, Krypton, Helium, Ozone and Hydrogen

The processes of animal life tend to increase the carbon dioxide concentration, but this is compensated for by those of vegetable life, which absorb it. Despite the influence of the oceans the balance of carbon dioxide has already been affected to a significant degree by Man's industrial activities, and such changes are being and ought to be carefully watched. But what is far more serious at present is the pollution that is found near all large cities. In the industrial areas many thousands of tons of poisonous and destructive exhaust gases and smoke are daily discharged into the air, as if it were a sewer.

The result is at its most unpleasant in New York or Los Angeles. If there are a few windless days in summer a vast cloud about 4,000 metres thick appears over these cities. It is a pearly grey colour with yellowish pink tints. It is dark at its base. It is formed mainly of motor-car exhaust gases. One cannot go into this smog without one's eyes smarting and without coughing. Not only does this smog damage life; it corrodes exposed metals and even stones and bricks. One gasps for wind.

The time has come when it is urgently necessary to ascertain the maximum extent to which the air may be used as a sewer, and to restrict exhausts and smokes to well below this maximum. These facts are as yet unknown: when they are known it will be possible for a global air pollution budget to be drawn up.

3. The Budget of the Oceans.

The Earth has been called the "water planet". 71% of its surface, or 360 million km², are covered by the sea, and only 29%, or 147 million km². are land. The oceans contain about 1,345,000,000,000,000,000,000 (1.345×10^{21}) tons of water, or 1,345 million cubic kilometres, for a cubic kilometre contains about a billion tons of water.[5] The oceans form a system in which there are huge inputs and outputs of water. These inputs and outputs are called the water cycle of the oceans. The following are the approximate daily inputs and outputs:[6]

Inflow of nearly fresh water into the oceans	100 km³
Outflow of pure water by evaporation	860 km³
Rainfall on the oceans	760 km³
Blown into air- space over land masses	100 km³
Evaporated from land masses	160 km³
The last two mentioned together rain down on land	260 km³
Of the last-mentioned there is returned to the oceans, completing the cycle	100 km³

The oceanic system, as we have seen does much to regulate the world's temperature. Enormous inputs and outputs of heat are involved, but we do not yet know much about them. They work in complicated ways. Just how complicated the "weather machine" can be is seen in an address to the Second International Conference on Oceanography, held in mid-1966 in Moscow. The paper was read by Dr. J. Bjerknes of the University of California. In examining the homeostatic or regulatory effect of the oceans he showed how heat applied at the Equator could cause a cold winter in Europe. The process is somehow as follows: heating up of the surface waters at the Equator leads, generally, to storms and strong winds. These tend to drive the warmed water from the Equator. To replace the water that has been driven away there occur upwellings of water at the Equator from deep in the oceans. This water, having been lying at-depth, is colder. In this manner the Equator atmospheric temperatures would tend to fall, and the normal temperature be restored. By processes too complex to be entered into here such a disturbance is, in the lecturer's view, likely to lead to a cold winter in Europe.[7]

Upwellings from the ocean depths often bring to the surface large quantities of nitrates and phosphates, the product of oceanic life that has "rained" down into the lifeless depths. When these enriched waters reach the upper, sunlit zones, they produce great increases in plankton; on the plankton feed tiny shrimps and fishes; on them feed larger fishes, whales, sea-birds and the life of the ocean takes a "great leap forward". Some of the most dramatic developments in the world of fishing have been the recent discoveries of how to exploit these upwellings. Two of the richest have been the upwellings of the Humboldt current off the coast of Peru, and a similar upwelling off the coast of South West Africa, and the neighbouring coasts of Angola and South Africa.

Little is yet known of all this, but no science is growing as rapidly as oceanography, and, perhaps in a generation, the global budget of the oceans will be, at least in its outlines, known.

4. The Fresh Water Budget.

Of all the water in the world, 97% is in the oceans, and only 3% exists as fresh water. Of this fresh water, 4/5ths is locked up in the polar ice-caps and glaciers. Another tenth is in the rock crevices and under the Earth. Only 0.32% of the world's water is in the lakes and streams, in the air and in living things.[8]

The water-vapour in the air, more than any other constituent of our planet, affects the image which we present to outer space, for we are a planet of dazzling whiteness ringed by the blue air. The whiteness is caused by the clouds, which make the Earth's albedo almost as white as that of Venus.

Life probably originated in water. At any rate, evolutionists are certain that the line of life existed in water at some time in the past. 80% of our bodies, by weight, is water. Our need for drink, though not so immediate as our need for air, is constant and will not be denied: thirst is one of the more terrible of sufferings. The correlation of water and life is seen perhaps most clearly in an irrigated land like Egypt. Flying over Egypt one sees the boundary of cultivation, starkly cut. Outside is the sterility of death; but inside it is the pullulation of green life, as in an oasis. The boundary is clear-cut, and it is possible to stand with one foot in the desert and one in the fertile land.

What is water? It is almost the only compound which exists naturally as a liquid on the Earth's surface. It is one of the simplest of substances. Two atoms of hydrogen are joined to one of oxygen to form a substance that is one of the few that are liquid at ordinary surface temperatures. At 0° it turns solid. Fortunately water shows one curious characteristic: at 4°C. it is heavier than it is when frozen at 0°C. This means that ice floats on the top of water. If this were not so, it is probable that many lakes and rivers in the cold parts of the world would never thaw, and would remain solidly frozen. This same might be true of the bottoms of much of the oceans, and the world might be a much colder place than it is.

Man is in love with water. Long ago the Romans put up little marble cascades in their principal cities, combining the functions of water-fountains and temples to the nymphs, adorable adult feminine water-babies. The Nymphaeum is one of the most attractive monuments left at Cuicul, Mauretania (now called Djemila, in Algeria). The Moors and Spaniards build their courtyards with a little fountain playing to give them the sight and sounds of water inside their homes even on the hottest days of summer. The sensuous yet cool caress of water on the skin of a swimmer is one of life's supreme experiences, and one hopes that the children and grandchildren of this generation will enjoy it to the full by discarding the little pieces of cloth hung irrationally round parts of the body and called "bikinis" and "trunks" which do little but draw attention to those parts of the body which they purport to conceal.

May I be permitted to speak personally for a moment and to give a series of pictures preserved in my mind which are associated with water?

As a boy I was particularly in love with the mountain water of the Cape Peninsula. It is not in the least muddy, yet had the colour of beer and the taste of peat. As a family we used to take weekly walks up these fragrant mountains, often with General Smuts and other friends. I would never miss the chance of drinking my favourite water with its sweet and metallic taste. Often I would swim in the rock pools, and marvel at the sight of bodies seen through the liquid topaz. There was at Stellenbosch a deep swimming-pool in a friend's garden. In it the water was unusually dark-coloured and one could not see more than a foot or two into it. Yet the underground water in these mountains often has a blue colour: witness the so-called bath of Lady Anne Barnard at Kirstenbosch.

Later in life some water-memories stand out. At school in England a chalk-stream with waving water-plants and trout keeping their station, waving in time with the water-plants. And mill-races where the upper water curved over a weir with a smooth mathematical curve.

Then, from later years, two others: swimming with a dear friend in the underground dolomite lake at Sterkfontein cave, hundreds of feet below the surface, while another friend, like Charon, held a high lamp to guide us back to the mysterious shore; and drinking the purest water I know, the water that runs gently from a fountain, green with water-cress and wild mint, into my house at Kubung in the mountains of southern Lesotho.

I mention these memories, not to write autobiography, but to try to awaken in my readers the same feelings of reverence and delight that pure water seldom fails to awaken in me.

Unfortunately, Man's need for water is now so great that the pure waters are being rapidly polluted. Compared with the atmosphere and the sea the world's fresh water is a small enough quantity to allow Man to do very much what he likes with it. And so, all over the world, hundreds of thousands of tube wells (boreholes) have been sunk and the underground water pumped out. Much of this water is geological water: that is to say that it has lain in its recesses for millions of years, and once mined will not be renewed. In addition, much of the replaceable underground water is being pumped out faster than it is replaced, and so the water-tables of the world are falling.

As the cities grow, so the rivers become aqueducts upstream and sewers downstream. One case shows this Man-domination with clarity: the Niagara Falls. Once a symbol of Nature's might, they are now reduced to being an urban utility. A century ago they became famous; the tourists flocked to see them, and sight-seeing at

Niagara became big business. The tourists needed accommodation, transport and souvenirs, and so right next to the falls a town grew up. To-day the town is a city of 150,000 inhabitants, needing, among other things, electricity. So canals were built that allow nearly the whole flow of the falls to be withdrawn and passed down to the level of the lower lake, Lake Ontario, through the turbines of a power-station. But the illusion of Nature's might must be preserved, so at tourist watching times some functionary switches the water over the falls circuit. At other times he switches the falls off: they go dry and the turbines begin to hum. The upper lake, Lake Erie, is slowly being turned by pollution into a stinking morass (see page 187), and Lake Ontario also is slowly filling up with sewage.

Water-shortages are occurring with increasing frequency in all the continents, and city-dwellers are drinking ever higher percentages of effluent. Two things are necessary if the descending graph is to be pulled upwards: pure water must be treated as something almost holy, which it is, and a world budget must be drawn up, which fortunately is being done.

Under the leadership of UNESCO there is already an International Hydrological Decade. It began on January 1, 1965. UNESCO has called in representatives of the United Nations, the World Meteorological Organisation, the World Health Organisation, the Food and Agricultural Organisation, the International Atomic Energy Agency and the International Council of Scientific Unions, to help map the Earth's water supply.

It is likely that the world's hydrologists will have a difficult task in drawing up the global water budget. When they have done so it will be necessary for a world water utilisation policy to be laid down. Since it is probably impossible for the present population of the world, with the best management possible, to enjoy clean fresh water at an American standard of living, it is to be hoped that the hydrologists do not rule out the only rational alternative: that the human population be held to a level at which every human being, and every animal will be able to enjoy one of the greatest pleasures that life can offer: pure spring water to drink and in which to wash.

The world's hydrologists' task will be considerably lightened by the national water budgets which are being drawn up in some countries. One of the countries where these studies are far advanced is Britain, and the main heads of the British national water budget are approximately as follows:

England and Wales 1964	Metric Tons / day
Mean yield theoretically obtainable from the rainfall	185,232,000
Total consumption (excluding cooling water)	22,700,000
The total consumption of 22,700,000 tons is divided as follows	
Total domestic demand	6,356,000
Total agricultural demand excluding irrigation	908,000
Irrigation demand	1,650,000
Industrial demand	13,786,000
	22,700,000

Consumption is increasing at a rate of about 4% a year. Hydrologists expect a domestic demand to level off at about 220 litres a day per person, or in tons for the country: 11 million. They also expect that irrigation might eventually extend to 500,000 hectares, an area ten times as big as that now irrigated, and that the amount of water-that would be required would be 12,076,400 tons. Industrial water consumption is also rapidly increasing, and by 1980 hydrologists are expecting an industrial demand of 45,400,000 tons. Agricultural demands are not expected, however, to go much beyond 1,000,000 tons. Tabulating the above estimates one gets the following table:

England and Wales 1980	Metric Tons /day
Mean yield theoretically obtainable from the rainfall	185,232,000
Total domestic demand	11,000,000
Total agricultural demand excluding irrigation	1,000,000
Irrigation demand	12,076,400
Industrial demand	45,400,000
	69,476,400

That is to say that the next fifteen years should see consumption at least trebled, and perhaps even approaching half of the total rainfall on England and Wales. This stage cannot be reached without some or all of the following technical practices becoming widespread: re-use of sewage, the desalination of sea water, the use of sea water for cooling power stations and the dumping of their ash into the sea.[9]

And so, as the population of England and Wales increases, and as their standard of living rises, one must, in the near future envisage empty rivers, heated lakes and shallow seas, and the discharge into the sea of ash, much of it radioactive. Perhaps some may remember, incredulously, that 400 years ago this was a "silver sea" that girt a demi-paradise.

In the United States some comparable figures are:[10]

1960	Metric Tons /day
Total domestic demand	124,720,000
Total agricultural demand	491,400,000
Total industrial demand	604,800,000
Total daily consumption	1,220,920,000

That is to say that the consumption per capita in the United States in 1960 of water was in the neighbourhood of 6.4 tons, compared with a consumption in England and Wales, in 1964, of 0.5 tons per capita.

British consumption, both actual and projected, is thus far less than the actual American consumption per capita.

5. Wildlife

Chapter 5 contained thoughts on the human global budget. As in the case of Man, it is now also necessary for there to be an accurate count of the higher animals. A real danger exists that the extinction of species might remove all the higher animals and that if Man should also become extinct the torch of consciousness would have to be taken up by the descendants of the rat, the goat - or the fire-ant. In the light of a wildlife count, action should be taken to rescue those in danger of extermination, and to re-establish a creative balance. Many organisations are exerting themselves already to this end but, as we saw in Chapter 3 such efforts, if they are to save the present remnants of the world's wildlife from slipping over the brink into the abyss, are going to need vastly more support that they are at present getting.

Not all such efforts will be directed towards conservation: for there are also cases of wild animals that will have to have their numbers reduced because they have become too numerous locally. In some cases it will be possible to move part of the surplus to other protected areas: an example is the exportation announced in September, 1966, of 40 African elephants from the Tsavo National Park in Kenya to a park in the United States. (Perhaps such moves hold out the best hope of rescuing species that are on the danger list, quite apart from relieving local pressures: an example is the successful move of a small breeding herd of the near-extinct Arabian oryx from Arabia to Phoenix zoo, Arizona). But where local pressures cannot be relieved by translocation it is in some cases already necessary to cull wildlife. Man has in so many places destroyed the predators that it is necessary that he should step in to keep the balance. The point was well made in an article "Wild

Life Conservation" by Dr. Fraser Darling, one of the leaders of the world's wild-life conservation movement.

I have myself seen the effect of giving total protection to large herds of elephant in the northern parts of the Kruger National Park in South Africa. Until about 1940 there were few elephants in this area. Then, suddenly, large numbers of elephant moved in, apparently from Mozambique. It is possible that news of the security to be found in the Kruger Park reached harassed elephants many hundreds of miles away, for, as Dr. Darling says in this article, "elephants are able to communicate factually as well as we can". As a result of this immigration, one of the world's largest concentrations of African elephants is now to be found in the Punda Maria area of the north of the Kruger National Park. Before their arrival, this area was savannah, with perhaps 200 trees to the hectare, a vegetation dominated by the mopane tree (Colophospermum mopane), and containing other trees as well, rising to a maximum height of 20 metres. But elephants specially relish the shoots of the mopane, many of which are too high for browsing; so, being Nature's closest approach to the bulldozer, they have been pushing the mopane trees over to get at the tender shoots. When I was last in Punda Maria much of the countryside resembled photographs of French woods in World War I, with shell-smashed trees, and the savannah was rapidly becoming grassland.

Similar problems exist in East Africa in the Serengeti, in the Murchison Falls and in the Tsavo National Parks. In all these reserves there have been mass immigrations of elephant. In the Serengeti "elephants first invaded the park, coming from both North and South, in 1958; a count last year showed that there were 2,200. Damage to the vegetation started in 1962, and in 1964 Dr. P. E. Glover discovered that in the northern part of the park destruction was going on faster than regeneration. Counts of the acacias (A. xanthophloeia) on six miles of the Seronera river valley, where 836 trees have been destroyed in four years, suggested that the present generation of large trees would all be destroyed in four or five years… Work is being done now on measuring elephant population trends and determining the rates of tree destruction…"[11]

In South Africa, too, in the Kruger National Park, an elephant census was held in 1964. For seven days helicopters photographed all the elephants that could be found. The total was 2,350, an increase over the previous year of about 600. At the time of this operation the number of buffalo was estimated at 10,000 and of hippopotami at 8,000. All three species were increasing rapidly, and were leaving the park authorities no alternative but to shoot some, in order to maintain a balance.

It is quite possible that such a transformation of vegetation is not harmful to the totality of life in the park, but it is also possible that it is. The hippos in the Queen Elizabeth National Park in Uganda have had to be culled because they began to destroy the soils and pastures of their habitat. The culling of the elephants is likewise inevitable. "Those of us who truly love the elephant," says Dr. Darling, "and who are deeply concerned for its survival should be ready to reduce the population in certain areas in ways which are going to hurt us emotionally. It would be unthinkable to harass large migrating groups in the dry season, killing some adults and making the herds hysterical. We must be prepared to work in the wet season when family groups are small, and to extirpate completely a family group so that the disturbance is minimal and none lives to tell the tale for, of course, elephants are able to communicate factually as well as we can, and I cannot see that their suffering is any less than ours. The task is easier with less intelligent and more phlegmatic animals like the hippopotamus".

Here we have a great conservationist, vice-president of the Conservation Foundation, speaking *with love* in an animal of marvellous beauty and intelligence that has multiplied to the extent that it is ruining its habitat, who recommends that Man extirpate completely... family groups... children, adults, all.

But Man is behaving precisely as these elephants are behaving. He too has multiplied to such an extent that he is ruining his habitat, the planet. Will it come to the culling of men? Shall we see complete human families extirpated, adults and children, in the name of mercy? Let those interests that oppose birth-control remember that horrors of this kind, and perhaps worse, are probably corning to us unless the tide of babies is stemmed.

6. *The Global Food Budget.*

Another important chapter in the overall global budget is that of Man's food. At present his food supplies are derived almost exclusively from the soil and the waters. Yet it has already been proved possible to synthesise protein from the hydro-carbons of the fossil fuels: from mineral oil, from coal and from natural gas. The transformation is achieved by bringing together the fuels and certain micro-organisms or yeasts that grow by eating the fuels. The yeast is then fed to the human or animal consumer, and it is said by those brave enough to have tried it to taste quite pleasant. It is highly nutritious. With developments like this we are probably on the edge of a breakthrough to a large exploitation of this new food source, yet at the time of writing it remains true that Man's food, almost without exception, comes from natural sources - from the world's farmers, fishers and hunters.

Like the global human budget, the global food budget is nearing a high degree of accuracy. The needs (output) are approximately known, and the production (input) is also approximately known. In certain developed countries these inputs and outputs are nearing a high degree of accuracy, but in the Third World, especially in those countries with an uneducated peasantry, there is as yet little accuracy in the figures, for no peasant can be compelled to report to an official each time he kills a chicken. Yet, even in backward countries, there is a growing need to know the production and consumption of food. And, more and more, these national food budgets are being collated and integrated into a global food budget.

Already a sketch exists for a global food-energy budget: it has been published by Professor David L. Linton, and is of the highest interest, as will be seen: "The energy content of the food we eat… for mankind in general… averages some 2,200 calories a day. Since mankind numbers some 2.350 million this implies a total yearly input of some 2.5×10^{15} calories. It is about one-sixteenth of the figure of 40×10^{15} calories a year that I mentioned earlier as the gross figure for inanimate energy (defined elsewhere by Professor Linton in terms that show he has in mind the total energy requirements of Man that are not met by foodstuffs) from all sources consumed in a year. Inanimate energy that in the ancient world was on an equal footing with the animate energy of the human population, now out-balances the latter by sixteen to one in the total energy budget. Probably we should add an amount not dissimilar to the energy value of our food for the energy consumed by work animals in order to obtain an estimate of the total vital energy, animate and inanimate, at the disposal of mankind".

For the global food budget increasingly accurate estimates are now possible, and the figures of the United States Department of Agriculture are perhaps as good as any others in the world. Their figures for the production of some foodstuffs over the last four years are of great interest, and they are appended overleaf.

Continent	Average 1960-64	1964	1965	1966
	In Millions of metric tons			
North America	49.6	53.6	55.8	59.7
South America	9.5	13.7	8.0	10.6
Western Europe	39.0	43.2	45.4	40.2
Eastern Europe	17.2	18.0	21.9	21.9
USSR	50.0	57.7	46.5	73.6
Africa	5.7	5.9	6.1	4.9
Asia	52.1	52.3	55.6	51.3
Oceania	8.5	10.3	7.3	11.6
Total	231.6	254.7	246.6	273.7

	1964-65	1965-66	1966-67
	Millions of metric tons		
Rice (excluding communist countries)	172	159	170
Feed grains		378	380
Maize			217
Barley			100
Sugar (Centrifugal)			66
Cocoa			1.4
Tea (excluding mainland China)			1

Wheat

World wheat production in 1966 is now estimated at 274 million metric tons, 7% more than the previous record of 255 million tons in 1964, and 11% larger than the 1965-66 crop. The harvest is 18% above the average production during the 5 years ended 1964.

In a more general aspect the need to think globally in food matters has been felt for some time. Arnold J. Toynbee, the historian, formulated this need clearly when he said: "In order to raise the world's food supply to its potential maximum, the whole habitable and cultivable surface of the planet will have to be thrown together into a single unit for the purposes of food production and food distribution. This is politically practicable. It was actually achieved for a few years at the end of the Second World War and just after it [12]. During those years, an international authority, the United Nations Relief and Rehabilitation Agency, was allowed to take control over the whole of the world's food supply and to ration it to the whole of the world's population. UNRRA made itself responsible for ensuring that no one in the world should starve, and it discharged this tremendous responsibility with remarkable success".

Something of the same sort is again being urged by the FAO. In a report published in 1965 a world plan for agriculture, designed to co-ordinate the world's food production and distribution is called for. This plan is called the "Indicative World Plan for Agricultural Development".

Such an overall plan is unlikely to be acceptable now to the rich food-exporting countries. But, by the end of the century, with a world population more than double the present population, such a plan will no doubt be necessary. No doubt it will be technically possible to feed adequately 7 billion human mouths, but the price to be paid will be heavy. Nearly the whole land surface would need to become farmland, with the once magnificent forests reduced to a few scattered copses, with pesticides levying their last toll on the remaining pockets of free wild life, with the waters controlled, canalised and altered by chemical additives. The cost to be paid in loss of beauty and freedom is certain. What is less obvious is the benefit, if any, that the doubling of the present world population would bring.

Toynbee's idea is obvious common sense, if we accept that the populations are to continue their speeding increase. Yet this is just what we should not do. Harrison Brown shows what might be the result of accepting fatalistically that the population increase is not stoppable: "If we were willing to be crowded together closely enough, to eat foods which would bear little resemblance to the foods we eat to-day, and to be deprived of simple but satisfying luxuries such as fire-places, gardens and lawns, a world population of 50 billion persons would not be out of the question. And if we really put our minds to the problem, we could construct floating islands where people might live and where algae farms could function, and perhaps 100 billion persons could be provided for. If we set strict limits to physical activities so that caloric requirements could be kept at very low levels, perhaps we could provide for 200 billion persons… A substantial fraction of humanity is behaving as if it would like to create such a world. It is behaving as if…it would not rest content until the Earth is covered completely and to a considerable depth with a writhing mass of human beings much as a dead cow is covered with a pulsating mass of maggots."[13]

7. Fuel.

If there is a danger of sudden food famines that can be understood and avoided by the drawing up of a global food budget and consequent action, the similar danger in the field of fuel of what Professor Linton terms inanimate energy, though less immediate, is probably more serious in the long run. Here, too, Professor Linton has drawn up a draft global budget. In the same address from which we have quoted, he speaks of the three sources of energy: the first of these is the radiant energy which comes to us from the Sun: second is the internal heat of our own Earth, and third the rotational energy with which our Solar System, both as a whole and in its various parts has been endowed. There is nothing that lives or works or moves on the face of the Earth - the winds, the tides, the flight of a bird, the sped arrow or the spoken word - but is kept living or is kept moving by the energy from one or other of these sources. But it is convenient to add a fourth category and set apart what we may call the vital energy of Man. This is not a distinction that a physicist or a bio-chemist would make but it is fundamental to the sociologist and the economic historian. Whether Man's activities are achieved by his own muscle power or that of his domestic animals, by windmills or watermills, steam engines or nuclear reactors, they differ from all other activities taking place at the surface of the Earth not in the ultimate sources of their own energy, but in the fact that the energy is purposefully controlled. "Vital energy" is a phrase we may use, not to denote energy of any special kind, but to mean energy in the service of Man.

Professor Linton then shows how, up till the Industrial Revolution, broadly speaking, Man used the inexhaustible, renewable energy of the Sun, and managed to balance his energy budget and live roughly within his annual income. Then came the Industrial Revolution that ushered in the second of the three great periods into which the history of mankind must be divided when we regard it from the point of view of energy relationships. The second or middle period is of course, the period of exploitation of fossil fuels - the brief bonanza of coal and oil in which the solar energy, stored by past vegetable and animal life through long periods of geological time, is being exploited and rapidly dissipated. My comment here is that these fossil fuels are useful not only as fuel, they are the basis of the rapidly expanding petrochemical industry, and provide the raw materials for most of the modern synthetic and plastic products, drugs and chemicals; they may even, as we saw earlier, become the basis of an important food industry. Our generation's thriftlessness will not be understood by future generations as they look at the empty and looted storehouses. It is as if we were to give the geological specimens in the British Museum to a speculative builder as materials for a new housing estate.

Professor Linton continues: "Energy is being consumed and dissipated at an unparalleled rate and the all-time peak will probably be reached during the lifetimes of the younger members of this audience. Present world consumption is of the order of 40 x 10 calories, of which coal, oil, and natural gas are responsible for four fifths. Consumption of these irreplaceable fuels was, in 1962, equivalent to 4460 million metric tons of coal, with oil and gas together slightly outweighing coal and lignite. The remaining fifth is from renewable sources, but is not supplied, as some of you may think, by hydro-electric developments. The larger part of it is, in fact, the energy used for cooking and heating by the poorer peoples of the world and is provided by burning dung and farm wastes. In the dry, treeless lands from Morocco to the Deccan the dried dung of cattle, goats, camels and buffaloes is the main source of inanimate energy and in the aggregate probably has a coal equivalent of at least 500 million tons - which is a good deal more than the yearly coal output of the USA - while corn cobs, corn stalks, and sugar cane trash in Latin America provide energy aggregating perhaps half this amount. Wood fuel in the land of the boreal and equatorial forests still provides energy with a coal equivalent of a further 200-300 million tons. Most of our energy from renewable sources is thus provided from farm and forest sources and the contribution from hydro-electricity had, in 1962, a coal equivalent of only 96 million tons… The production of nuclear power… amounted to… a coal equivalent of rather less than a million tons.

"If the second or middle phase in the history of mankind is that of the exploitation of the fossil fuels the third is obviously the long future that will continue after their exhaustion. How soon the third phase will be upon us cannot readily be forecast, for any figure that we may offer is the quotient of a very uncertain estimate of total Earth resources, divided by a rate of exploitation which itself depends on other unpredictable factors. Chief of these is, of course, the rate of growth of the world's population, and hardly less important, the attitude which mankind adopts towards its dwindling fuel reserves. Both of these are essentially matters of policy, World population now about 3,479 million (mid-1958) - is confidently expected to double by the year 2000 and, indeed, there is little mankind can do that it is prepared to do to prevent this happening. But the growth of population in the twenty-first century will have to be a matter of decision, and the decisions must be made in the coming generation if matters are not to get out of hand… In such a situation regulated use of the fossil fuels is likely to be enforced and the period of their usefulness may be considerably extended".

My comment here is that there exists another factor, fully as important as the actual world population. Elsewhere in Professor Linton's address it appears that the per capita consumption of energy in the United States is 6 tons per annum of coal equivalent, while for the human race as a whole it is about 1.3 tons. But (a) attempts are being made everywhere to raise world standards to American standards, and (b) there is a close correlation between energy consumption and standards of living. If, therefore, the world could suddenly attain an American standard, the fossil fuel requirements would be quadrupled. And if the world attains American standards at the end of the century, when the world population is double the present total, the annual requirements will be *eight times* the present consumption, of 35,000,000,000 tons of coal equivalent.

Since existing proven oil reserves are only 33 times current annual oil consumption, it is most unlikely that at existing population growth rates the human race will attain present American standards on the fossil fuels now known to exist. And what will American standards in America be at the end of the century?

Professor Linton is, however, more optimistic than I am in the foregoing paragraphs for he judges that "oil is assured in plenty for this century and, under sensible population and extraction policies, perhaps for much of the next. Coal is generally thought to be available for considerably longer, though recent estimates have been less optimistic than earlier ones".

He then speaks of the growing use of nuclear power and shows how important it may become, "provided the problems of radio-active wastes on a vast scale can be solved. If so, a period of several centuries may supervene in which our profligate civilisation, having run through its inherited fortune of fossil fuels, runs through a second fortune of radio-active ores before settling down with a regulated energy budget to live within its annual income". This means (as would have been clear if I had not presented Professor Linton's address so summarily) that in the long run we shall probably have to live within the limit of the amount of solar energy reaching the Earth annually.

As in the case of other chapters of the overall global budget, the broad outlines of a budget are already visible, but effective action is a long way off. The necessary world regulatory bodies do not yet exist. Yet, as in the domain of demography much can be done by forward looking governments even now. Obviously much can be done to-day to limit the calls on the fossil fuels since nothing is more certain than their exhaustion in the foreseeable future.

There should be a general move to raise the price of motor fuel. One glance at an advanced modern community shows that there is far too much going to and fro much of it unproductive and pointless, and it is quite clear that motor fuels are, almost everywhere, far too cheap. Governments everywhere should raise the taxes on these fuels, devoting the proceeds to better highways and to making motor transport more efficient. The oil-producing countries should, in concert, raise their prices. The mechanism lies ready to hand in OPEC, the Organisation of Petrol Exporting Countries. OPEC succeeded, notably in the 1965 agreement, with the major oil companies in slowly raising the price of oil. But OPEC is seriously weakened by the political disunity of the Arab world. Here is a challenge to constructive Arab statesmen: unity in OPEC will not only be good for immediate receipts, and for the poorer part of the world, but a higher oil price would break the present profligate use of this irreplaceable heritage.

Just how important OPEC could be is shown by the following facts from the Economist: "More that 60% of all the oil at present known to exist in the world lies under the Middle East. Counted more practically: of all the oil reserves presently being drawn upon for international trade to any significant degree, the Middle East possesses three quarters. About two thirds of the oil Britain uses comes from there; 60% of the European Economic Community's oil supplies, three quarters of Japan's… As of to-day, the Middle East still deserves the name of the place where Reynolds first struck commercial oil there just 57 years ago - *Maidan-i-Naftun,* the Plain of Oil. As of to-morrow, too, - oil - and gas will be found elsewhere, probably nearer to market. Nuclear energy is coming down to the costs of a practical workaday fuel. Technology gets more and more production out of all kinds of fuel. Nevertheless, postulate the rates of economic growth that we all expect nowadays, and the world's energy needs grow almost alarmingly… Over the next generation, energy demand may grow 2.5 times; and until, say, close to the end of those twenty five years, oil will probably have to supply the biggest part of that increase. And as Mr. John Loudon, who is retiring as senior managing director of the Royal Dutch Shell Group, said in the Cadman lecture "On current evidence the largest proportion of the increase required will have to be supplied from the Middle East".

From the facts such as these does OPEC derive its present and its probable future importance especially as the growth in the use of oil is faster than is that of other fuels. The petroleum committee of the International Labour Office has reported that the consumption of oil doubled between 1950 and 1960, and that it is still doubling each decade.

Price increases could do much to restrain wasteful uses of oil. Another desirable change would be the encouragement by all transport authorities of the use of electric traction instead of diesel and petrol traction. The trend has been heavily in favour of diesel and petrol recently: even to the extent of railway companies in the United States tearing down their electrification installations. And in many cities the electric trolley-bus has given way to the diesel bus, ousted by the greater flexibility and cheapness of diesel power. Quite apart from the unpleasant effect that this change-over has had on the atmosphere of many cities, its rightness can be questioned on almost every score. Diesel engines require petroleum-based fuels, but of all fossil fuels it is the petroleum reserves that are most endangered. Electric traction can be powered by the more abundant coal, or by replaceable hydro-electricity or by the much more abundant nuclear power. Electric traction is relatively noiseless. It is likely that private transport will have, in the future, to be exclusively by means of small electrically-driven cars, so short that they can be parked nose on the curb, for our cities cannot endure an unlimited growth in the number of petrol-driven standard motor cars. If local authorities would look forward more than a handful of years to the coming dearth of petroleum they would halt the present trend towards diesel traction, and would encourage the use of electricity, in private as well as in public transport.

There is little doubt that the future of motor transport lies with electric traction. The electric car has the immensely important advantages that it is silent and that it does not emit noxious gases. In addition, the development of electric batteries and fuel cells is proceeding at great speed and a car powered by a zinc-air battery is already nearly as efficient and cheap as a conventional car. Electricity will probably have overtaken petroleum as the major motor fuel by the turn of the century.[14]

Another desirable change would be for the makers of automotive machinery to develop a cheap and effective coal-powered smokeless, gas turbine for long-distance transport. And a further change would be for more oil-from-coal plants to be built. The urgent need at present for fuel statesmanship is for almost any technique to be developed that will ease the pressure on the remaining petroleum reserves.

The above are just a few ideas out of many hundreds that could easily be put forward for leaving something of this heritage of fossil fuels, and in particular of the oil deposits, for our grandchildren and their grandchildren.

8. Soils

Soil, that seems so solid, is also in a process of constant use and renewal. Soil is manufactured by plant life and micro-organisms, and by oxidisation and weathering of rocks. Soil is removed by erosion, partly naturally but mostly as a result of Man's activities. Before Man learned agriculture these two processes were in creative balance, but as agriculture and pastoralism have spread, so this balance has been destroyed. Fertile soils are disappearing to-day far faster than they are being made.

In 1943 I wrote a booklet which attempted to draw attention to the dangers of soil erosion, a task much more ably accomplished by a galaxy of writers (Vogt, King, Lowdermilk and Bennett) who have influenced, and who have deserved to influence, the course of human affairs.[15]

Despite much research it is not yet possible to estimate accurately the amount of soil created each year, nor even the amount of soil washed away. But the problem presses, and the drawing up of a soil budget is a necessary pre-requisite for action to save the soils of the World.

Pending a budget and pending accurate information, all governments ought to be pursuing rigorously conservationist policies towards their soils. Unfortunately few governments are doing so: perhaps the only governments to have decisively reversed the progress towards ruin are the governments of the United States and Israel. Even in Europe, the home of soft rains and skilled farmers, though the land is comparatively safe from erosion, the process of soil degradation and the consequent silting of the rivers continues at a rapid pace. And in other countries, sometimes through impulsive or doctrinaire state decisions, vast areas of bush or prairie are laid open through tractor-ploughing to the harsh scourging of the elements. This happened under Russian Socialism in the so-called virgin lands, and under British socialists in the unsuccessful ground- nut scheme for Tanganyika.

Unfortunately most of the world's farms are under the control of unskilled and ignorant farmers, and as the populations in their countries increase, so they are going to be under heavier temptation even than formerly to mine the soil.

The above does not mean that careful farming is a monopoly of the men of the 20th century. Perhaps the most careful farming ever seen was the traditional farming of China, Japan and Korea, marvellously described early in this century by an American agriculturalist.[16] Every scrap of compostable matter was composted, and returned diligently to the soil; canals were drained methodically, and the fish shared out among the people, and the mud carried from the canal to the nearby fields; the use of human wastes and excrements was much more intelligently and economically handled than it is to-day in the glittering European and American metropolises; the scarce fuel, wheat straw, was used with the greatest care for cooking and heating the houses; the sloughed-off skins of the silkworms laid reverently in the mulberry-grove and worked back into the soil.

As a result these farmers had tilled their soils for 4,000 years without loss of fertility. In their agriculture lie many, many lessons for the men of the tractors and combine harvesters who so far have not been able to farm without impoverishing their soils.

This great subject has only been touched on. What is certain is that we must use our soil all over the world knowing how precious it is, knowing what losses and gains are being scored, and doing everything to preserve it for another "forty centuries" at the least.

Conclusion: The Basic Unity of Science.

Early in mathematics one learns that one cannot add together apples and pears. *A fortiori* one cannot add men to animals, units of radiation to tons of water. And so these various chapters of the global budget can never be combined in one great overall statement. The units are disparate, yet there is an underlying unity. For on the global intake of energy depends the global weather. On the global weather depends the food production. Similarly intertwined are the human population, the soils, the fuels. The more one looks at the totality of the life of the World the more it is seen to be a multiplicity of facets, with an underlying unity. From a strictly scientific viewpoint too, a unity is imposing itself.

Professor Lloyd V. Berkner, of the Graduate Research Center of the Southwest, at Dallas, Texas, has written an article "The Unity of the Geophysical Sciences" to make this very point.[17] The more you look at, say, vulcanology or seismology, hydrology or meteorology, the more it is seen that these sciences cannot be considered in isolation. Professor Berkner writes: "With the advance of physics, and especially electronics, in our own lifetime, powerful new tools for observation, measurement and analysis have become available. Employment of such new and excellent means from the physical point of view has created the recent science of geophysics, which has given a new order of power in analysing our planet. Extended to chemistry and biology in our time, the word 'geosciences' has come to describe the complex study of our own planet.

"It is therefore fitting that we summarise briefly the state of geophysics, or, more generally, the sciences of the Earth as a group of unified sciences.

"Since the geosciences employ mathematical and analytical methods applied to all aspects of planet Earth as well as the other planets, they embrace a wide variety of scientific disciplines. Geology, the descriptive science of the accessible surface of the Earth, not only provides clues to the history of the Earth, but also to the evolutionary emergence of the living species. Among the more analytical researches, giving Man insight into the nature, origin, and history of his planet are: (1) geodesy and gravimetry, concerned with the figure of the Earth; (2) seismology, dealing with wave motion in the Earth and the resulting inference of interior structure; (3) tectonophysics, involving the internal forces producing surface irregularities; (4) vulcanology, geochemistry and petrology, concerned with the analysis of rocks and other volcanic products and of meteorites; (5) geochronology, dealing with the dating of terrestrial, planetary and meteoric matter; (6) oceanography, the science of the oceans and their waters; (7) meteorology, the science of the lower atmosphere; (8) hydrology, the science underlying the Earth's basic supply of fresh water; (9) aeronomy , involving the outer atmosphere, ionosphere, and exosphere, and including many terrestrial aspects of space science; (10) geomagnetism, the study of the magnetic field of the Earth; (11) cosmic-ray physics in its geophysical aspects involving the behaviour of high-energy particles; (12) solar physics, and (13) interplanetary physics".

Professor Berkner then gives many examples of the ways in which the Earth and atmosphere and oceans interact, and convincingly shows that none of these sciences can be considered *in vacuo,* but only as one of a group of unified sciences.

If there is a growing unity of the earth-sciences, unity is coming to science in other ways too. One of the effects of the study of ultimate particles has been to unify physics and chemistry, and to draw them closer to astronomy. One of the effects of molecular biology has been to draw together biology and chemistry and physics. As more becomes known of the nature of matter, so all sciences meet, at least at the level of the ultimately small.

In another way, too, a unity is imposing itself on science. The body of knowledge is now so colossal that it is no longer possible for, say, a biologist to keep abreast of happenings in other disciplines, though often these may be pregnant with importance for him. Thus, a recent proposal which has been well received is for there to be a "science of science", a body of knowledge which will concern itself with maintaining in accessible form, knowledge of science and making it available to those who might need it.

In a political way too, unity is imposing itself on science. Political and linguistic boundaries are one of the real barriers to the progress of science, and to an ever-increasing extent the World's scientists are learning to ignore them. Some of the greatest achievements in recent times have occurred when, in effect the scientists have told the politicians to mind their own business and that they intended to share their knowledge on a global basis. An immense step forward of this kind was taken when the International Geophysical Year was inaugurated in 1957. Almost for the first time scientists from all major countries cooperated as brothers on a world-wide scale to deepen our knowledge and understanding of our planet-home.

Now something similar is planned by the biologists. It is known as the International Biological Programme. It has as its main task the study of the biological basis of productivity and human welfare. Commenting on the programme, Science Journal, December 1966, says: "(It is) perhaps the most ambitious (programme) to be undertaken by Man for peaceful purposes (and) will shift biology from the nineteenth century to the twenty first… IBP, with the entire biosphere as its stage, is geared to answer the increasingly pressing problems of how best to use the Earth's biological resources to support overpopulation by the dominant species, Man". Fifty eight nations were involved by December 1966, 38 of which were firmly committed to carrying out IBP studies.

The global budgets of all substances whose input and output make life possible, budgets firmly founded on a growing unity of all the sciences, are thus necessary to us to be able to take stock of life's assets and liabilities. The interests of Man, of the biosphere, and of the planet itself demand that this work be done; and Man's greedy looting of the assets makes it imperative it be done quickly.

REFERENCES

(I)   *The Observer,* 1 May, 1966.

(2)   *Larousse Encyclopedia of the Earth,* London, 1961; p. 16.

(3)   *The Observer,* 1 May, 1966.

(4)   *Jeune Afrique* 22 May, 1966. (My translation from the French).

(5)   *Larousse Encyclopedia of the Earth,* London, 1961; p.93. Note that billion here is understood as million million, not as is now conventional a

thousand million. *Editors.*

(6)   Water and Life, by L. and M. Milne, Deutsch. 1965.

(7)   *Le Monde,* 9 June, 1966.

(8)   Water and Life, by L. and M. Milne, Deutsch. 1965, p.131.

(9)   From "Making the Most of our Water" by Peter C. G. Isaac, Professor of Public Health Engineering, University of Newcastle-on-Tyne.

(10) U.S. Department of Commerce.

(11) *Oryx,* April 1, 1967.

(12) There was a proposal by Lord Boyd-Orr that the arrangement continue, in the form of a world food board, but this proposal was defeated in the FAO, allegedly by the "rich countries" which wished to preserve a free market.

(13) The Challenge of Man's Future, by Harrison Brown.

(14) The Electric Automobile, by George A. Hoffmann, *Scientific American,* October, 1966.

(15) The Enemy, by "Melanchthon", Morija Printing Works, Basutoland.

(16) Farmers of Forty Centuries, by King.

(17) Transactions, American Geophysical Union, Vol. 45, No.3 Sept. 1964

7 Bacillus Sapiens

THE GLOBAL budgets, as we saw in the last chapter, display a disturbing overall picture of human improvidence and greed. And, looking to the future, we saw that the probable increases in the human populations threaten to double and quadruple the harm done by our improvidence and greed. Looking back in history and pre-history we tried to spotlight the really important developments: the developments that gave us the weapon, agriculture, the state, and science. These we termed super-events. Each of these super-events produced evil and cruelty. Yet each, too, produced good: perhaps if the killer-ape had not learned to murder his brother, Bach's music might never have been written.

Bach's music, however, does not abolish evil. Is it possible that human power is intrinsically evil, that with each advance in power and knowledge evil gains a lead over good? Are the graphs of human development pointing to a future human who shall be a learned titan - and a devil?

Most people will reject such an idea, for it hurts our own self-esteem, and it conflicts with the optimism of many scientists, of the Christians (original sin having been defeated through Christ), and of the Marxists (exploitation having been defeated through scientific socialism). Nevertheless it is our duty to look at truths even if they conflict with our pre-judgements and with our self-esteem. The hypothesis that knowledge and evil go together is the only hypothesis that seems to explain satisfactorily the most important events of history. It is also the only hypothesis that seems to explain satisfactorily the intrinsic nature of Man.

The proof of the pudding is always in the eating. Can one say that Man himself, the product of a million years of human history and pre-history, is intrinsically a repellent being? Clearly, if one could ask the remnant of the wild animals, the answer would be yes, for they have special reasons to resent the being that has taken the world from them and that has persecuted them cruelly and remorselessly. If one asks Man himself, the answer would be no, but then one should not ask one of the parties to a civil case to be judge. Let us therefore try to imagine the look, the smell, the feel and the total impact of Man as they might be sensed by an entirely unbiassed observer. Since no such observer exists on this world, let us try to imagine how a visitor from another extremely distant world might react to the human race. Let us imagine that a spaceship from a planet of the nearest star, Alpha Centauri, has just landed in the park of a great English country house. Out of it steps an intelligent being, able to communicate with us, sent here to make a fair assessment of the true nature of Man. He is immediately welcomed and given hospitality by the owner of the house who spends some time in briefing him. After some days he has drawn up a programme with his host, and out he goes into the wider world, able to range far and wide and to see all the aspects that he feels are needful for his assessment.

The first thing he would do is to look at the outer aspect of human beings, to watch their behaviour and to listen to their noises and their talk. Perhaps the first note in his notebook would concern human babies. Why, he would wonder, do they, alone of young things, spend so much of their waking time in tears and screaming? He would compare them with a day-old leveret or any other young animal and see a happy young thing obviously in harmony with its surroundings and with its mother. Only human babies howl. Why? Why is the entry into human society so painful, so much a matter of despair? Could it be a painful impact with the accumulation of a million years of evil?

He would notice that, alone of young things, only the human kind seem to have constantly-running noses and to be naturally dirty. Looking at the larger children he would notice how instinctively cruel they seem to be to their own kind. Passing up the age-scale, he would notice that human adolescents, unlike growing animals, are subject to acne, rashes of pustules on their faces: And, looking at the human race in general he would notice that it is Man alone who is built incapable of excreting cleanly. He would notice that

Fig. 4. Five week old gorilla baby

it is only men and pigs (who resemble men so closely in anatomy and in habits of feeding) that produce thoroughly unpleasant-smelling excreta. He would notice that, alone of animals, it is the human gastrointestinal canal that so often goes out of action with psychosomatic faults.

Passing even further up the age-scale, the Alphacentaurian would notice that, alone of animals, Man is ravaged by the aging process. Other animals, it is true, show physical signs of the passing of the years. The great ears of the African elephant become torn, for example, by the thorn trees, and the old lion's teeth become blunt. But in no other species is the aging process so closely correlated with ugliness. How few of us are able to age with beauty or serenity! The human infant is beautiful', and normally displays the undamaged character of the DNA-encoded pre-social inheritance. Some of us preserve this beauty into early middle age. But as the decades roll on, as Man-manufactured society distorts and presses on the individual, there are few who do not show the marks in their faces and bodies.

If anyone should doubt the truth of this let him look round in a bus, let him look at those lack-love apathetic, greedy faces; this being was once potentially near-perfect, cradled in its mother's arms. And if he should still doubt its truth, let him look, if he is middle-aged, in his own mirror.

Our visitor would note the extraordinary distribution of human hair, betraying perhaps Man's curious irresolution about his own nature, as if he did not know whether he is an animal or not. The male head in youth is hairy, yet in age is often bald. He would see, with distaste, that many men grow hair, sometimes mats of it, on parts of their bodies.

He might find beards and moustaches funny. Or perhaps, in general, repellent, since in most countries men shave once a week rather than daily, giving them a dirty, dishonest, tramp-like look. The pubic hair is ugly and serves no purpose, being, indeed, somewhat counterproductive. And the armpit hair is ugly and aggravates the *hircus alarum,* the pungent odour which in all ages has been found offensive. One can see the beauty in a hairless human body: the Greek statues are the ideal of this type of beauty. And one can see the beauty of a furred animal, such as a sleek tiger or a well-bred horse. But our visitor would be puzzled and perhaps amused by the betwixtness and betweenness of the human body as it really is with curious tufts of hair in curious places. And, looking at the masses sunning themselves on the bathing beaches he would likely compare them to their disadvantage with the seals sunning themselves on their rookeries.

Man's bad smell is not limited to the armpits. Alone of animals his general smell is repellent. A horse smells sweet, even after it has sweated heavily. It is true that some of the predators smell unpleasant when they have been caged, and that some pigs smell bad when they are enclosed in filthy sties. (It has recently been discovered that if pigs are given a sty in which they can excrete cleanly they will do so, and will train the young generation to do so as it comes along). No animal bodies stink in the way in which unwashed human bodies stink. None has the immediacy of our own body odour. There is only one odour that can rival ours in Nature: the repellent odours *deliberately* ejected by skunks as a defence mechanism.

But our visitor is level-headed, and would not wish to dwell too long on the merely physical aspect. He might at this stage say: "all right, I can see that this human biped is dirty, tufty-haired, noisy and shuffles his way through life. It is possible that his glory lies elsewhere, so let's consider his culture".

Here he would be partly right, for Man has to his credit many achievements of the greatest value. The visitor would no doubt react favourably to the best human music, buildings, sculptures poems and paintings. Then he would notice that most of the best had come down from earlier times, and he would note that at present there is a cult of ugliness and obscurity. For five centuries Europe (to take but one of the continents) produced masterpieces, both at the level of high art and at the level of popular and peasant art. Yet to-day Beethoven and rustic dances and songs are without successors, and our composers of to-day create the vulgar howling of "popular" music, which is often an incitation to immorality, and sometimes even to criminality and drug-addiction.

A similar phenomenon is visible in the fields of sculpture and painting. Here an incomparable tradition rooted in the most ancient past of Egypt and Greece, has died, and has been replaced by the follies of picassoism. And there is a status-seeking vogue which cultivates pop-art and non- representational art. Perhaps it could be more correctly termed "non-significant art".

The use of new materials, and the need to house the new tidal waves of people have, of course, necessitated new architectural styles. Yet here, too, the ugliness cult has moved in, and many modern buildings have but one virtue: to proclaim how thoroughly their architect had broken with all tradition.

In literature and poetry similar trends have appeared. Deliberate obscurity has been practised, and on this obscurity a modern esoterism has been established, coteries of adepts who are able to claim - in appropriately obscure language - understanding of their authors' delphic writings.

Is this cult of the obscure based on a desire not to reveal ourselves, on a defence-mechanism set up against the pervasive, invasive power of a mechanised society? In an excellently pessimistic article in the SUNDAY TIMES Lord Eccles, speaking of sexual relationships, believes that we do not, nowadays, commonly reveal ourselves to one another, and that in armouring ourselves against mechanised society we also armour ourselves against the love we are offered.[1] Most of us, perhaps will agree, and will look back to our idea of the Greek Arcadia with the sadness of having missed a supreme terrestrial joy, the sadness of knowing that *homo scientificus* is probably unable to give himself to that joy.

A somewhat related phenomenon is the increasing fogginess and imprecision of the English language. Anyone who has listened to a telephone conversation between two Americans will know how imprecisions are used to conceal meaning. The same process is at work on the other shore of the Atlantic, and British English is becoming a language that our grandfathers could not understand. A whole new language is being built up to hide behind. The core of this new language is the new compound verb: how many of the following verbs existed a century ago? And how many have a clear meaning to-day?

TO CHECK in, on, upon, out, with: a checking account;

TO KEEP out, in with, at, on at: up with;

TO KNOCK in, off, out, over, at;

TO SET in, out, at, make a set at, out, out to;

TO COME off (succeed), on (improve), over, out (in spots), off it, to, at, up with, on in;

TO GO off, off at, to at, away with, on, on at, over, under;

TO LIVE on, off, it up, it down, up to, out, in;

TO CRACK down on, up (break up or praise);

TO PACK in, off, up;

TO KNOCK in, off, out, over, at;

TO PUT up, out, up with, in, in for, over;

TO CAST down, out, away, up;

TO DO for, in, down, away with, up, with;

TO HOLD up, over, away from, out, under, out of.

These verbs are the pidgin of modern man, weasel words, words that hide behind the cigarette and the mumbling lips, words of the scared corporation-man. Compare this contemptible pidgin with the language of the Authorised Version of the Bible; or with the manly simplicity of a Bantu language; or with the clarion words of the Iliad or the Aeneid; or with the cantering rhythm of the Odyssey.

Surely in this linguistic field the degeneracy of our modern times could be statistically assessed.

Why are these cults of ugliness? It is difficult to reply, but elements of the answer seem to be that our age responds unusually strongly to two drives: the drive to belong to an avant-garde, and the drive to admire something new. In the cultural field and in the field of fashion these two drives merit, perhaps, a new word: neomania the unbalanced passion for the new, a passion closely coupled with Man's obsession with sensation.

Our visitor would note as perhaps Man's main characteristic this unquenchable passion for the exploration of the senses. It takes root in the need which all life experiences to explore the unknown, for how else does a species know accurately and fill completely its evolutionary niche? But Man the extremist carries all to extremes. And so our visitor would learn that the ancient Romans, when they could afford it, used to have their meals twice, to enjoy twice the pleasures of the stomach. In order to make room for the second meal they would retire to their vomitorium where their slaves would help them to vomit up their first meal.

In our times we have not yet returned to this Roman custom, but otherwise we seem to have tried everything. In particular Man has spent much energy exploring abnormal sexual pleasures. And he has also developed the use of drugs to an immense extent. Two drugs alcohol and tobacco, have become almost as necessary as bread to hundreds of millions. And other drugs, such as Indian hemp *(Cannabis indica)* or marihuana cocaine, morphia and other opium derivatives are becoming more and more used. Then there are the new synthetic drugs such as amphetamine (purple hearts) dexedrine and the hallucinants, which are becoming the vogue of the sixties in the advanced societies.

In Britain "the number of heroin addicts has risen dramatically from 62 officially recorded in 1958 to 670 in September 1966. They grow younger: none under 20 in 1959, 145 in 1965. The use of cannabis has shown a marked increase since 1960. To-day it is described on the Continent as "The British problem". The misuse of amphetamine - the active ingredient of purple hearts" - has been rising since the 1950's. Once confined to London, it now exists in almost every part of Britain. Most barbiturates misused are got legally on prescription, Phenobarbitone is probably the best known. Consumption leaps every year. It doubled between 1953 and 1959.[2]

Even such drugs are not enough, and the ultimate control of pleasure is being approached. Pleasure-centres have been found in the brain, and these can be cheaply stimulated with small electric currents to give exquisite pleasure of a degree unattainable by the use of drugs.

Our visitor would note, with some surprise, that to an increasing extent people are turning to outrageous behaviour to "give them a kick". Some motor car drivers drive in a manner to risk their own and other lives "for a kick". Others destroy telephones and other public property "for fun". And others, particularly in America and Britain, have rediscovered the old Roman amphitheatre: killing people as the ultimate in "kicks".

There have been many such cases: perhaps the most noteworthy was the case in which a young British couple, Ian Brady and his paramour Myra Hindley, killed children for the fun that it gave them. They were charged with murder in April 1966 at Chester in England. Evidence showed that the two had been connoisseurs of murder and torture, that they had captured and assaulted sexually two children and a 17-year old youth. They had murdered them slowly, and had chopped up the body of the youth. To enhance the pleasure of it all they had recorded the proceedings on their tape-recorder, so that they might savour, perhaps during future long winter evenings, the screams and pleas of their victims. One of the highlights on this tape was the fruitless prayers of one of the little girls who begged to be allowed to go home, as otherwise her parents would "give her hell". These tapes were played over in court.[3]

The English pride themselves on being connoisseurs of quality, but for sheer quantity no nation, as is well known, can rival the Americans. In the United States our visitor would note that there exists an obsession with murder, killing and crime. He would find that, since 1939 there have been eleven cases of group-murder by civilian murderers.[4] He would also find that a recent book *In Cold Blood* can become a best-seller simply by recounting in detail the commission of one of the nastier murders. This book was acclaimed not only in America, but in France also where *l' Express* gave a 12-page review. What is perhaps important is that the rave publicity given to this book and its author in *Time* magazine preceded by only a few days the most shocking group killing of all, the indiscriminate slaughter of 16 people in the university of Austin, Texas. It is well known that great publicity given to sensational deeds encourages others to imitate them, yet it is unlikely that the editors of *Time* will find themselves arraigned as aiders and abettors of the Austin killings. Yet is there so much difference between the exaggerated publicity that they gave the book *In Cold Blood* and the man, who in a crowded theatre, shouts "Fire!"- Judge Oliver Wendell Homes's classic example of the lengths to which the doctrine of free speech do not extend?

Apart from these most shocking bulk killings in the United States, some 17,000 people are annually killed in that country by firearms; 5,000 murders and 12,000 suicides and accidents.[5] Since 1900 it appears that civilian-owned guns have brought death to about 750,000 people in the United States, more than the 530,000 who died in all America's wars during the same period.

The problem here is that the American constitution permits anyone to own arms, and that with typical commercial energy and ingenuity, the American arms market is well stocked with an excellent variety. One young fellow in that country bought himself an anti-tank bazooka, and went around his district shooting down the pole transformers that reticulated the electricity to his neighbours. He did thousands of dollars' worth of damage before he was caught.[6]

Crime is almost unknown in the simpler societies: for 150 years the islanders lived on Tristan da Cunha with no magistrate and no prison. But everywhere that there is "progress" crime flourishes and grows. The statistics in the rich countries show more clearly the unmistakable correlation between knowledge and evil. Here are some crime statistics from England and Wales:

FIGURES OF INDICTABLE OFFENCES

Offence	1938	1961	1962
Breaking & entering	10,853	36,240	42,760
Larceny	56,092	107,235	119,034
Receiving, fraud	5,333	13,589	15,310
Sex offences	2,321	6,150	6,068
Violence to person	1,583	11,519	11,986

The total of indictable offences in England[7] and Wales was 283,220 in 1938 and the total for 1964 was over a million.[8]

Yet, "crime figures for 1966 would be the highest on record, Mr. Jenkins, Home Secretary, told (a meeting) at the Home Office."[9] And, in Britain, there is "an unprecedented wave of arson. The Ministry of Technology's fire research station at Boreham Wood said yesterday that the number of wilfully started fires had increased six-fold in 10 years."[10] And there were, in 1965, 34,351 hoax fire alarms in Britain, compared with 124,188 genuine fire alarms.[11]

In America, the technological leader of the Free World (a term which apparently includes South Africa) the increase in crime has become the concern of all. President Johnson appointed a 19-man commission on Law Enforcement in 1966 to advise him on ways of saving society from the very real threat of crime. The following facts appear on their report. One American boy in six will turn up in a juvenile court for a non-traffic offence before he is 18; in some urban areas nearly half of the residents stay off the streets for fear of attack; the overall crime rate has been spiralling year after year: it shot up 13% in 1964, 5% in 1965, and 11% in 1966. In 1965 alone there were almost 2,500,000 recorded burglaries and major thefts: one for every 80 citizens. Among Afro-Americans the arrest rate for murder is 10 times as high as it is for whites, and for burglary it is 3.5 times as high.

The report made it clear that their figures dealt only with detected crime, and that much crime, being unreported or undetected, was not included in the above figures.[12]

In the same country a new crime is very much on the upgrade, a crime which combines the anonymity and the technique of so much of modern life: the anonymous telephone call. During 1966 the monthly total of obscene or threatening telephone calls *which were reported* increased from 46,000 to 56,000. As a result there is a move to have this crime declared a federal offence.[13]

In almost every country the graph for the more unpleasant forms of crime pursues, year after year, its relentless march upwards. Criminologists tinker with its causes, but few dare face the truth: that crime is inherent in our nature, and has been so ever since we ceased to be animals, and that freedom and crime are inseparable. Apart from normal violent crime the most developed countries have produced a new form of violence which is increasing rapidly: the "battered baby" problem. To a growing extent, adults, usually parents, are brutally and often murderously assaulting tiny babies. Here is a report on this new phenomenon from America: "Suddenly, across the United States… there is an upsurge in discoveries of brutal cases of child beating… "If we had the real figures", says Dr. Frederic N. Silverman, a Cincinnati radiologist, "the total could easily surpass auto accidents as a killer and maimer of children… "Mostly, parents say, they are just getting the child to behave. Almost all the victims are under 3 years of age. And one in ten of them will die. Among those who survive, 15% suffer permanent brain damage."[14] According to another report, such cases now amount to 10,000 annually in the United States.[15] This plague extends to England too, and in London pathologists on the lookout for battered babies are having X-rays taken of all infants found dead at home, dying unexpectedly, or bearing trivial injury. This examination is carried out before a post-mortem, Professor Keith Simpson, Home Office pathologist, told a meeting of the Royal Society of Health… They were on the watch for cases where parents had the cunning to lie effectively when a catastrophe like a fracture or a brain injury demanded explanation.[16]

What would we think if we had landed on Mars and found the Martians behaving like this? We can imagine the effect on our visitor. As he looked at this key question: what is crime? he would find that with the rise of so-called civilisation crime had been growing, as we have already noted. He would compare the bulging prisons and mental hospitals with the fact that such institutions do not exist in many of the simpler communities. In pre-conquest Bantu South Africa there were no prisons, and there was a system of justice that was in many ways fairer more logical, and gentler than the white man's system that replaced it. In Bantu law the aim of the court was to repair the damage, to fine the offender with the aim of compensating the plaintiff, not so much with the aim of exacting retribution and inflicting pain and punishment. Our visitor would note that life in cities produces more criminals than life in the countryside. In the city of Washington, DC, for example, the incidence of serious crime increased 116% between the years 1959 and 1967.[17] And here are some more revealing figures from the United States:

Rates per 100,000 population for crimes known to the police in urban and rural areas, United States 1960

OFFENCE	RATE	
	Urban	Rural
Murder and non-negligent manslaughter	4.9	6.4
Forcible rape	10. 3	6.8
Robbery	70.7	11. 3
Aggravated assault	88.7	42.2
Burglary - breaking or entering	568.9	210.9
Larceny - theft ($ 50 and over)	340.9	102.8
Automobile theft	243.7	42. 1

More criminals in the cities than in the country; more criminals in the developed countries than in the undeveloped countries. But everywhere the effort is to develop the under-developed countries. And everywhere the countryside is emptying itself into the city. Here we see again the correlation between Man's knowledge and power on the one side, and the growth of evil on the other.

The correlation is not true alone of so-called civilised men and so-called uncivilised men; it is true of Man as a whole compared with the animals. Though the field of study is new it is becoming apparent that animals are gentler and more moral than men. Such was the message of one of the BBC talks in the series LIFE which was transmitted on 9 January 1966. The message of this wonderful talk was that Man's behaviour is worse than that of the animals, and that as he grows more civilised he grows crueller, and that as the pressure of population grows, so the behaviour grows worse, in both men and animals.

The programme began with pictures of animals fighting against members of their own species, and the discussion led off with statements by the distinguished scientists who participated that, nearly everywhere in Nature, animals had evolved non-fatal ways of fighting against their own species. Many of the fights were ritual, and even when there were injuries these rarely ended in the death of either of the combatants. This moral pacifistic behaviour was contrasted in the programme with the limitless cruelty of Man. "The truth is," said Dr. Desmond Morris, the introducer of the programme, "that unlike Man and certain animals that he's tampered with like these fish (Siamese fighting fish shown on the screen) or fighting cocks or Spanish bulls, most natural species keep physical violence down to a minimum. They simply can't afford to go around tearing one another to pieces. Now, if animals manage to control themselves better than we do, then it's time we took a close look at them to see what we can learn…" The programme then showed pictures of various species fighting their own kind and it became clear that even an animal like the wolf, so long a symbol in Man's mind of cruelty, is gentler than Man. Then a consultant psychiatrist, Dr. Anthony Storr, was brought into the programme and, in reply to questions said: "One of the really peculiar features of human aggressive behaviour is our extreme vindictiveness towards enemies. I mean, we've seen from these films that when an animal fights another of the same species the loser isn't usually harmed. The loser retreats and the victor is quite satisfied with his Victory, but human beings are so extraordinary in this way that, that they pursue their victims to the end; then they do all sorts of unpleasant humiliations upon them. "I would call (this) the paranoid tendency in human nature". Later, Dr. Storr spoke of "the sadistic behaviour in human beings… the apparent pleasure that people get in inflicting pain on one another or in fact putting one another to death…" He then instanced the case of a fifteenth century Frenchman, Gilles de Rais, who murdered more than a hundred and forty children, apparently one by one, and for pleasure.

Some of the other contributors to the programme put forward the thesis that human cruelty is a product of overcrowding, but this was questioned by Dr. Storr who pointed out that Gilles de Rais was a Marshal of France, and a big landowner, a man to whom overcrowding simply didn't apply.

Nevertheless the others produced impressive evidence to support the view that overcrowding is indeed an important factor in cruelty. They showed how even gentle wild things could, through overcrowding, develop an almost human degree of cruelty. Conrad Lorenz, in addition, had shown how a turtle-dove (the very symbol of gentleness) had flayed another alive when the two had been caged together in a small space and neither was able to flee.

Dr. W. M. S. Russell, a contributor to the programme, a zoologist who has spent his recent years looking at men, said: "If you crowd animals - if you don't give them enough space - there are certain activities they can't perform, then, even if they have plenty of food so that they're materially affluent, nevertheless their society breaks down and they become violently aggressive. This, of course, fits in extremely well with what's known of human societies… from 1950 - 1960 the rates of violent crime in London were very definitely located in areas where the population was extremely dense and living conditions bad… It has now been shown in several species that when their population in an enclosed space reaches a certain point they begin to kill their young." Dr. Russell then instanced the "battered babies" problem already mentioned.[19]

Finally, Dr. Leo Harrison Mathews, Scientific Director of the

London Zoological Society, also touched on this problem. He said: "Animals are very careful not to use (their weapons) fatally against each other (of the same species) normally, but when we get into conditions of overcrowding… then things start to go wrong". Dr. Mathews was asked what, in view of the fantastic increase in human numbers that is now occurring, he thought was going to happen. He replied: "Something very unpleasant, I think. There will be too many people, there will be too much competition for food, and territory and space - eventually for standing room, and either a new virus will mutate and there will be a terrific epidemic, or there'll be a, famine, or somebody will get trigger-happy and press the button and let off atomic weapons".

The whole trend of this calm and dispassionate discussion was that human malevolence had indeed increased with "civilisation", and was likely to increase with the increase in population.[20]

Another zoologist, Dr. S. A. Barnett, has made the same point: "Predatory animals, such as water-beetles and pike, eat other animals of different species, just as we eat cattle or game; but what of their relationships with each other (those of the same species)? Man has war and riot, revolution and murder: what are their counterparts in animal communities? The short answer is: none. The dealings of one animal with another of its own species are nearly always regulated so that severe direct injury is avoided."[21]

At this stage it is necessary to remember that even in human communities there are saints. And there are normal individuals who are truly good, people whose faces shine with an inward light. Nothing in this book should be taken to be an absolute, total condemnation of humankind. The thesis is simply that, on balance, evil triumphs over good; on balance knowledge and cruelty go hand in hand. At this stage a defender of the human race might object: "But you cannot possibly weigh these two things, particularly over such vast periods of time. What you are saying betrays more about your own prejudices than it does about Man. Granted that in some ways Man is getting worse: in others he is becoming better. Think of the improvements in hygiene and in medical care. Think of the thousands of benevolent societies. Think of the abolition of slavery".

The first sentence of this objection is obviously true, and that is why the book opens with "Some Saving Clauses". If we are to see the road behind us and the road ahead we are still obliged to use more insight than statistics, for the simple reason that the statistics simply do not yet exist. If one is lost in a forest at night, a glow-worm's light is better than no light at all.

As to the prejudices of an author, of course his prejudices matter, his background too, his experiences, and his psychology. Having said all this is not necessarily to invalidate his thesis, for he has the duty to defend it with the best evidence available. It is entirely possible that Archimedes was drunk or unbalanced when he rushed out of his bath. It is entirely possible that his nurse had given him an Oedipus complex by frightening him with a toad in his infancy. The fact is that his principle works, that his insight was correct no matter what his own imperfections may have been.

Medical care and hygiene are of course among the great achievements of the present age. Yet to what extent are they *technical* achievements, and to what extent are they *moral* achievements? No one can doubt Man's technical excellence: it is the thesis of this book that as it improves so does evil. Medical advances are clearly a mixture of morality and technology, so that the progress of medicine is a fact which will not, with clarity, either support or weaken the main thesis.

As for the benevolent societies, it is clear that they are one of the great hopes of the world. They are the vehicles which allow the vision of the few to act in the world. They have probably done more to improve the morality of the human species than all other agencies. It is exceedingly encouraging to note how many there are for forwarding the cause of conservation and of animal defence, for the prevention of cruelty to children and so forth. Whether they have stemmed the tidal growth of massive cruelty can only be judged by insight. Whether they are able to do much outside the cosy middle-class world of the rich countries is also an open question. On both issues a healthy scepticism is in order. As for slavery, it is a mistake to speak of "the abolition of slavery". Slavery continues to-day, and if anything, is stronger now than it was thirty years ago. There is a small and valiant society in London, the Anti-Slavery Society, of Denison House, SW1, which was founded more than a hundred years ago, and which continues to attack slavery wherever it may be found. Its recent experience may be of interest in assessing human morality and the effectiveness of the benevolent societies in the modern world. Thanks to it and to other like-minded groups, a conference on the subject of slavery was held at Geneva in July 1966. The aim of the society was to get a special United Nations commission set up to counter slavery. (There are to-day between 250,000 and 500,000 slaves in the world.[22] In Saudi Arabia, for example, the price of slaves has risen greatly with the rise in personal fortunes derived from the oilfields, and it is alleged that some rich muslims from West Africa take with them on their religious pilgrimages to the holy places a young impecunious relative, a living traveller's cheque, whom they sell in Mecca. Interpol is powerless to act, for Interpol is only able to act on local police information, and the countries where slaves are found are unwilling to admit that they exist).

At Geneva, the whole issue was dealt with as a political issue in which the Third World, aided by the communist states, made common cause against the westerners who made the allegations. At first it was alleged that it would be too expensive. Then the Tanzanian delegate ended the debate by criticising the motion on the double grounds that chattel slavery did not exist, and that in any case the *apartheid* of the South African government was a much worse invasion of liberty. No commission was set up.

So slavery continues, though, of course, not on the scale that it used to. For this we must be grateful, and must honour the selfless men who devoted themselves to the cause of abolition which was one of the great credits in history. Again, whether this credit brings down the scales on the side of good is very arguable.

The Alphacentaurian felt that he wished to look at unarguable evident weighable facts, and so at this stage of his investigation he looked at the standards of cleanliness observed by the human race. He noted that, alone of all the animals Man defiles his environment with all sorts of unpleasant and dangerous garbage.

As a result, the normal environment of perhaps half the human race is littered and polluted with undisposed food garbage, with broken bottles, rusting industrial wastes such as old tins and motor cars, with excreta and stale urine. He found that the atmosphere is heavy, near Man's towns, with exhausts and smokes, and that the sea is of growing importance to Man as a huge garbage-dump and as a sewer. He noted that many captains of oil tankers have made a habit of flushing out their empty crude-oil tanks with sea-water, with no thought of the damage that this does to the beaches of the world or to life as a whole. Occasionally there is a catastrophe, as when the giant tanker Torrey Canyon was wrecked on the Scillies and both Britain and France received the curse of the Black Tide, followed by the applications of millions of pounds of detergent in an attempt to cleanse the sea and the beaches. Both the oil and the detergent caused immense damage to the sea and its life.

Some days ago I saw the results of some of these human habits on the beaches near Skikda, in eastern Algeria, They are some of the loveliest in the world: to the east of the little port lie twelve kilometres of golden sands, and to the west steep mountains plunge down abruptly into the blue Mediterranean, and little crescent-shaped sandy beaches alternate with vertical cliffs. The sea-bottom below the cliffs is a patchwork of brilliant emerald and sapphire, as sand alternates with rocky bottoms. Out towards the horizon the blue dominates, as the sea mirrors the sky.

Going down to the sealine I expected the delights of a sea bathe. But I was not alone: many people, mostly noisy children, had got there first. The grown-ups had many transistors... Some of the children pelt visitors with sand. The rocks are their public latrine, and on the sand and in the shallow pools lie broken bottles and discarded sardine-tins. Old newspapers float on the surface or slowly drift along the sea-bottom. Yet all these unpleasantnesses are secondary: for the beach has been spoiled, and for years, by the tarry waste from the passing tankers. Pieces of rounded tar lie liquescent in the summer sun, and one cannot approach the sea without walking in some of it.

The sea is being polluted in so many ways. The Marine Resources

Council set up by the Food and Agricultural Organisation of the United Nations (FAO) recently condemned the widespread opinion that the sea is "an ideal place to deposit any unwanted by-product of civilisation and industrialisation". Some of the examples of pollution found by this council were that DDT had been found in the Antarctic penguins, that similar poisons had been found in the flesh of tunnies (oceanic fish) and traces of lead tetraethyl also in tunnies - the poisonous anti-knock lead additive in modern motor car fuels.

Any mention of the dangers to which the use of pesticides has led must include an admiring tribute to the late Rachel Carson, whose wonderful book *Silent Spring* profoundly moved the world and produced much effective action, How fortunate the world is that her cruel illness allowed her time in which to get her saving message published.

Pollution is much more serious on land than it is yet in the sea. The size of the terrestrial problem is already very grave, and is fast growing, as is reflected in statistics given by two American bodies, the National Academy of Sciences and the National Research Council. Together they produced a report called "Waste Management and Control", and in this report occurs the following passage: *"Man is the messiest of beasts* (my emphasis), and when his kind congregates in vast numbers, the mess multiplies to barely manageable proportions. These facts and projections, although they apply to the United States, have a sharp relevance for every industrialised country. Pollutants such as carbon monoxide, sulphur oxides and hydro carbons, produced by the burning of fossil fuels, are being dumped into the atmosphere at the rate of 125 million tons a year. That amount is expected to double by 1989 and redouble by 2000. By 1980 sewage and other water-transported wastes will be enough to consume, in dry weather, all the oxygen in all the 22 river systems in the United States.

"Per capita production of rubbish has increased from 1.25kg a day in 1920 to 2kg a day in 1965. The rate is believed to be increasing about 4 per cent a year, and already in certain areas is much higher. Studies of the San Francisco Bay area indicate a total of 3.5kg per person per day". The conclusion of the report is that "the right amount of pollution must be planned with criteria set somewhere between the ideal of complete cleanliness and the havoc of uncontrolled filth". But the cost of cleaning up the mess will not be light, and the committee estimates that adequate facilities for sewage treatment alone would cost the United States between $20 and $30 billion. [23]

Such a report is most welcome, but its recommendation is sadly unambitious. In their own words, if it were possible for "the havoc of filth" to be controlled, they would find that this was tolerable. It is only the *uncontrolled* filth that evokes the committee's condemnation.

But (always being grateful to the committee for the relatively radical nature of their report), is this really the best that the Americans can do? Given the present population of the United States (196.9 million in mid-1966), and the fact that this population is due, on present trends, to double itself in only 44 years, it is fairly clear that unless trends are radically altered, the citizens of the world's richest and most powerful state are indeed condemned, for the foreseeable future, to live amongst the "havoc of filth", whether controlled or uncontrolled. It is clear then that the price that the Americans must pay if they wish to escape from this filth is a radical reversal of population trends, and that only when they have reduced their population will they be able to hope to live away from the "havoc of filth".

Lest the above be thought to be exaggerated, here are some facts about the pollution of one of the greatest fresh-water lakes of the world, Lake Erie: Twenty per cent of the world's fresh water is found in the Great Lakes of North America. One thinks of them as vast reserves of blue, clear cool water. But now, writes a commentator, "Lake Erie is making headlines: it is so polluted that it is literally dying. Industrial wastes and sewage poured into the lake by cities and factories in five states has robbed a good part of the water of its oxygen. All the desirable fish have gone; so has a commercial fishing industry. Instead, choking growths of algae, thriving on phosphates in the sewage, threaten to turn the already shallow lake into a swamp… The worst offenders are the Cities of Detroit (which discharges nearly 1. 5 million pounds, or 600 tons, of wastes a day into the Detroit River, a tributary of the Lake), Cleveland and Buffalo. But cities some distance away contribute their bit through filth-laden rivers which eventually flow into the Lake and many of the heavy industries along the shore dump in raw acid, oil, iron, and other substances which consume oxygen… To clean up Lake Erie may cost each of the five states – Indiana is involved as well as the four which border the lake – around a billion dollars". It seems at last as though the Americans are going to do something about it, though whether, even after they have deployed their best efforts, Lake Erie will contain clear, cool blue water is at the very least doubtful.[24]

It has recently been made known that even if all pollution were to cease flowing into Lake Superior tomorrow, it would take five centuries before the natural flow of water would be able to remove the existing filth.

So far I have dealt with what one might call "conventional" pollutants, that is to say, sewage, acid, metals, detergents and pesticides. The picture revealed by an examination of nuclear pollutants is even more disquieting, since the dangers from nuclear pollutants are still largely unknown. The twenty-two years since Hiroshima have not been sufficient to enable scientists to determine accurately the harm done to life by nuclear wastes.[25] According to a French monthly "it is urgently necessary that research programmes be set up, not only to investigate the harmful effects of ionising radiations on living organisms, but also on the career of a radionuclide as it passes through the whole of Nature. But in both of these fields our ignorance is great. And, paradoxically, such studies are poorly supported in national as well as international budgets."[26]

This article shows how, from the beginning of time, there has been a certain level of radioactivity on the surface of the world. Some of this comes from outer space. For instance, the inhabitants of La Paz, Bolivia, living as they do at an altitude of 3,600 metres, receive an annual dose of 270 millirads of radiation, compared with an annual dose of 50 millirads received at the mouth of the Seine. Again, some natural radiation comes from radioactive substances inside the earth. For instance the inhabitants of Kerala, southern India, who live near naturally radioactive thorium sands, receive an annual dose of radiation 10-15 times larger than that received elsewhere.

To this level of natural radioactivity one must now add the artificial radioactivity due to nuclear explosions and nuclear wastes discharged by nuclear installations. When a nuclear bomb (uranium or hydrogen) is detonated, an immense quantity of fission products is liberated - about 170 different elements and isotopes. Among these is Strontium 90, and also Caesium 137 and radioactive zinc, cobalt, and manganese. These radioactive metals are particularly dangerous, since they are readily taken up and stored by marine organisms and fish. These fission products are thrown up into the stratosphere (up to 80km high). They fall back to the earth's surface more or less quickly. It is estimated that, between 1945 and 1962, the testing of nuclear arms liberated into the atmosphere 193,000 tons of fission products. Many of these are known to be extremely harmful to human life, and the UN Scientific Committee, the US Federal Committee, and Professor Linus Pauling have estimated that the tests which took place between 1945 and 1963 probably have already caused malformations in 160,000 children, and are likely to cause malformations in the future to 16 million children.

At this point let us look away from figures, and let us consider just one child born with a malformation. Let us imagine that we had been born with a malformation, and let us imagine the burden that this would have thrown on our parents and friends. Then one must multiply such suffering by 16 million. And then one must remember that this figure is for one species alone, and that there are three million species in the world, most of which are sensitive to ionising radiation. And then one must attempt to assess the refusal of the Chinese and the French to sign the test-ban treaty, and their continuing tests in the atmosphere.

The dangers of strontium 90 are well known, "By behaving like calcium, ^{90}Sr is taken up by the bones of children, there to subject the children's tissues and bone marrow to ionising radiations. It has a half-life of 28 years, so that this radiation will continue right through childhood and into adult life. It is of interest too to note that the experts judge that, even if all testing were to stop under the treaty, the concentration of ^{90}Sr in the world's crust would go on increasing until it reaches a maximum in 1966-1970.

So much for the dangers of military nuclear contamination. Similar dangers exist also as a result of the peaceful use of atomic energy. The dangers of radioactive wastes are given great attention by the atomic power authorities, but, in the absence of adequate information about the effects of these wastes on soils, waters, the sea, and on macro- and micro- fauna and flora, it is not surprising that the question is giving thoughtful people much concern, especially as the number and size of atomic power-stations continues to increase.

As in so many new developments, what is lacking is the spirit of conservatism, the spirit that would wait until the harm is known. In place of such a wise spirit, we have the spirit of competition and haste, a race to install nuclear capacity. The engineers hope that to do so will not irrevocably destroy the sea and the land, but they act without certain knowledge that great damage will not be done.

In all this consideration of pollution we have rather forgotten our Alphacentaurian visitor, but he has been present all the time, looking at the lakes and rivers, sea and land. After seeing the results on city life his desire now is to take a look at the cities, the source of most pollution, "where Man's kind congregates in vast numbers". He would be told how sudden their great growth had been, how over two centuries, the cities of the rich world had grown because they had created wealth, and now how the cities of the poor world were growing because men were fleeing rural poverty and backwardness.

The real nature of the modern city was well described by the nineteenth-century German sociologist Tönnies who understood that in the modern city the old links of friendship and love that had subsisted between villagers had been dissolved. He preached that, in the modern city, men lived closely together not because they belonged together in one community (*"Gemeinschaft"*), but because it was profitable for them to live together in one association (*"Gesellschaft"*), Tönnies showed how *Gesellschaft* could not meet Man's deepest needs, and that the modern city is a psychological and sociological monstrosity. Developments, both in the rich and in the poor countries since Tönnies wrote have justified his concern, and it is difficult to know whether it is better to compete killingly in the competition of the New York "rat-race" or whether it is better to be half-employed in the vertical bidonville apartments of Calcutta or in the *favelas* of Recife: both ways of life have been divorced from the meaningful community and from Nature.

It is probable that close contact with the soil and with Nature is necessary for full mental health. For millions of years the human line has lived in the closest relationship with the soil, first as a food-grubber and a hunter, and then as a farmer. Our fear and happiness reactions have over many thousands of generations been related to real dangers and joys. Now, in the city we are cut off from these real dangers and joys, and through television and other mass media we are subjected to the sight and sound of many hideous and terrifying things, and many other things that would be joys. Yet they are only simulacra on screens or on paper, and have no real power to hurt or to make happy. Their only power is to stimulate, and it seems probable that the human mind has now learned to respond to ersatz stimulations with ersatz reactions. Perhaps in this fantasy world lies one of the reasons why the modern city is psychologically and sociologically ill.

Our visitor might see all this, yet he might enquire whether conditions in cities were not improving. In some cities they undoubtedly are. But, in cities as a whole, "a piped water supply is available to a dwindling proportion of the world's population", as Mr. René Maheu, Acting Director General of Unesco, told a special meeting of experts in Paris in February 1963. He said, "less than 10% of the 3,115 million people on earth have piped water."[27]

For the rich too, all is far from being well with water-supplies. "More than a third of the (American) population drink water that has been used before so recently that public health officials are beginning to worry."[28]

Water and air: the two substances most immediately necessary to life. Our visitor would look up at the air above the modern city, and would notice that the air, too, had become a vast sewer. Each owner of each factory, each driver of each vehicle, has taken the right to pour out poisonous gasses and smokes and oily soots into the common air. In America most apartments have their own incinerators. Much has, it is true, been done in England and elsewhere to control smokes, and much is being done in America to prevent motor-car exhausts from emitting harmful gasses. But at the present rate of improvement matters are still likely to be worse a century from now.

He would notice the noise. Common law forbids a man to assault the body of another, yet almost nowhere is there any efficacious law to protect a citizen's ear from the battery of willful and dangerous noise. Some noise is perhaps unavoidable as the machinery and traffic of a great modern city performs its functions. Yet there is another, more socially dangerous noise, the noise made deliberately by one person to draw attention to himself, by driving cars and buzz-bikes that have been equipped to maximise their noise.

Another extraordinary modern habit that is largely due to the need to assert oneself is the cigarette habit. It is now years since satisfactory statistical proof has been available that cigarettes cause lung cancer and death. They also greatly inflate the statistics of death from emphysema, heart disease, and circulatory disease. If one ten-thousandth as many people had died from eating, say, a kind of table-salt there would have been a national scandal, and the salt forbidden by law. Yet, despite hundreds of thousands of cigarette-induced deaths in America each year, people are smoking more cigarettes. The number smoked in the United States has increased from 440 thousand million in 1952 to 560 thousand million in 1965.[29] Such a habit must fill an acutely-felt psychological need. There is, of course, a certain drug effect in nicotine which can, with study, become pleasurable. But such pleasures do not go far in explaining this habit. If the behaviour of addicts is closely watched, and if the advertising propaganda that hooks them is analysed, a revealing picture of modern mental poverty is revealed.

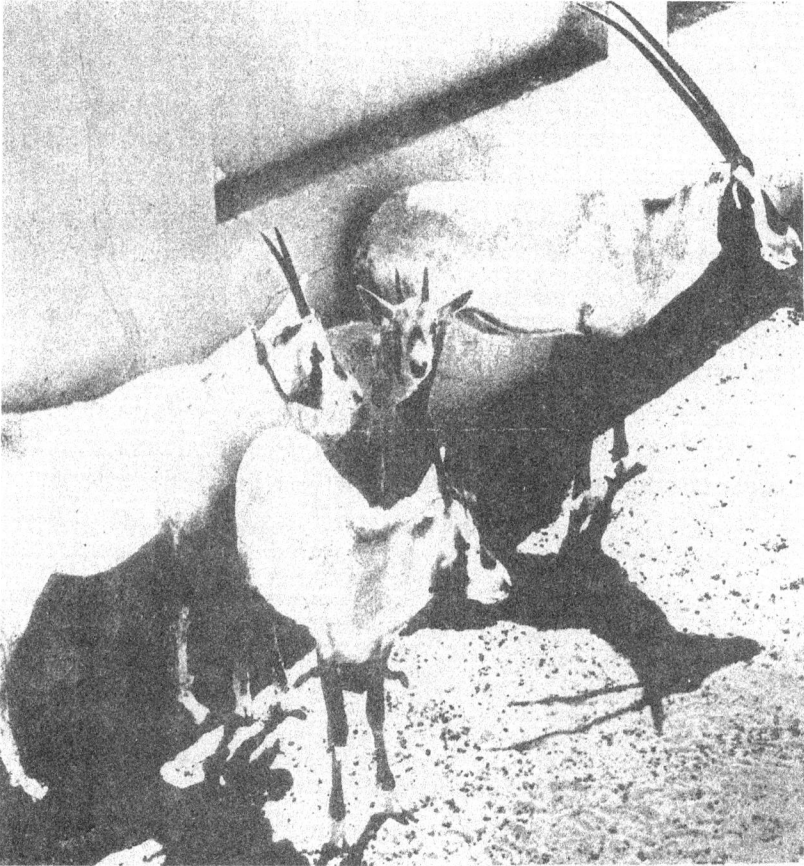

Fig. 5. Saved from the threatened extermination in their native country! Arabian oryx in Riyadh awaiting export to Arizona (Chap. 3). (World Widlife Fund)

Cigarettes are smoked because, through a fortuitous combination of circumstances, and a brilliantly orchestrated publicity campaign, they give assurance. They give assurance to the young who wish to seem more adult than they are; and they give assurance to those who feel lost and crushed by the cruel impersonality of the modern city, and frozen by the coldness of Tönnies's Gesellschaft. Such unfortunate persons have been persuaded that, in the tilt of a cigarette, in the skill with which it is lit, in the generosity with which the pack is shared, lie sources of self-assurance, adulthood and prestige. For these artificial psychological props they are prepared to shorten their lives.

In addition a cigarette enables a smoker to commit the same aggression against his neighbour as does the playing of a transistor radio. The smoker can impose himself on his surroundings, can compel those present to breathe his used breath, his brand of tobacco mixed with his acrid brand of burning paper. Many smokers do not actually "consume" more than a tenth of their cigarettes; instead, they hold a cigarette so that the smoke blows across those who are with them.

The modern city is indeed sociologically ill. If any further proof is necessary, one should consider the revolt of the young against modern industrialised life. Sometimes it is called "juvenile delinquency". Sometimes it is seen as an all but unbridgeable gulf that separates fathers from their children. The older generation, both in the Communist world and in the liberal world, is shocked and amazed, and blames itself.

In the Third World the problem is, of course even more acute than it is in the rich countries. The birth-rate is so high in the Third World that neither the parents nor the teachers can adequately educate the young. The home is not large enough, nor has the mother enough energy to cope with her brood. She sends them into the street and it is here that they receive most of their education. As a result a typical street south of Naples, east of Lima, and west of Singapore rings all day with the bullying mots d'ordre of the street leaders. The little mobs dominate traffic and play football. Society and its policemen are quite impotent. As I write this in

Constantine, Algeria, the noise from the street is so overwhelming that unless one closes the windows one cannot hold a conversation in this fourth-storey flat. What sort of a world it will be when this generation takes over hardly bears thinking about, and one trembles for the future both of Algeria and of the world.

Is it surprising that suicide is on the increase? In line with the present thesis the higher rates are found in the more developed countries. According to the 1963 UN DEMOGRAPHIC YEARBOOK, the countries with the highest rates are Austria, Finland and Czechoslovakia, closely followed by Denmark and Sweden. As our visitor learned this he prepared to leave, and to undertake his long journey home. Taking his leave of his host, he climbed into his spaceship, and soared vertically away from the earth.

Settling back in his gravity-couch for the long month of acceleration, he looked through the mass of material that he had collected, and his eye lighted on an article by Alan George, "A Medical Aspect of the Population Problem" [30]. In it he read: "I suggest... that there are some interesting analogies between the growth of the human population of the world and the increase of cells observable in neoplasms. To say that the world has cancer, and that the cancer cell is Man... (is not proved) but I see no reason that instantly forbids such a speculation... The destruction of forests, the annihilation or near-extinction of various animals, and the soil-erosion... illustrate the cancer-like effect that Man, in mounting numbers and heedless arrogance, has had on other forms of life on what we call "our" planet... Finally I submit that if some of the more thoughtful cells in... a rapidly-growing cancer of the stomach could converse with one another, they might... hold... a "discussion on the population problem".

Looking back for a last look at the Earth he saw one of the great cities below him, and realised that in truth he was looking at a sort of cancer, a world-cancer of which the agent is Man, this astonishing and terrible newcomer, Pulling out his note-book he noted the fact and tentatively named the organism *"Bacillus sapiens"* the intelligent microbe.

REFERENCES

(1)   15 January 1967.

(2)   *The Observer,* 12 February 1967, page 21.

(3)   *Newsweek,* 2 May 1966.

(4)   1929, Chicago: 7 gangsters of the Moran gang executed by a rival gang; 1946: 7 probably killed by a student named Heirens; 13 killed in 12 minutes by an ex-soldier named Unruh at Camden, N.J.; 1956: Taborsky and Culombe kill 6 to rob them in Connecticut; 1956: an engineer, Baier, kills his family of 6, and then himself, at Parsippany, N. J.; 1958 Starkweather and his 15-year old mistress kill 11 in cold blood in Nebraska and Wyoming; 1959: Smith and Hickock kill a family of 4 to rob them in Kansas; 1966 the "Strangler of Boston" kills 11 women in 2 years at Boston, Massachusetts; 1966: Richard Speck kills 8 nurses in a nurses' home in Chicago; 1966: a student kills 16 people in the university at Austin, Texas, and then commits suicide; 1966: a mother kills four members of her family, and then herself, at Milpitas, California. - see *Le Monde,* 3 August 1966.

(5)   *Time* Magazine, 29 July 1966, p. 64: review of *The Right To Bear Arms,* by Carl Bakal, McGraw-Hill, 1966.

(6)   Ibid.

(7)   pp. 614-615, *Whitaker's Almanack,* 1965 (taken at random).

(8)   *The Round Table,* No. 224, October 1966, p.399.

(9)   *The Times,* 26 January 1967.

(10) *Sunday Telegraph,* London; 2 October 1966.

(11) *New Scientist,* 2 February 1967, p.254.

(12) *Time,* 24 March 1967.

(13) *Newsweek,* 30 January 1967, p.6.

(14) *Life Magazine,* 14 June 1963. See also p. 21 below.

(15) *Time* Magazine, 18 November 1966, p. 35.

(16) *The Times,* 25 January 1967.

(17) *The Times,* 3 January 1967.

(18) Federal Bureau of Investigation figures quoted at P. 238 in Metropolis*: Values in Conflict,* ed. C.E.Elias; Wadsworth, Belmont, Ca1. 1964.

(19) cf. VII 16.

(20) *Life.* A BBC Talk; telediphone recording by courtesy of BBC, 9 January 1966.

(21) *New Scientist,* 26 May 1966, P. 536: "Is there a human aggressive instinct?"

(22) *Le Monde,* 17-18 July 1966.

(23) *New Scientist,* 7 April 1966.

(24) *The Economist,* 28 August 1965.

(25) *Science et Avenir,* May 1966.

(26) *Science et Avenir,* May 1966.

(27) *Water and Life,* p.59; by L. and M. Milne, Deutsch, 1965.

(28) *Water and Life,* p.72; by L. and M. Milne, Deutsch, 1965.

(29) *The Economist,* 10 September 1966, p. 1020.

(30) *Science* 121: 681-682, quoted in *Population, Evolution and Birth Control,* p. 73, ed. Garrett Hardin; W.H.Freeman & Co. 1964.

8 Extrapolation

"The hour is very late, and the choice of good or evil knocks at our door."
 - *Norbert Wiener,* (The Human Use of Human Beings, p. 186)

THE FOREGOING chapters contain a gloomy view of Man, gloomier than that of Pascal, which earned him Voltaire's stricture; "It seems to me that in general the spirit in which Mr. Pascal wrote his *Pensée* was intended to show Man in an odious light."[1]

But Voltaire, though one of the brightest human spirits ever to illumine our world, lived in the age of Enlightenment when it was generally believed that human goodness would inevitably grow in harmony with human knowledge. However if he were to return he might acknowledge that Pascal's view had much to justify it.

Despite the pessimism of the foregoing chapters there is, of course, much good in the world. Some of it is growing more, and some of it is growing less. Will the sum of the good increase or decrease over the next two generations? Will the sum of evil increase or decrease? In other words, if one attempts to extrapolate the graphs of good and evil, do they point up or down? And irrespective of the reply to this question, what can be done to "fight the good fight"? In the field of ethics these are the central questions which every autonomous person must ask.

These questions involve so many factors that it is not possible to reply exactly to them. They cannot be quantified and processed by any computer. Thus the autonomous person must attempt to reply to them with the best information available to him and with his intuition. It is certain that his answer will contain much of himself, and much of the prejudices of his age. No matter: he must still reply. Many thinkers have recorded their views. So far as European thought is concerned the general consensus a hundred years ago was that things would improve. Man's knowledge and power were evidently increasing and it was felt, with Voltaire, that his goodness would increase *pari passu*. Jules Verne's science fiction glowed with optimism.

Such a view is now out of fashion and the most influential writers are gloomy when they survey our future prospects. And, it must not be forgotten, influential writers are influential partly because they reflect, as well as create, opinion. It is thus safe to say that the easy optimism of the Enlightenment has quite disappeared.

In Europe, in fact, ever since the unreal euphoria of 1918 faded, the belief has grown that the future will be more unpleasant, and that Man will be less good than in the past. And a strongly held view of the future is important, for it is often self-fulfilling. Often something is brought to pass simply because many people believe that it will happen. One has only to think of the Stock Exchange. If a great number of people believe that there will be a drop in the value of the shares of Company X, then there is a drop in their value, below what it would have been in the absence of the belief. This is only one instance in human affairs where belief in trends produces the trend itself, and where "that which I have feared greatly is come to pass".

It is therefore disquieting, and important, to know that, for at least a generation, influential writers have expected the graph of goodness to head downwards in the future.

Any short list of such influential forecasts must include Aldous Huxley's "Brave New World". In this work he hit on the brilliant device of describing the world of the future by the extrapolating of trends generally believed in the nineteen twenties to be "good", such as artificial birth and control over life, antisepsis, happiness drugs, immunity from the caprices of nature, hovering flight, orderly government. To the horror of the reader this world of the future which should have been a heaven, is instead a hell.

The list, of course, must also include George Orwell's "1984". Here, too, there is an extrapolation, but mainly in the field of politics. Orwell continued the graph of political autocracy, the control of the individual by the tiny anonymous group of leaders, right through to total control by the state. His England of 1984, ruled by "Big Brother" has already become a potent symbol in the mind of all thinking men.

The apprehension that we may be approaching an era of total control by governments of individuals is brilliantly explored in "Fahrenheit 451", by Ray Bradbury. This is a book that is not as well known as it ought to be. Cast in a normal science fiction mould, it has the pessimism of Swift, a writer whom the author evidently much admires. In a way, "Fahrenheit 451" is in the same genre as "Gulliver's Travels" for since the total land surface of the globe is now quite exposed, and since it has lost most of its mystery, Gullivers have now little choice but to voyage into the future.

Bradbury's world is a democracy, since there are free elections for the president. Yet it is at the same time a tyranny of almost infinite cruelty, far crueller than Hitler's or Stalin's. The horror resides in the fact that it is so obviously the state towards which we are, at present tending, and the direction in which people want to go. That is to say, in "451" television has become so refined that it is able to envelope the viewer in an illusion so strong that all reality is quenched. In addition, miniaturised radios, inserted like earplugs, are able to bathe the listener in a never ending tide of music. Books, being obvious foci for free thought and discontent, have been replaced by "digest-digests and digest-digest-digests", also by three-dimensional sex magazines. The democratic tyranny has forbidden anyone to possess books and special squads of firemen are sent out to burn books, and with the books the house and, if necessary, the owner. Books and deviationists are smelt out by Bradbury's most brilliant device, a mechanical eight-legged hound, equipped with a deadly needle to inject massive doses of procaine into its victims. It has a chemical memory and the ability to spoor its victims at very high speeds with its electronic sense of smell.

In this hell all is done in the name of "happiness". As to-day in the world of Vance Packard, it is the happiness of the conformists.

This hell is, of course, totally destroyed in nuclear war. Yet he clearly welcomes the destruction of so monstrous a thing, for its removal makes room for a renaissance which looks as though it may be more gentle, more rural and more pleasant.

I have read no more powerful warning against what is thoughtlessly termed "progress" than this small book.

Another powerful protagonist for pessimism was H. G. Wells, whose "Shape of Things to Come" pioneered science fiction in England, and who was, in the First World War, optimistic about the future. That war, he believed, would mark the end of an intolerable oppression upon civilisation. Yet, by 1945, in his "Mind at the End of its Tether", he had lost all hope. "The writer sees the world as a jaded world devoid of recuperative power. In the past he has liked to think that Man could pull out of his entanglements and start a new creative phase of human living. In the face of our universal inadequacy, that optimism has given way to a stoical cynicism… Man must go steeply up or down, and the odds seem to be all in favour of his going down and out."[2]

This was the considered pessimism of a writer who had predicted in 1914 in "The World Set Free", thirty years ahead of realisation, the invention of the atomic bomb. It is an opinion which because of the unique accomplishments of H. G. Wells, is of the utmost importance and cannot be shrugged off as the embittered reactions of an ill and disappointed man. It is the considered judgment and the final reply of H. G. Wells to the questions mentioned above.

Much the same pessimistic extrapolation is implicit in most of the rest of science fiction which is now being written. Few science fiction works depict personal liberty in a world of nature. Nearly all depict societies of man-like robots and robot-like men, societies ruthlessly controlled by oligarchies or dictators, societies in which the word "joy" seems as out of place as a poppy would be in a science fiction wheat field. Science fiction depicts worlds in which contemporary men would wish to commit suicide.

A film that imprinted itself deeply, perhaps because of its hopeless pessimism, on the thinking of the nineteen-sixties, was "Dr. Strangelove". In this film the happy ending demanded by the Victorians of their plays is replaced by the destruction of the world by an atomic "doomsday machine".

Nevil Shute's "On the Beach" made a similar impact somewhat earlier perhaps because its brilliant description of the end of the world confirmed contemporary man's worst fears about the inevitability of nuclear war. Certainly Man's limitless folly in key situations, and his millenary inability to win the longed-for victory over war itself, can only lead to the greatest pessimism when one attempts to answer one major question about the future: is it to be peace or nuclear war?

It is unnecessary here to enter into detailed descriptions of what nuclear war would mean to the world. Others have done so admirably, and all thinking men have a fairly clear picture of what the effects would be. We have reached the stage when our rulers are seriously calculating the potential dead by the hundred million, maybe even by the billion. Has despair about the future ever been greater, in any age?

Since nuclear destruction would mean the end of this age and the destruction of the conditions for which this book is written and might mean the end of the world as we know it, let us assume that it does not in fact happen. Are the other indicators hopeful or pessimistic about the future?

Chapter 7 described the repulsive side of man. Let me repeat that in almost every way, this repulsive side is getting worse. The crime graphs point up: the graphs of kindness point down. The graphs of cultural beauty point steeply down: the graphs of drug-taking point up. The graphs of road deaths point steeply up: the graphs of human concern with road deaths point down, as familiarity breeds apathy. The graphs of wild-life point steeply down: the graphs of pollution of the globe point steeply up. The graphs of human dignity, courtesy, even beauty, though extremely difficult to assess, probably point down: the graphs of cruelty, callousness and of noise point sharply up.

In this chapter let it be said, then, that the extrapolation of nearly every graph is a matter for pessimism about our future, and that the authors whom we have looked at have been right to be gloomy. Can we find any basic reasons for these appalling trends?

I suggest that the basic reason is the growth of human power, which is inherently evil. Also that the whole problem is greatly exacerbated by the growth of human population.

Another reason for extreme pessimism is the swiftly growing ascendancy being gained over the individual by external groups, including governments. This ascendancy is, to a small extent, politically organised by the traditional methods of governmental intimidation of the individual. But to a much more important degree this ascendancy is nowadays being achieved by an actual invasion of the innermost recesses of the personality by external manipulators. Sometimes this invasion has scientific curiosity as its aim; sometimes it has commercial profit as its aim; and often it has political power as its aim.

The penetration of the individual soul is frankly the aim of the psychologists, and its manipulation is frankly the aim of the psychiatrists. The fashion is spreading rapidly, especially in the rich countries. In North America there are over 40,000 active, professionally recognised psychologists and psychiatrists - with what positive results it is difficult to judge, especially if one compares the mental balance of the Americans with that of the so-called primitive peoples.

Even where psychoanalysis may succeed in restoring mental health, has it not been done at immense cost: the surrendering of the autonomy of the soul over the individual life?

The purpose of the growing practice of hypnotism is precisely this: the replacement of the authority of the individual soul over all provinces of its own being by an external authority. Where this growing practice will end is uncertain, for in an alarming experiment on the BBC, it was found possible for a vast television audience to be hypnotised by one man. The power that such mass hypnosis would give to a small and ruthless group of rulers can easily be imagined.

In another field, somewhat more commercialised and sordid, the manipulation of the innermost sancta of the individual by salesmen is now with us. Dichter has shown how profitable it can be to blur the border of what is within the province of the individual self and what is outside it. Vance Packard's "The Hidden Persuaders" gives us a clear and somewhat startling account of how far Madison Avenue has gone down the road of subliminal suggestion and commercialised psychology.

Governments have not been slow to grasp the possibilities inherent in the manipulation of the masses. Up till now they have not gone much further than using mob psychology to pressure the individual. Yet the results have been important. Man as a member of the mob has always been Man at his most malleable - and his most repulsive. In our times mobs have swollen to sizes never before imagined, through the power given to a few men by microphone and loudspeakers. The mob has been used as an instrument of government by Hitler and Stalin, by Fidel Castro and Mao Tse Tung. To-day's dictators regard a mob of one million as a normal sized mob, while in China they have boasted of mobs of three million. The mob is a brainless polyp: it responds only to the threat; and it can express itself only by dominating or by being dominated, by intimidating or being intimidated. A new generation of political leaders has taught the mob to howl its hatred of the leaders' enemies, enemies that are often purely fictitious.

In consenting to join one of these mobs the individual abdicates his control and hands it over to the ferocious pressures of the mob-mind which itself is manipulated by the rulers.

Beware of the mob! Mobs even larger and more ferocious are now growing up in the streets of the Third World. Poor illiterate parents have produced families that are too large for them to control or bring up. And so, day after day, the young of the Third World are playing in the streets the whole day long. In the streets they form a mob and respond only to threats. The streets of the Third World are loud with the threats of the street bullies dominating the mobs and building up their gangs. This is happening almost unnoticed by political observers and commentators. In the years, when these young thugs are fully grown, they cannot fail to be an important factor in the world, and a danger to all their neighbours. The manipulation of young Chinese gangs in the autumn of 1966, their constitution into the "Red Guards" to intimidate those opposing their manipulators, is a foretaste of a phenomenon that is likely to become widespread.

The manipulation of the soul has also proceeded along more

directly mechanical lines. One way of invading and manipulating the innermost self is the implantation of electrodes in selected areas of the brain. A tiny current applied to one area of the brain can stimulate a human being to move a limb involuntarily or to a violent transport of anger without cause. In another area it can produce an effect of exquisite pleasure so overwhelming that the subject seeks its repetition as opium is sought by an opium addict. Other electrodes can be connected with an electro-encephalograph and the activity of the brain monitored, recorded and analysed. Naturally the most radical of these experiments have been on animals. Dr. Lawrence R. Pinneo has reported that he inserted tiny probes into the brains of monkeys and cats, in such a way that an electric stimulus at selected spots in the brain elicited a particular movement of the animals. By stimulating different parts in sequence, the animal was forced to make movements as desired by the experimenter. The animal, in fact, became a marionette, and was controlled from outside. Some of the movements imposed may be quite complex.

After locating the sites within the brains, Dr. Pinneo implanted up to six probes in the brains of three squirrel monkeys. Electric pulses were sent through the probes in various sequences, building up complex movements of various kinds, some like those seen in nature and others quite abnormal. *The stimulus overrode any natural movement which the animal happened to be making at the moment,* and worked whether it was asleep, awake, or anaesthetised. Some of the stimuli produced group movements.

Control of the individual by implanted probes could take several forms. As suggested by the experiments on monkeys and cats, stimuli could be used for the direct control of movements and perhaps thoughts. Then, using pleasure and pain stimuli as rewards and punishments, the individual could be educated to perform acts pleasing to the manipulator.

With the miniaturisation of radio receivers it would now, technically, be possible to attach a receiver, connected to probes implanted in each child in infancy. The parents could, in collaboration with the manipulators, build up in the infant behaviour-patterns pleasing to the manipulators. Indeed the parents, themselves probably being wired to a central control, would have little choice but to collaborate. It is thus already technically possible for a central manipulator to press a button and to produce a sensation of exquisite pleasure instantaneously to a whole nation numbering many tens of millions.

Judging by the popularity of transistor radios the wiring up of everyone in this manner to a central station might be welcomed by a majority.

Another possibility is opened up by experiments conducted by Dr. Harry Wiener of the Pfizer Laboratories in New York. The experiments led him to postulate the existence of potent external chemical messengers whereby the mere presence of one person can profoundly affect the behaviour and even the psychological state of others. The experiments concern the apparent influencing by one person or experimental animal by means of smells. "I suggest," writes Dr. Wiener, "that in mice, in monkeys and in man, external chemical messengers are present, and have potent effects which so far have been overlooked in man, recognised in animals, and thoroughly studied in insects." The New Scientist comments: "If Dr. Wiener is right, the implications for man (are great), for here is a possible clue to the little-understood factors regulating group and mass-behaviour. Might dictators of the future not maintain control by the use of appropriately formulated aerosols, piped from a central behaviour plant to every factory, office and home?"

Another way in which control of the individual might be increased is by the use of brain operations for political purposes. It is known that prefrontal leucotomy and lobotomy can radically alter the personality, in the direction of destroying initiative and turning the subject into a human vegetable. Hitherto, so far as is known, such operations have only been used for the purposes of neuro-surgery, for removing destructive tensions. In schizophrenic patients the operation is used to reduce his abnormal worries, but there is no reason why such surgical intervention should not also be used on normal subjects for political purposes. Many dictators would welcome a means of removing the initiative from some of their opponents, and of reducing them to the level of human cabbages. Leucotomy could be used discreetly on dangerous opponents to neutralise them. A dictator might, in this way, even get a reputation for humanity, for after such an operation the opponent could safely be allowed home from the internment camp.

As Sir John Eccles, the Australian who won a Nobel Prize for physiology, said recently: "What worries me is the idea that brain research may reveal techniques by which people could be made to be efficient members of a totalitarian society, never rebelling but doing exactly what they are told. They might be made to perform the most complex tasks… but they would do these with a motivation which was always under the control of the operator. I am sure that this has been seriously considered in parts of the world and it seems to me that if control were used in this way it would be more dangerous than the atomic bomb."

Political leaders have not, in the past, shown themselves slow to seize technical developments that allowed themselves to manipulate the individual. It is unlikely that, in the future, they will be reluctant to use the newest developments. Thus it would seem merely a matter of time before political leaders seize on some or all the above-mentioned techniques for reducing their citizens to a total dependence and a total obedience. The obedience of the millions would greatly increase the power of the rulers.

There are few signs that political rulers are becoming more moral: on the contrary. And so the probabilities are that small groups of totally amoral rulers will establish control of their populations by means of mass hypnotism, implanted electrodes, external chemical messengers, drugs, neurosurgery, as well as by the extremely effective traditional methods of manipulation. Is it any longer open to doubt that such methods are already able to produce robot-like, fearless armies of super-fanatics? Such armies would pose a deadly threat to all their neighbours.

Not only do such new methods favour the control by small groups of men of vast numbers of human beings: other new methods have enabled the rulers to eavesdrop on the individual at any time, and listen in to him in his most private conversations. New developments in electronic listening-devices mean that man may no longer assume that the police are not hearing his conversations.

In the past the ability of the police was mainly limited by the difficulty of screening out the few seditious sentences from the thousands of harmless sentences uttered each day. Thanks to computers this screening can now be done mechanically, and the phone-tapping recorders can now be programmed to become activated only when key-words or combinations are spoken.

Thus the very citadel of the soul is nowadays subject to unprecedented invasion and manipulation. Hence stems much of the pessimism of thinking men, for from the beginnings of philosophy, the autonomy of the self and individual freedom have been among the *summa bona* and the supreme purpose of life.

Freedom is also menaced from directions other than the psychological. It is menaced as we have seen by the brute political, military and economic strength and size of the super-states. But it is more insidiously menaced in quite non-political ways. As men congregate in their megalopolises, so their movements approximate ever more closely to the movements of physical particles in gases and fluids. Just as a physicist can predict that, under certain conditions, a certain number of molecules of moving gas will pass a certain point, so an urbanist or a sociologist is able to predict that at a certain moment a certain number of people will enter, say, an urban railway station. Neither prediction will be absolutely accurate: both are subject to a certain statistical imprecision. As the size of the city increases, so the percentage margin of error shrinks. In traffic, the shape of the roads and passages designed for optimum human flow tends more and more to resemble the shape of the passages built for optimum fluid flow. For instance an air photograph of a motorway bears an unmistakeable affinity to a cross-section of the penstocks and tunnels that carry water to a hydro-electric station. And, as traffic density increases, as the police enforce ever more strictly the speed limits, and as motorways widen, so does the movement of vehicles resemble the movement of molecules in a gas flow. Just as hydro-static pressure is exerted by a fluid on the walls of a containing vessel, so does a human mob press against the barriers which confine it.

Urban man submits to molecular status principally at rush hours, or when he travels at high speed on motorways. But as the giant cities grow - and all are expected to grow spectacularly - so molecular status will become to a growing extent, a condition for life in the city.

Fortunately such a prospect need not be painful. For by that time it is probable that instant happiness will be obtainable either by happiness drugs, or by a little electrical stimulation to the brain's pleasure-centres.

If psychologists and politicians are trying to "engineer" the soul, biologists are already planning to engineer the genes. Now that the genetic code has been cracked the possibility of manipulating the DNA molecules to produce an artificial message exists. In this way utterly new forms of life could be produced by human volition. Such is the speed of development that the first such manipulations have already been performed and completely new types of *drosophila* fruit-flies have been produced.[3]

The way lies open for the creation of a new species including new species of men: super-men, and perhaps sub-men. Molecular biologists will probably soon achieve two hitherto unimaginable breakthroughs: the synthesis of life itself through the synthesis of coded DNA molecules; and parthenogenesis, the production of an offspring from a female ovum which has not been fertilised by a male spermatozoon. The resulting girl-child would have the same genetic make-up as her mother and would resemble her at a comparable age, as closely as would an identical twin. In this way immortality, at least on the physical level, could be achieved down the ages. We are also on the threshold of being able to produce and to control human conception *in vitro*.

Medicine has already partly conquered death and the re-animation of corpses is now a daily event. Medicine also enabling us to remake our bodies and their secretions in accordance with our conscious desires. The surgery of spare parts is only at the beginning of a spectacular leap forward which will occur as soon as the immune reaction is understood and controlled. It is already possible for a man to father a child years, perhaps centuries, after his death if his spermatozoa are preserved by freezing. And the prospect of preserving human beings in deep-freeze indefinitely and then reviving them is now on the threshold of possibility.

It is not too early to begin to consider what the effect of these god-like powers will be in the fields of politics, law and morality.

The effect of such powers on law and morality will probably be devastating, for law and morality, as is now becoming evident, are based on certain beliefs which science is dissolving before our eyes. These are: that natural death is inevitable and beyond our control; that the nature of the human species is immutable; that the sex and nature of the individual are immutable; that birth takes place as a result of coitus within marriage.

As to the political effects, it is highly probable that these tremendous powers will be used for the obtaining of political advantages for their possessors, and for moulding the human race into shapes profitable and pleasing to their possessors.

A second deplorable political result of these god-like powers is that they are likely still further to render rich and powerful the rich countries without doing much to end the weakness and poverty of the Third World. In this way the world's political equilibrium, already unstable, is likely to become even more precarious.

At this stage the objection might well be made: if the equilibrium is so unstable, if man is moving into such danger both from nuclear destruction and from a surfeit of scientific development, and if his populations are so excessive, and if man is so evil, what is there to worry about? Let nuclear war come. Let there be a hot and fiery pruning of man's excess numbers, and a repression of the evil side of his nature in a nuclear doomsday. One author even welcomes the prospect since the radiation that would be released would be likely to produce new mutations in man, some of which might be valuable, and from some of which there might be evolved a new race of supermen.

I find this suggestion atrocious, if only for the reason that, even if all men deserve to die or be maimed by radiation sickness other forms of life do not so deserve, and a nuclear doomsday would damage all forms of life, non-human as well as human, innocent as well as guilty. No, the path into the future may be difficult and dangerous, but it is unthinkable to call in a nuclear *deus ex machina* to solve the difficulties.

In these eight chapters I have sought to show, dispassionately and scientifically, that our world and ourselves are in danger; that man inherited a heaven, and is busy creating a hell; that man is morally wicked, though very clever; and that, armed with godlike powers, he has chosen the path that leads down to the depths. These chapters demand detachment and impartiality from the reader, qualities without which the truth cannot be known. They demand that the reader be courageous enough to see the human image truly in the mirror, and to know the truth about man at all costs.

As Gandhi said: Truth is God. Let us sacrifice our all to this God who is Truth. Only if we do so can we know our destiny, where we have come and where we ought to be going.

REFERENCES

(1) *Lettres Philosophiques,* letter 25. My translation.
(2) "The Man who Invented Tomorrow" by Malcolm Muggeridge; *The Observer,* 11 September 1966.
(3) *Genetics,* Vol. 53. p. 897.

9. Man and Earth

"The power wielded by scientists is increasing at a terrifying rate, but the growth of any adequate scientific ethos and philosophy is almost imperceptible."

- Editorial in *New Scientist,* 30.3.67

"Science carries within itself the need for a new system of ethics, if only because it destroys traditional systems of ethics. But Science, through its search for truth, through its knowledge, can cover only one aspect of this new ethic. Science is not able to cover human emotions."[1]

- *Francois Jacob,* French molecular biologist and Nobel prize winner

"Science must therefore play its part in the elaboration of this (new system of) ethics of which the need is evident."

- *Jacques Monod,* his colleague also a Nobel prize winner

"What mankind needs to-day is a new objective - if you like, a faith - that will make life more worth living."[2]

- *Professor J. W.S. Pringle,* professor of zoology at Oxford

I HAVE TRIED to show that Man is on the wrong path, and that a change of direction, perhaps a radical change of direction, is necessary. But, even if it is not certain that Man is on the wrong path, it is evident that he is lost and bewildered, and that there is no agreement about the direction that ought now to be taken. To return to the image of the forest with which we opened this book, the procession of life under Man's leadership is seeking, sometimes desperately, to find the best way forward.

I have also tried to show that our age has two principal needs. The first is a largely acceptable system of ethics to prevent human society from falling apart. And the second is that the destruction of Man's environment must cease, the destruction of the non-human life of the biosphere, and of the atmosphere, soil, and waters of the planet itself. In this final chapter I shall attempt to show that these two principal needs can be met by a single development: the establishment of a geocentric, earth-centred ethic, in place of the present anthropocentric, Man-centred ethic.

Let us look first at the need for a system of ethics. The view that a new system of ethics is needed is widespread, and the quotations that head this chapter typify the manner in which some of the most distinguished men of our times formulate this view. What is an ethical system? It is, surely, a system of values logically worked out, resting on a firmly-held, widely-held belief about the nature of the Universe, which can serve as a frame of reference for everyday acts, both important and unimportant. Having such a system allows us to know whether such acts are right or wrong without each time having to return to fundamentals to assess their rightness. It is a system that allows us to assess an act done by someone in a limited volume of space and in a limited duration of time, against a much wider context, thus enabling us more easily to see the long-term effects of what we do. An ethical system is moral geography, moral astronomy, moral history. Without such a system it is difficult for the average man to live a life of integrity.

In the rich countries more and more people are living without an ethic. The proof that in the long run it is not possible for them to do so lies in the rates of crime and suicide and insanity which are highest in the richest countries. There is little doubt that these tragic figures will increase still further, for many men and their rulers are still living within the ruined walls of the religious cathedrals of their grandfathers, guided to an extent by memories of the old ethical systems. These memories will scarcely outlast this generation, and our children and our grandchildren are already being sent out on the vast ocean of life without charts.

Geography and astronomy help us to locate a point accurately in terms of other points, both on the surface of the earth and in relation to space as a whole. Similarly, since no act, however private is ever entirely self-regarding, and since even the most private acts affect the nature of the self and therefore affect its relationship with its environment and with other selves, and since we are all members one of another, leaves on the simple great tree of life, an ethical system locating every act accurately in terms of other acts, and in terms of time and space is needed.

The wider the time-and-space-scale, the more absolute is the ethic. If we were able to extend out the ethical graph to infinity - and this is what the religions did - then the ethic is absolute and its imperatives are absolute. The problem is that if a religion loses its authority, then the ethical graphs based on that religion also lose their authority, and it is no longer possible to extend the graph to infinity or to have absolute imperatives.

In the workaday world, however, men are accustomed to work without absolutes, contenting themselves with "rules of thumb". Most men, in their day-to-day lives, are guided by ethical systems that are small scale. The family, the round of acquaintances, the business circle, sometimes the tribe or the nation, these are, for most of us, the widest scale which is felt to be important in terms of space. And, in terms of time, a few days or months are felt to be long enough. In the workaday world an act which will benefit a man's family or business for a few months is felt widely to be a "good" act irrespective of longer-term side-effects.

In traditional Christianity, the individual maintained his integrity by living with God's eyes on him all the time. He sought to do things pleasing to God, and when he failed he sought to maintain his relationship by confession, by laying aside his fault, and by being absolved from its consequences by the priest.

In traditional Confucianism, the reasonable and attractive ethical system laid down by K'ung and Futsze five centuries before Christ, patterns of moral behaviour were imprinted on the child's mind, and if a man wished to acquire integrity and merit he would relate each little daily act to the imprinted ethical grid.

Neither Confucianism nor Christianity has come undamaged through the ordeal of science. In China the Confucian temples have been emptied, and many have been destroyed as part of the immense attempt to brainwash the Chinese people into the Marxist-Leninist ways of thought. And in Christendom the temples have been nearly emptied as the intellectual authority of the bishops has been rendered almost irrelevant by the advance of science.

The other traditional religions have fared little better: Islam, Buddhism, Hinduism, and African animism. All have withered or are about to wither, at the touch of science. All have faded, or are about to fade, under the blaze of the light of scientific truth.

With the crumbling of the traditional religions, their ethical grids have lost their authority. As we have seen, the erosion of these ethical systems has left a vacuum which must inevitably be filled by some new system of moral astronomy and geography.

What is needed now is quite simply a world-sized ethical system. Yet width in space is not of itself enough: an ethical system must also have duration in time. And even if it has this duration and this width, unless there is a general agreement on the direction in which affairs ought to be moving, no morality can be established. Unless there is a consensus of opinion of the direction, not enough people will agree to create enough social pressure to make the ethic enforceable.

We are constantly using the words "good" and "evil" without a proper definition, without establishing in advance this consensus without which such words are meaningless. I take an example almost at random. There was a report recently about a strange new sect named "scientology", the leader of which is a certain Ron Hubbard, and the headquarters of which is at East Grinstead. At this place supporters of the movement are lodged while they are "processed".

During 1966 the established residents of this somewhat, conventional small town took exception to the strange behaviour of the people who were being processed. They would walk around East Grinstead, for example, in a daze with a notice hung round their neck saying that they should not be spoken to as, they were being "processed". These conventional residents tried to get the British government to investigate "scientology". The minister to whom they addressed themselves wrote that "further enquiry is not necessary to establish that the activities of this organisation are potentially *harmful*". And an earlier enquiry undertaken by the government of Victoria, Australia, had apparently concluded that "scientology is evil; its techniques *evil;* its practice a serious threat to the community, medically, morally and socially, and its adherents sadly deluded and often mentally ill."[3]

I have no desire to defend this cult, particularly as Mr. Hubbard once intervened in a manner unfriendly to the South African democratic movement, but merely to point out that unless one has a clear idea of the direction in which mankind is going and ought to be going such judgments are meaningless. For instance, Mao Tse-tung might well say that if "scientology" harmed the petty bourgeois way of life of Victoria, then it must be a force that helped, rather than hindered the progress of the human race along the glorious path laid down by Marxism-Leninism. The words "harmful" and "evil" are often used in the above manner, without there being any agreement between speaker and listener on how the harm was being inflicted, on what, and which direction of human affairs was being blocked by the activities complained of.

Religions dared to erect ethical frameworks of infinite range, infinite in space and in time, and to specify quite clearly certain directions as being "good". By revelation, prophets would tell their followers that such and such an act, seen *sub specie aeternitatis* (in the glare of eternity) was, or was not, pleasing to God. Such absolute ethics have, however, largely disappeared, leaving the ethical vacuum which Monod and Jacob speak of, and which needs filling.

The traditional religions have disappeared, or are in the process of disappearing, because they were inadequate. Not only were they shown as inadequate by the rise of the scientific method, but as soon as ordinarily percipient minds learned to free themselves from the spells and incantations of the religions, and to look at life without prejudice, the religions were often seen to be foolish and often harmful.

Some may regret the damage done by science to the religions. Of course, in all religions, there were beauties which transcended all other art forms. Many of these things will live forever: one thinks of Bach's Mass in B Minor and his Passions. Yet one cannot, because of such beauties, call off the corrosive attack on all unscientific systems by the scientific method. The scientific method itself is almost religious, for the self is excluded as rigorously from scientific experiments just as much as it is mortified rigorously by religious exercises. As Gandhi said: "Truth is God", not God is truth.

Despite the beauties of the Christian religion, it is clear that, at least in the rich countries, the churches are to an ever-increasing extent regarded as irrelevances. Jesus may have been one of the most admirable figures of history. Yet Christianity is more than just the personality of Jesus. Christianity is the church, with all its incrustation of incredible miracles and, incomprehensible dogmas. Insofar as the philosophy of Christianity can be summarised, it is a statement that God became man, otherwise than by the normal process of birth, and that this man, Jesus, by his death and resurrection ensured to his followers and to them alone eternal life. This statement is so extraordinary that the onus of proof is unavailable and must surely remain unavailable.

And Christianity is more than the example of Jesus and the dogmas of the church, based on the New Testament: it is also the cult of Jehovah, the God of Abraham and Isaac. The Old Testament is an integral part of Christianity, as much as it is of Judaism. And what a repulsive cult it is! To understand how repulsive one must read the whole Old Testament, and not merely the selected pieces that are read as lessons from the brass lecterns. Jehovah's character was violent. As he has told us himself, he was "jealous."[(4)] He incited his chosen people to commit crimes of genocide on a Nazi scale, apart from the minor crimes of fraud that were committed in his name.

Read, for instance, what happened when the children of Israel were fighting to make their home in Palestine, after they fled from Egypt. One of the tribes that stood in their way was the tribe of the Midianites who were the original "natives". "And the LORD spake unto Moses, saying "Avenge the children of Israel of the Midianites: afterward shalt thou be gathered unto thy people... And they warred against the Midianites, as the LORD commanded Moses; and they slew all the males.

And they... took all the women of Midian captives, and their little ones, and took the spoil of all their cattle, and all their flocks, and all their goods. And they burnt all their cities wherein they dwelt, and all their goodly castles, with fire. And they took all the spoil, and all the prey, both of men and of beasts... And Moses was wroth with the officers of the host, with the captains... and Moses said unto them, Have ye saved all the women alive? Behold these caused the children of Israel through the counsel of Balaam, to commit trespass against the LORD in the matter of Peor, and there was a plague among the congregation of the LORD. Now therefore kill every male among the little ones, and kill every woman that hath known man by lying with him. But all the women children, that have not known a man by lying with him, keep alive for yourselves."

It is no coincidence that there has always been a high correlation between Christianity and conquest, Christianity and slavery, and, in our times, Christianity and the maintenance of colour discrimination. During the American civil war and before it the southern churches were a bastion of slavery. And to-day, in the United States, eleven o' clock on Sunday mornings is the most segregated hour of the week.

It therefore seems to me that Christianity is inadequate to be the guideline that our age is seeking for.

Nor can I believe that Islam is adequate. The book on which Islam is founded is transparently a work of fiction, as bogus as is the similar "Book of Mormon". And if Christianity correlates with conquest, surely Islam correlates with dirt, poverty, the oppression of women, and a social system that imprisons its members.

Nor, surely, would Hinduism be adequate as a generally accepted guideline. There is its repulsive pantheon of many-armed gods and demons. There is the horrible cult of Jagannath (Juggernaut), an avatar of Vishnu, one of the forms of Krishna. An idol of Jagannath used to be paraded in a huge chariot under, which, as reported by the early European travellers, devotees would fling themselves to achieve a holy death. There is the absurdity of the sacred cows, 220 million of them in the land of famine, devouring foodstuffs desperately needed by productive men and animals, and blocking urgently-needed economic channels. There is the religion-backed caste system which is an ancient system of colour-discrimination. The word "varna" in Sanskrit means "caste" and it also means "colour". The Indo-European conquerors of the dark-skinned Dravidians imposed on them a sort of multiple apartheid. Even to-day many Indians are colour-conscious, and their religion is largely responsible for this.

Other cults were even worse: the cult of Huitzilopochtli, the ancient Mexican god of war was quite diabolical. Making allowances for the propaganda that the Catholic conquerors made against their Aztec opponents, it is clear that each year many hundreds of young people were sacrificed on the god's altars. The manner of their death was ritual: the priest would cut open the living body of the victim and wrench out the still-beating heart.

Then there was Moloch, the Canaanitish god whose favourite diet was the burnt bodies of young children.

Then there was the pantheon of Greece and Rome, reasonably kindly and amusing in comparison with the other systems which we have mentioned. Yet it was this humane system that induced Lucretius, the calm and scientific Roman epicurean poet, a hundred years before Christ, to call out in a protest that has echoed down the ages:

Tantum religio potuit suadere malorum (5)

There is another cult in the modern world, the near-religion of Marx. For over a century its devotees have kept alive the otherwise outmoded custom of solving problems by having recourse to scriptures. Yet the authority of this cult is fading with the others. Even in the Soviet Union leaders of opinion are no longer satisfied to look for answers to problems in the real world in their Marxist scriptures. As one participant to a Soviet conference on historical methodology said in 1964: "Can one really limit oneself, when explaining one or another set of historical phenomena, to a few statements from the classics of Marxism that were based... on a study of sources and literature accessible to them at that time, before the appearance of a great deal of new factual data?" (6). In the course of the same article the author says: "The scientists have virtually won (in the Soviet Union) their battle for objective, apolitical inquiry." 'As one of the most distinguished Soviet scientists informed me', writes Leopold Infeld , the Polish physicist, 'physicists no longer read the Soviet philosophical journals and they don't care a damn what the philosophers have to say.'(7)

Two super-powers claim to have based their societies on these Marxist scriptures, so the social effects of the intellectual fall of these scriptures may well be important.

There is another guide which, although it is not a religion, is felt by many to be capable of replacing the religions, and guiding the human race into the future. This is humanism. Humanism exists in two somewhat distinct forms: the first is the unformulated belief held by most people round the world, that the interests of the human race are always paramount, and that the ultimate aim is the maximisation of the power and happiness of men. That is to say, a man in most countries will take the right to kill any animal that inconveniences him or that competes for food with him. This form of humanism I have termed for convenience "*de facto* humanism". The second form of humanism is the formalised body of beliefs which is often called "evolutionary humanism". Those who have formulated this doctrine take the view that all non-human forms of life have gone down cul-de-sacs, and that it is only in the human race that evolutionary progress is being made. Therefore, in the interests of this progress, Man's needs have a value that transcends the needs of other forms of life. In the case of both forms of humanism Man is placed at the centre of the system.

De facto humanism is nothing other than the old Law of evolution, of the filling of the living space. Hitherto human affairs have been ruled by this law, though at certain periods religion and morality have moderated some of its worst harshnesses. The Jains and Hindus, for example, have nobly tried to abstain from harming other forms of life. Apart from a few such exceptions, governments, whether they call themselves socialist states or "the free world", are humanist governments. It will be interesting to see whether humanist governments will be any more able to restrain the greed and cruelty than were religion-backed governments, of those in power.

Humanism, then, has long ruled the world. It is therefore responsible for the present state of the world. It is no coincidence that in general it is the leaders of humanist thought who are most satisfied by the present direction of progress, and that those who are least satisfied by the present direction of progress are those who are the least favourable towards humanism.

I am one of the latter, and believe that humanism, like the religions and cults, is not adequate as a guideline into the future. All forms of humanism must glorify Man, since he sits at the centre of their systems. Yet this descendant of the killer-ape, this Cain who has conquered the world by being the most successful murderer, is not a fit character to sit at the centre of any ethical system.

Again, there is no proof that Man is the most valuable object known to us, and a system of ethics ought to take, as its centre, the thing of greatest value. Man is but one species, though there are more than three billion members of that species. Apart from Man, there are three million other species, divided among 200,000 genera, in addition to the plants and micro-organisms.

It is, of course, true that Man is powerful enough to do what he likes with these other forms of life, but to base an ethical system on this fact is to base an ethical system on the principle that might is right. As Dr. Frank Fraser Darling, the ecologist, wrote in a memorable article, "We should be ready to admit that animals exist in their own right and not by our permission" [8].

It is of course true that animals seem to us to have either no culture or only a poor culture. But we are only just beginning to understand their languages, and it is probable that when we do we shall acquire a greater respect for them than we now have.

A compelling reason for disliking a Man-centred system of ethics is the aesthetic argument. When one visits truly Man-free parts of the world one is overcome by a feeling of beauty and holiness. It has been my great good fortune to have experienced this supreme delight in three very different spheres: under the sea, in the Sahara, and in the East African craterland.

When one dives under the sea, assisted by flippers and goggles and a snorkel, one becomes a sort of postulant cetacean as weightless as a cosmonaut. One enters a new world as foreign as might be the life on another planet. One is surrounded by a flora and a fauna seemingly quite unrelated to those of the land surface. Round one are schools of bright fish, many of them interested in the visitor and unafraid. One glides through forests of tall waving seaweed. Here is a world not yet dominated by Man. Its beauty and its rightness overwhelm one and compel one's adoration.

Yet even in this watery Eden there is a snake: already Man the hunter is hunting and terrorising the fish of the reefs. Already there are schemes for turning all this other worldly beauty into undersea farms. Already the technical difficulties in the way of human immigration into this magic world are being solved.

In the Sahara desert, too, I have been privileged to walk in a Man-free world, sometimes barefoot, sometimes riding on a camel. This world is a world of brilliant orange seas of sand, clinically clean, free of footprints, with harsh sandstone hills, utterly free of human wastes and garbage. It is a world of silence, of dazzling sunshine, of dark blue skies and pure air. Fromentin, the French Algerian writer, once wrote: "One of the most subtle charms of these lonely and empty lands (is that they)… give us clearer perceptions, and open for us the unknown world of the infinitely small noises, and reveal a large extent of inexpressible joys."[9]

Even for those who have not experienced these "unknown worlds" the planet must be a better place because they know that the solitude is there if they should ever need it. Solitude and the knowledge that it exists are not merely desirable: in an increasingly crowded, dirty and noisy world they are essential elements of sanity.

Yet here, too, one learns that there are many schemes for

"reclaiming" the desert. More accurately, such schemes are schemes for encouraging human immigration into these "unknown worlds". And with the human immigrants, of course, would come the rats, cats, goats and dogs; the filth and the tumult.[10]

Best of all, there is the Man-free world of the forest and bush, of the wild animals and the birds. Such an Eden still exists in parts of Africa. I have had the joy of visiting African wildlife reserves. Perhaps the most miraculous was when my wife and I visited the crater of Ngurdoto near Arusha in Tanzania. Ngurdoto is one of many craters in East Africa, many of which have lakes on their floors. When we went to Ngurdoto we were the only human beings in the crater. We, the motor in which we travelled, and the motor road, a mere track through high forest, were the only factors in the situation that would not have been there a million years ago. We were able to leave the car, and to walk hand in hand along the path, and to see, to hear, and to smell the world as it was before Man conquered it. From the thickly forested rim we looked down on the open grassland of the floor of the crater and on its shallow pools. We looked down on herds of elephants and rhinoceros, on the strange giraffes, and on the antelopes and the lions. We saw, high above the clouds, the glaciers and snows of Kilimanjaro's 6000-metre peak, an astonishing backdrop to this equatorial scene.

Ngurdoto is not far from another, more famous crater, the Ngorongoro crater. Unfortunately Ngorongoro is already compromised, as Masai graziers are allowed to share it with the animals. The authorities there told me that they were optimistic that the crater could be shared forever by the Masai graziers and the wild animals, but I felt that their optimism was quite unrealistic. Fortunately no human occupation has been allowed in Ngurdoto, and may it be preserved for ever.

Fortunately in Mwalimu Julius Nyerere a leader exists who has so far been courageous enough to bar the way to human immigration into such holy places. In the absence of such a barrier, as has been seen in Europe, Asia, and America, the human immigration-tide would soon flood into Ngurdoto, converting its animals into meat and trophies, and its streams into sewers. How does humanism explain the holiness of these Man-free worlds? Usually by saying that these reserves are necessary for Man to be able to enjoy the world fully. But that is not the full story. Anyone destroying Ngurdoto would not merely deprive the human race of a source of enjoyment: he would have destroyed something that has nothing to do with Man, something that was there before Man, something that carries its own raison-d'être within itself, something that has as much right to life as has Man, though unfortunately not the power to preserve it without the aid of enlightened men.

Another weakness of humanism is that although its theoreticians purport to understand, and for the most part approve the direction in which affairs are moving, they do not in fact have any clear idea of what the future holds. Professor Jacques Ellul of Bordeaux University, France has drawn attention to the poverty of their teleology in his remarkable book *The Technological Society*. Towards the end of this book he tells of a series of contributions made to the weekly *L' Express* by some of the humanist leaders who had been asked to describe what, in their opinion, the world would be like in the year 2000. Ellul describes the contributors as "American and Russian scientists, Nobel prize winners, members of the Academy of sciences of Moscow, and other scientific notables whose qualifications are beyond dispute." Ellul then summarises the picture - a remarkably consistent picture it must be admitted- they paint of the year 2000 which Ellul sarcastically terms the "golden age". He continues: "If we take a hard unromantic look at the golden age itself, we are struck with the incredible naivety of these scientists... They seem incapable of grasping... that what they are proposing... is in fact the harshest dictatorships. In comparison, Hitler's was a trifling affair. That it is to be a dictatorship of test tubes rather than of hobnailed boots will not make it any less a dictatorship. When our savants characterise their golden age in any but scientific terms, they emit a quantity of down-at-heel platitudes that would gladden the heart of the pettiest politician. Let's take a few examples: 'To render human nature nobler more beautiful and more harmonious'. What on earth can this mean? What criteria, what content, do they propose? Not many of our theoreticians,

I fear, would be able to reply. 'To assure the triumph of peace, liberty, and reason'. Fine words with no substance behind them. 'To eliminate cultural lag'. What culture?" Ellul's angry words are applicable generally to humanists.[11]

There follow my two main objections to humanists. The first is that I believe firmly that this material world is not the whole story. Somewhere, still concealed from our eyes, is the key to creation and the secret of the universe. One day we may learn it, but we do not yet know it. We may well approach towards it along the new pathways that are being opened up by science, but we are still at an immense distance from actual discovery. Humanism is essentially the denial that this secret exists, the denial that there is "something behind" the material world. Often this denial is expressed aggressively and overconfidently, and merely serves to repel genuine and earnest seekers after truth.

My other objection was simply and clearly expressed by Jesus when he said: "Whosoever will save his life shall lose it."[12] That is to say, self-centredness is self-destructive. Humanism is the worship of Man by Man, the setting up by Man of a golden image in his own shape. This worship is different from the love that human beings ought to feel for one another, the love of a man for his neighbour. It is the setting up of our all too imperfect race as the measure of all things. Humanism thus becomes narcissism, and inward-looking self-worship.

For all the above reasons I dismiss humanism, as I dismissed the traditional religions and the cult of Marxism, as an adequate guideline into the future. The first essential now is to move Man away from the centre of the ethical system. In the words of Alan Gregg, "if Copernicus helped astronomy by challenging the geocentric interpretation of the universe, might it not help biology to challenge the anthropocentric interpretation of nature?"[13]

Yet the need for an ethical system remains. Is it possible to envisage one of the traditional religions, or the cult of Marxism refurbishing themselves and thereby regaining moral authority? Evangelists such as Billy Graham seem to have such an aim for Christianity. I think that the answer is no. For even if one of the traditional religions were, by a tour de force, able to harmonise its thinking and dogmas with science, and to regain its earlier hold on its erstwhile adherents, for political reasons none of the traditional religions could appeal to other continents and peoples. Let us assume for the sake of argument that under the influence of Mr. Graham Christianity were able to become again the creed of Europe and America. Would this revival make Christianity any more acceptable in Asia and Africa? Almost certainly not, for historical and political reasons. In those continents it will not be forgotten that at the same time as the European political and military leaders were colonising the Asians and Africans, European missionaries were trying to evangelise them into the fold of the Christian churches. Asians and Africans found it difficult to see the difference between the two processes.

And just as Christianity is almost certainly unacceptable to-day outside the racial barriers of the European world, Islam is almost certainly unacceptable outside the peoples who are traditionally members of Islam, Buddhism outside the traditionally Buddhist countries, and Hinduism outside India.

Yet, with the development of communications, one of the primary desiderata of a new ethical system is that it must be acceptable to a large majority of the human race in all continents.

A refurbished Marxism might have a better chance of becoming a universal faith, especially as its attractiveness for the young remains great. But the intellectual respectability of Marxism is waning fast, and it is difficult to imagine ways in which it might be given a sufficient face-lift.

If it is unlikely that any of the traditional religions or that the cult of Marxism will regain strength, to the extent that it might become a world-faith, on which a world ethical system might be built, is it likely that a completely new faith might arise and conquer the world? Might some new Buddha or Christ be born, and lay down the foundations for a new world religion and world ethical system? Certainly there are evidences that the world is thirsting after some new revelation. There is the Cao Dai cult in Vietnam, the Soka Gakkai cult in Japan, the religiosity of the Californian "hippies", the Zionist Christian sects of Southern Africa, and the modern "Christian" sects of the United States such as Christian Science, Mormonism, and Aimée Semple McPherson's church. No body of beliefs, no ceremonial is too weird to repel these hungry and thirsty seekers after God.

Yet can we fold our hands, and wait for a new Messiah? Such great prophets are as rare as are supernovae in our galaxy, appearing perhaps once in a millennium. Surely we must do what we can now to save ourselves. If a prophet is to be born, he is more likely to be born to a world that is trying to help itself: "Ho tsosoa Khomo e itekang" (the cow that tries is saved) as the Basotho say.

Yet what can we do?

I believe that there is something that we can do, and that there is a path out of the predicament described above. I believe that such a path might very well be generally acceptable. The solution, as I see it, is that we should work towards a new harmony between Man and his environment, the whole surface of the world in which life lives. The solution, as I see it, is that Man be removed from the centre of the ethical system, and that the earth be placed there; that a geocentric ethic replace the accepted humanistic, Man-centred, anthropocentric ethic.

This is the solution, but it is not going to happen tomorrow. What we can do now is to propagate the idea.

The fundamental proposition of this new ethical system is that the words "good" and "bad" shall come to mean "what is good (or bad) for the Earth and for its rocks and waters; for its biosphere with all its non-human and human life, the human life always being seen as part of the whole". And the decision on what is good or bad must be made in the light of at least the next three generations.

Man would, of course, be the most important part of the totality since the power to sustain, change or destroy it lies *de facto,* in his hands. Yet this power must always be used with a sense of responsibility to the whole.

In replacing the traditional religions (or supplementing them), this new ethical system would not attempt to answer questions in terms of the absolute: it would be frankly a provisional ethic for

Fig. 6. Arabian gazelles, almost exterminated in Jordan by motor raiding parties from neighbouring oil states (Chapter 3)

the next hundred years. If we could establish such a provisional ethic, we might be enabled to buy time, time during which later, perhaps truer and more efficacious, ideas might be put forward.

Such an ethic might appropriately be called "geism". The word comes from "ge", the root of "geometry", "geology" and many other words that relate to the earth. The word is short and simple and would translate easily into almost any language. It is formed on the analogy of "theism" and "deism", eighteenth-century words describing a monotheistic, non-dogmatic system of thought. It should be pronounced with a soft "g" and should have as its corresponding adjective the "geist" to rhyme with "theist".

Now merely to proclaim the desirability for an ethic is not enough. Nor is it merely enough to describe an ethical system. Men do right because they love the good, and this love is the mainspring of any ethical system. The mainspring of the traditional religions was the love that the adherent felt for the gods and the prophets of these systems. And so, if the solution here put forward is the correct solution to our present predicament, the first thing to do is that the love of Man for the world must be strengthened, above all in the young.

If Man loves the world, he will come to understand that this world is indeed the most valuable thing of which we have knowledge, and that it is therefore right that it should be the centre of the system of values that is to be the new ethical system. It will be easier for Man to move himself away from the centre. And it will be also easier to obey the geist moral imperative if the love of Man for the world should grow stronger.

Man's love for the world, it is true, exists already. Yet most of us take its beauties, its softness, its mildness and its security for granted. The very first act, if these ideas here put forward have any value, is that each reader should try to open his own eyes to the beauty of the world, and that he should stop seeing it with eyes glazed and dulled by familiarity. Then he should attempt to awaken the new vision and the love of our home, in those around him, especially in the younger generation. Then he should do what he can to propagate the idea in a more formal manner.

A parallel is the nineteenth century love of country that so powerfully changed the history of Europe. Most men love their own country. Patriotism built on that cult, and consciously propagated this love. The child absorbed it in his earliest days, and honoured it through his life in all manner of ceremonies and symbols. I am not, of course, saying that nineteenth-century patriotism was a manifestation that could or should be retained for the remainder of time: I am merely using it as an example of how, when the time has come for a cult of the world to be established, it can be built consciously, on the existing foundation of a previously-existing state of love for an object.

In fact the love and cult of the world could do much to repair some of the damage done by the earlier cult of patriotism. All men of all nations do already share in this love of the world, and could consciously work to strengthen it. In this love there could grow to ripeness a deeper union of the various branches of the human race [14] and a union of human and non-human life. In this love would be de-emphasised the hurtful divisions of race, colour, creed, class and nation. And in this love would be furthered the conservation of the imperilled soils and waters.

In this love we could experience emotionally what science is now discovering, that there is no sharp dividing line between Man and the animals, between the molecule and the virus and the higher forms of life. All are part of one great creation, and therefore all owe love and loyalty to all others. That all life is one is ancient Buddhist Wisdom, ancient wisdom that the modern scientists are daily confirming in their experiments.

In this love would come the planning of an optimum level for the populations of men and animals, living in a clean, calm world, a world of safe waters, a world with room for the wilderness, a world giving to each being a sufficient niche in which its full genetic potentialities might be realised, a world in which the utmost variety of living forms is safeguarded, for evolution needs variety in order for its task to be best accomplished.

Although the state of affairs is depicted here as a short-term aim, it will nevertheless be exceedingly difficult to attain. For it would involve nothing less than the repeal of the old evolutionary law. Under this law Man has unconsciously tried to fill his niche, just as all other forms of life have tried to fill theirs. But to-day Man's niche has become the whole world, and if he were to fill this completely it would be a disaster.

Man must therefore repeal this old law, and must replace the simple principle of expansion with the much more demanding principle of restraint.

Put somewhat differently, the old evolutionary law is the law of self-love, while the principle of restraint is the law of love for the other, a law in which incidentally the self finds fulfilment. The change required is vast. How is the progress to begin? It seems to me that all such changes must begin with the birth and development of an idea; the idea that Man must love the world.

As I have said, the change would involve mankind in a great act of self-renunciation. If such a change should prove impossible, then I think that Man and the Earth do not have a future: all will be destroyed by the human doomsday thunderbolts. But there is no place for despair: the survival of the human line into the present time has been extraordinarily difficult, and the lesson of evolution and of history is that almost everything is possible, if only Man puts his mind to it.

Yet the self-renunciation would only be apparent, and only in the short run. Only by some such renunciation can a new harmony with the environment be established, and only by a new harmony can Man enter into a symbiosis with the biosphere, and only thus can there be any guarantee of survival and of happiness for Man or for non-human life.

Love leading to the renunciation of self is more than love: it is adoration.

This state of love and adoration would permit men to subject their problems, and to make their decisions in the light of their love for the world. Many of these problems are international, and the existence of this state of love for a shared object must make these problems more easily soluble.

In no sense would this cult deny the existence of God. Nor for the adherents of the traditional religions or of Marxism, would it be inconsistent with their practising their faiths. The position of geism is simple: that until there can be a generally accepted religious revival there can be no efficacious ethical system based on religion. Yet the need to-day is for a generally accepted ethical system ". The ethical system based on geism would be a stop-gap, an interim system, until something better can be found. Yet it would always be firmly based on scientific truth, and would always be in harmony with the truth as progressively revealed by science.

Not only would geism be scientific: it would be rational, for there is nothing irrational in men loving this beautiful planet. There is nothing unreasonable in men making all their decisions in the light of their love and devotion to the world. Religions used to demand that men act remembering that the eyes of God were on them all the time. And already there are millions of people who do act, all the time, in the interests of the world, people who do not throw litter and garbage about, who do not act unreasonably towards their fellow-men because they understand that such behaviour harms life as a whole. And they do this without necessarily having formulated the reasons why they act thus.

The central idea of geism is not new: it appeared with clarity in the thinking of the Saint-Simonians, the followers of the French political idealist Claude-Henri, Comte de St. Simon, According to the Saint-Simonians whose thought flourished in the 1830's, the planet was "the mystical centre towards which all their gestures converge, all their actions, and all their thoughts, even the least of them."[15] And one of the Saint-Simonian writers was the source of this wonderful invocation: "O terre, tu m'as donné ta vie et ils disent que je ne te donnerai que mon cadavre! Non, je te donnerai et te donne sans cesse tout mon amour, tout mon sang; tu es ma mère! tu seras glorifiée, embellie, parée par ton enfant; tu seras bénie dans le fruit de tes entrailles, parce que je te rendrai meilleure encore pour tous que tu ne l'as été pour moi. Et je vivrai dans la forme que je t'aurai donnée, je serai le lait de tes mamelles fécondes, la douceur de ta caresse pour tes enfants; Le *Globe,* voila notre fiancée, notre mère pour le moment: caressons la terre."[16]

Teilhard de Chardin sensed with great clarity the embryonic growth of the geist idea, though as a Christian he disapproved it. He wrote in 1933: "By all the roads of experience and of thought we have realised the unitary grandeur of the Universe and the organic meaning of Time… Henceforward there exist for us a Past and a Future that is to say a growth of the World. Around us and in us the Universe is seen to be not only a wide, static association of objects given together, but as a specific Whole, endowed with an organised power of development… And the World, when it is seen to possess a sort of natural unity through time, gains not only an extra dimension in the eyes of intellectual researchers, it also becomes, in the eyes of the human individual, an object of superior value and dignity, to which one ought submit and to devote oneself. It makes the strings of adoration vibrate in us in sympathy with the undeniable attraction of a tangible and close humanity…"[17]

The Saint-Simonians realised clearly the need for an emotive side to their faith, and that any ethical system must appeal no less strongly to Man's emotions than it does to his reason. And so, if geism is to grow, it will need to cultivate the emotions no less thoroughly than did any of the traditional religions. Fortunately the hymns and prayers that can do this lie ready to hand: all the songs and poetry and literature, all the symphonies that praise the beauty of the world. Such music and poetry has arisen among all cultures, in all countries. And, just as General William Booth of the Salvation Army looted the music-halls for good tunes, because he did not see why the Devil should have the good tunes, so much of the glorious religious music that we have might be used to increase Man's love of the world.

There is a secular work which comes to mind at this stage, Gustav Mahler's "Lied von der Erde", an unforgettable art-nouveau tone-poem, perhaps the noblest musical farewell ever taken in the world. Mahler composed it knowing that his death approached. He set to music a series of songs freely translated from the Chinese. In his song-cycle are heard flute contentedly sighing, reviving happy memories of Mahler's fugitive springtime; and also the funereal tolling of muffled gongs. The work ends with a final farewell, diminuendo, as the contralto almost faints away with the word "ewig" (forever) on her lips.

Especially in youth, Man's love for the world can be an image of sexual love, as is suggested in this untranslatable extract from "Soleil et Chair" by Rimbaud, France's adolescent poet, written when he was only fifteen and a half:

Le Soleil, Le foyer de tendresse et de vie,
Verse l'amour brûlant à la terre ravie,
Et, quand on est couché sur la vallée, on sent
Que la terre est nubile et déborde de sang;
Que son immense sein, soulevé par une âme,
Est d'amour comme Dieu, de chair comme la femme,
Et qu'il renferme, gros de sève et de rayons,
Le grand fourmillement de tous les embryons!

… Et tout croît et tout monte!
… … O Vénus, ô Déesse!

Je regrette les temps de l'antique jeunesse…
Où les arbres muets, berçant l'oiseau qui chante,
La terre berçant l'homme, et tout l'Océan bleu
Et tous les animaux aimaient, aimaient en Dieu!
Je regrette les temps de la grande Cybèle…
Je crois en toi! Je crois en toi! Divine mère.

There are, of course, many other poems and songs of this kind, and also paintings that celebrate the paradisiac beauty of the earth. This is a language understood by all men. And the love of nature has drawn many people, oppressed by the irrelevance of much that they are given in contemporary religion, to seek communion in the open air of the good countryside, communion with their deeper selves, with other men, and with life as a whole.

One does not have to be grown-up to feel these things: a seven-year-old child wrote the following lines unaided:

I love you, Big world.
I wish I could call you
And tell you a secret;
That I love you, World. [18]

Parents and teachers would have little difficulty in building the geist ethic on the natural love that this little poem expresses. Thus could be harnessed to morality the loving emotions of tiny children, emotions without which morality is merely a dusty learning-by-rote.

Just as patriotism had, and still has, its ceremonies and festivals, so it would be natural for geism to have them, and they could be drawn from an all but inexhaustible reservoir: the earth-centred thinking of the ages. There need be no fear of syncretism, and the cults of Demeter and Ceres, the worship of the Great Mother, could merge harmoniously with the Anglican harvest festival, and the American Thanksgiving.

Thus could be established, within each person a "yes" to life, and a focus for love. At present we are able mainly to say "no" because so much has gone wrong. We say "no" to war, "no" to racism, "no" to crime, "no" to soil erosion, and all the other ills that beset us. But "no" is less powerful than "yes". "No" is a word of conflict, while "yes" is a word of peace. So geism would say "yes" to the earth and to all its life, and from this "yes" would flow controls that would only exceptionally need to be externally reinforced. Is the answer to the swelling crime rates not to be found somewhere near here?

Geism might become the long-awaited "religion of science" foreshadowed at the beginning of this chapter. While never attempting to transcend the area of scientific knowledge geism could still be compatible with mysticism, and extra-sensory perception. Here there are potentialities for a "new frontier" of knowledge that might well startle the more materialistic of our thinkers.

There are signs coming with increasing frequency from all round the world that something like geism is "the wave of the future". Everywhere there is increasing concern with the need for a generally acceptable ethical system. Everywhere there is a rising interest in the conservation of beauty, soil, water and wildlife. Everywhere there is a growing understanding that the great City, though it enriches Man materially, is killing his soul. And science preaches with ever-increasing insistence the unity of the whole.

Nevertheless any system which is put forward however modestly, and with however much cogency, will always arouse objections, and no doubt the ideas here put forward will be contested. One can imagine the form that some of the objections will take.

The principal objection that is likely to be made is that geism, being a cult of something less than God, is a retreat from monotheism, the precious concept distilled with such difficulty from the older polytheisms; that geism therefore sacrifices something infinitely precious for the smaller, hypothetical advantages of a new and doubtful ethic.

The reply to this objection is that I do not see that geism would set itself up to deny God in order to worship the planet in his place. It is to me self-evident that God exists at the very least in the sense of being the Essence of the Universe. Yet it is unarguable that the traditional roads between Man and God are breaking down. Yet on them depend the ethical systems. And also, it might be added, on them depends Man for the exercise of his numinous sense, the need to worship. If this numinous sense could be exercised in a geocentric cult and if an ethical system could be built on a geocentric cult, why not? Geism would not, as I see it, deny any greater truths, providing that they are the truth. It might even one day be a step which might lead to a greater truth.

A further objection might be that Man, having defeated all other forms of life, has rendered them all unimportant, and that it is unnecessary and unprofitable for him to consider any interests that are external to himself. "Let us assume", thus might run this objection, "that the world were damaged by something that profited Man. There could be no conceivable objection to this thing being done. The lessons of evolution and history are plain: that the phenomenon of Man is so important that human considerations outweigh all other considerations".

The reply to this objection is a reply in space and in time. In space, we cannot know all the needs of all the forms of life which are met by the planet at the present time. Therefore we cannot know the extent of the damage that our present activities are inflicting on these forms of life. And, in time, we cannot know what will be the needs of our distant descendants, nor of the unimaginable forms of life that will one day fill the world. How, then, can we assume that these interests must be subordinated to Man's present-day needs? Man does not own the planet. He is a tenant. He has inherited the right to live in Eden, yet he is no more than a steward. Since he cannot know all the needs of life now and in the future, he must behave as if there were a sacred duty on him to hand on to future ages what he took over from the past without asking too many questions. Yet to adopt such a stand is to accept the principal theses of geism.

A further objection might be: "Why stop at the planet? If Man is to be dethroned, surely the whole universe is the only object that can replace him." In a way this is true, and in the fullness of time there may again be an ethical system which places something infinite at the centre. Yet we cannot do this to-day. We know too little about infinite time and space. We cannot love what we do not know, and it is essential that the centre of the ethical system be an object which is known and loved. We are aeons away from the moment when the ordinary person can *love* the surface of Venus or of the moon.

The sun is, of course, in a different class. We cannot know much about the surface of the sun, yet we can see the manner in which its rays give life to our earth. We can understand the ideas that gave rise to the sun-worshipping religion initiated by Akhnaton of Egypt, and we can sympathise deeply with them. They, too might form part of a geist cult, for the earth without sunlight is no longer alive.

A further objection is that the idea of a cult is retrogressive, and, *a fortiori,* that there can be no cult that is in harmony with science. Science, so might run this objection, has rid the world of cults. Surely the reply to this objection is that cults are necessary and probably always will be necessary in order for men to be strengthened by loving in common. The parallel with patriotism has been noted. And to deny the importance of the emotional side of Man is to deny perhaps his greatest and finest side.

There may be other, perhaps more weighty, objections, yet I launch this idea with some confidence that it may survive them. To return to the image with which this book opened, the image of the journey through the primeval forest, I believe that in geism we have found the vantage-point towards which the next march should be taken, the vantage-point which, even though it may not be a final direction, will yet help us to discover that direction. To march towards it is in the interests of all men, and to march together towards it might once again give meaning to human affairs.

The baffling question: what is Man here for? is posed ever more insistently by every new advance in medicine, in automation, and in most other fields. If geism is found acceptable there will be found in it a partial answer, an answer that will last several generations, even though it may not be the full answer. Man is here to pursue the search for scientific truth. Man is here to create a world brotherhood which shall include all forms of life. And Man's highest purpose is to contemplate, to love, and to tend the world, and to establish between it and Man a creative balance and harmony.

In the firm belief that these ideas are able to be helpful to all at the present time, I offer them with modesty for the consideration of all.

REFERENCES

(1)   *Le Monde,* 9 December 1965.
(2)   *Biology and Human Affairs,* Vol. 30, No.3, summer 1965 "Biological responsibility in a Technological Society".
(3)   *The Observer,* 5 March 1967.
(4)   *Exodus* 20.
(5)   How much harm has been done because of religion! *De Rerum Natura,* Book 1, line 102. Lucretius lived from about 99 BC to about 55 BC.
(6&7)   *Foreign Affairs,* October 1966, p. 104 et seq. "The Rise and Fall of

Scientific Socialism", by Arthur P. Mendel, Professor of Russian History, University of Michigan.

(8) *Wild Life conservation;* The Conservation Foundation 1964; page 7.

(9) *Algérie Tunisie:* Les Guides Bleus; Hachette 1938; page 353 cf. v. 25.

(10) cf. Chapter 5.

(11) *The Technological Society;* by Jacques Ellul; Knopf. New York, 1964 p. 432.

(12) *Mark 8*: xxxv.

(13) "A Medical Aspect of the Population Problem", Alan Gregg, in *Science,* 121: 681-682.

(14) As Szent-Gyorgyi, the Hungarian-born American biochemist beautifully expressed it: "I feel closer to a Chinese colleague than to my own postman", a statement felicitously quoted by one of his fellow-Nobel prize winners, Dr. Max Perutz, in *New Scientist* 16 March 1967.

(15) Mentioned in the biography of Henri Duveyrier, *Un Prince Saharien Méconnu,* by Rene Pottier; Plon, Paris; 1938, page 3.

(16) Ibid. Probably Charles Duveyrier, father of Henri. Charles was the "poete de Dieu of the Saint-Simonian religion, 'New Christianity' " "O, Earth, it is you that have given me your life, yet they say that I shall give you nothing but my corpse! No - I shall give and do ceaselessly give you all my love, all my blood; you are my mother! You will be glorified, embellished, and adorned by your child; you will be blessed in the fruit of your womb because I shall leave you lovelier for others than you have been for me. And I shall live in the form which I shall have given to you; I shall be the milk of your exuberant breasts, and the sweetness of the caress you give your children; the *Globe* is our betrothed, our mother; let us caress the Earth."

(17) *Vie Intellectuelle,* T. 24, 25 October 1933, pp. 219-222, quoted by Yves Congar in *'Informations Catholiques Internationales,* p. 27, 15 April 1967 (my translation).

(18) *Time,* 6 January 1967, in a review of *Miracles;* collected by Richard Lewis; Simon and Schuster.

Supplement: World Population Data Chart	Population estimates Mid-1973 (millions)[2]	Birth Rate[3]	Death Rate[3]	Annual Rate of Population growth (percent)[4]	Number of Years to Double Population	Population Projections to 1985 (millions)[2]	Infant Mortality rate[5]
Region or Country							
WORLD	3,860 9	33	13	2.0	35	4,9333[9]	-
AFRICA	374	46	21	2.5	28	530	-
NORTHERN AFRICA	95	44	17	2.7	26	140	-
Algeria	15.5	50	17	3.3	21	23.9	86
Egypt	36.9	37	16	2.1	33	52.3	118
Libya	2.1	46	16	3.1	23	3.1	-
Morocco [10]	17.4	50	16	3.4	21	26.2	149
Sudan	17.4	49	18	3.1	23	26.0	121
Tunisia	5.6	38	16	2.2	32	8.3	120
Western Africa	110	49	24	2.5	28	155	-
Cape Verde Islands [11]	0.3	39	14	2.5	28	0.3	121
Dahomey	2.9	51	26	2.6	27	4.1	149
Gambia	0.4	42	23	1.9	37	0.5	125
Ghana [10]	9.9	47	18	2.9	24	14.9	156
Guinea	4.2	47	25	2.3	30	5.7	216
Ivory Coast	4.6	46	23	2.4	29	6.4	159
Liberia	1.2	50	23	2.7	26	1.6	137
Mali	5.5	50	27	2.3	30	7.6	190
Mauritania	1.3	44	23	2.1	33	1.7	187
Niger	4.2	52	23	2.9	24	6.2	200
Nigeria	59.6	50	25	2.6	27	84.7	-
Portuguese Guinea [11]	0.6	41	30	1.1	63	0.7	-
Senegal	4.2	46	22	2.4	29	5.8	-
Sierra Leone	2.8	45	22	2.3	30	3.9	136
Togo [10]	2.0	51	26	2.5	28	2.8	163
Upper Volta	5.7	49	29	2.0	35	7.7	182
EASTERN AFRICA	106	47	22	2.5	28	149	-
Burundi	3.9	48	25	2.3	30	5.3	150
Comoro Islands [11]	0.3	-	-	-	-	0.4	-
Ethiopia	26.8	46	25	2.1	33	35.7	-
Kenya [10]	12.0	48	18	3.0	23	17.9	-
Malagasy Republic	7.5	46	25	2.1	33	10.8	102
Malawi	4.8	49	25	2.5	28	6.8	120
Mauritius	0.9	25	8	1.7	41	1.2	65
Mozambique [11]	8.2	43	23	2.1	33	11.1	-
Reunion [11]	0.5	30	8	2.2	32	0.7	58
Rhodesia	5.6	48	14	3.4	21	8.6	122
Rwanda	3.9	52	23	2.9	24	5.7	133
Somalia	3.0	46	24	2.2	32	4.2	190
Tanzania	14.3	47	22	2.6	27	20.3	162
Uganda [10]	9.3	43	18	2.6	27	13.1	160
Zambia [10]	4.7	50	21	2.9	24	7.0	159

MIDDLE AFRICA	**38**	**44**	**24**	**2.1**	**33**	**52**	-
Angola	6.1	50	30	2.1	33	8.1	192
Cameroon	6.2	43	23	2.0	35	8.4	137
Central African Republic	1.6	46	25	2.1	33	2.2	190
Chad	4.0	48	25	2.3	30	5.5	160
Congo (People's Rep of)	1.0	44	23	2.1	33	1.4	180
Equatorial Guinea	0.3	35	22	1.4	50	0.4	-
Gabon	0.5	33	25	0.8	87	0.6	229
Zaire (Dem. Rep. Congo)	18.7	44	23	2.1	33	25.8	115
SOUTHERN AFRICA	**25**	**41**	**18**	**2.4**	**29**	**34**	-
Botswana	0.7	44	23	2.2	32	0.9	175
Lesotho	1.1	39	21	1.8	39	1.4	181
South Africa [10]	21.7	41	17	2.4	29	29.7	138
Namibia (Southwest Africa) [11]	0.7	44	25	2.0	35	0.9	-
Swaziland	0.5	52	24	2.8	25	0.7	168
ASIA	**2,204**	**37**	**14**	**2.3**	**30**	**2,874**	-
SOUTHWEST ASIA	**84**	**44**	**16**	**2.8**	**25**	**121**	-
Bahrain	0.2	50	19	3.1	23	0.3	-
Cyprus	0.6	23	8	0.9	77	0.7	26
Gaza [11]	0.5	44	8	3.6	19	0.8	-
Iraq	10.8	49	15	3.4	21	16.7	104
Israel	3.1	28	7	2.4	29	4.0	23
Jordan	2.6	48	16	3.3	21	3.9	115
Kuwait [12]	0.9	43	7	9.8	7	2.4	39.
Lebanon	3.1	-	-	-	-	4.3	-
Oman	0.7	50	19	3.1	23	1.1	-
Qatar	0.1	50	19	3.1	23	0.1	-
Saudi Arabia	8.4	50	23	2.8	25	12.2	-
Syria	6.8	48	15	3.3	21	10.5	-
Turkey	38.6	40	15	2.5	28	52.8	119
United Arab Emirates	0.1	50	19	3.1	23	0.2	-
Yemen Arab Republic	6.2	50	23	2.8	25	9.1	-
Yemen, Peoples Republic of	1.4	50	21	2.9	24	2.0	-
MIDDLE SOUTH ASIA	**828**	**44**	**17**	**2.6**	**27**	**1,137**	-
Afghanistan	18.3	51	27	2.4	29	25.0	-
Bangladesh [13]	83.4	-	-	-		123.3	-
Bhutan	0.9	-	-	2.2	32	1.2	-
India [10]	600.4	42	17	2.5	28	807.6	139
Iran	31.1	45	17	2.8	25	45.0	-
Maldive Islands	0.1	46	23	2.3	31	0.1	-
Nepal	12.0	45	23	2.2	32	15.8	-
Pakistan [13]	68.3	51	18	3.3	21	100.9	142
Sikkim	0.2	48	29	1.9	37	0.3	-
Sri Lanka (Ceylon)	13.5	30	8	2.2	32	17.7	48
SOUTHEAST ASIA	**313**	**43**	**15**	**2.8**	**25**	**434**	-
Burma	29.8	40	17	2.3	30	39.2	-
Indonesia	132.5	47	19	2.9	24	183.8	125
Irian, West [11]	1.0	-	-	-	-	1.3	-
Khmer Republic (Cambodia)	7.8	45	16	3.0	23	11.3	127
Laos	3.2	42	17	2.5	28	4.4	-

241

Malaysia [10, 17]	11.8	38	11	2.7	26	16.4	-
Philippines [10]	42.2	45	12	3.3	21	64.0	67
Portuguese Timor [11]	0.6	43	25	1.8	39	0.8	-
Singapore	2.3	23	5	2.2	32	3.0	11
Thailand [10]	39.9	43	10	3.3	21	57.7	-
Vietnam (Dem. Republic of)	22.5	-	-	-	-	28.2	-
Vietnam (Republic of)	19.1	-	-	-	-	23.9	-
EAST ASIA	**978**	**29**	**12**	**1.7**	**41**	**1,182**	-
China (People's Republic of)	799.3	30	13	1.7	41	964.6	-
Hong Kong [1,11]	4.5	20	5	2.4	29	6.0	19
Japan	107.3	19	7	1.2	58	121.3	13
Ryukyu Islands [11.14]	1.0	22	5	1.7	41	1.3	-
Korea (Dem. People's Rep. of)	15.1	39	11	2.8	25	20.7	-
Korea (Republic of)	34.5	31	11	2.0	35	45.9	-
Macau[11]	0.3	-	-	-	-	0.4	-
Mongolia	1.4	42	11	3.1	23	2.0	-
Taiwan (Rep. of China)	15.0	27	5	2.2	32	19.4	18
NORTH AMERICA	**233**	**16**	**9**	**0.8**	**87**	**263**	-
Canada	22.5	15.7	73	1.2	58	27.3	17.6
United States [15]	210.3	15.6	9.4	0.8	87	235.7	18.5
LATIN AMERICA	**308**	**38**	**10**	**2.8**	**25**	**435**	-
MIDDLE AMERICA [16]	**75**	**43**	**11**	**12**	**22**	**112**	-
Costa Rica	2.0	34	7	2.7	26	3.2	67
El Salvador	3.8	42	10	3.2	22	5.9	53
Guatemala	5.6	43	17	2,6	27	7.9	88
Honduras	3.0	49	17	3.2	22	4.6	-
Mexico [10]	56.2	43	10	3.3	21	84.4	69
Nicaragua	2.2	46	17	2.9	24	3.3	-
Panama	1.6	37	9	2.8	25	2.5	41
CARIBBEAN [16]	**27**	**33**	**11**	**2.2**	**32**	**36**	-
Bahamas [12]	0.2	28	6	4.6	16	0.2	37
Barbados	0.3	22	9	0.8	87	0.3	42
Cuba	8.9	27	8	1.9	37	11.0	36
Dominican Republic [10]	4.8	49	15	3.4	21	7.3	64
Guadeloupe [11]	0.4	30	8	2.2	32	0.5	45
Haiti	5.6	44	20	2.4	29	7.9	-
Jamaica [10]	2.1	35	7	1.5	47	2.6	39
Martinique [11]	0.4	27	8	1.6	44	0.5	35
Netherlands Antilles [11]	0.2	23	6	1.7	41	0.3	-
Puerto Rico [11]	2.9	25	7	1.4	50	3.4	25
Trinidad & Tobago [10]	1.1	24	7	1.1	63	1.3	40
TROPICAL SOUTH AMERICA	**165**	**40**	**10**	**3.0**	**23**	**236**	-
Bolivia	5.0	44	19	2.4	29	6.8	-
Brazil	101.3	38	10	2.8	25	142.6	-
Colombia	23.7	45	11	3.4	21	35.6	76
Ecuador	6.7	45	11	3.4	21	10.1	91
Guyana	0.8	36	8	2.8	25	1.1	40
Peru	14.9	42	11	3.1	23	21.6	-

Surinam [11]	0.4	41	7	3.2	22	0.6	30
Venezuela	11.9	41	8	3.4	21	17.4	49
TEMPERATE SOUTH AMERICA	**41**	**25**	**9**	**1.7**	**41**	**51**	-
Argentina [10]	25.3	22	9	1.5	47	29.6	58
Chile [10]	10.4	26	9	1.7	41	13.6	88
Paraguay	2.7	45	11	3.4	21	4.1	
Uruguay	3.0	23	9	1.4	50	3.4	43
EUROPE	**472**	**16**	**10**	**0.7**	**99**	**515**	-
NORTHERN EUROPE	**82**	**15**	**11**	**0.4**	**175**	**90**	-
Denmark	5.1	15.8	10.2	0.5	139	5.5	14.2
Finland	4.8	12.7	9.6	0.3	231	5.0	11.3
Iceland	0.2	19.7	7.3	1.2	58	0.3	13.2
Ireland	3.0	22.4	11.2	0.5	139	3.5	19.6
Norway	4.0	16.6	10.0	0.7	99	4.5	12.7
Sweden	8.2	13.8	10.4	0.3	231	8.8	11.1
United Kingdom	57.0	14.9	11.9	0.3	231	61.8	18.0
WESTERN EUROPE	**151**	**14**	**11**	**0.4**	**175**	**163**	-
Austria	7.5	13.8	12.6	0.1	700	8.0	25.1
Belgium	9.8	13.8	12.0	0.2	347	10.4	19.8
France	52.3	16.9	10.6	0.6	117	57.6	13.3
Germany (Federal Republic of)	59.4	11.5	11.7	0.0	-	62.3	23.2
Berlin, West [11]	2.1	9.1	19.0	-1.0	-	1.9	28.0
Luxembourg	0.4	11.8	11.9	0.0	-	0.4	13.6
Netherlands	13.4	16.1	8.5	0.8	87	15.3	11.4
Switzerland	6.5	14.4	8.7	1.0	70	7.4	14.4
EASTERN EUROPE	**107**	**17**	**10**	**0.7**	**99**	**116**	-
Bulgaria	8.7	15.3	9.8	0.6	117	9.4	25.8
Czechoslovakia	15.0	16.5	11.5	0.5	139	16.2	21.6
Germany (Dem. Republic of)	16.3	11.7	13.7	-0.2	-	16.9	17.7
Berlin, East [11]	1.1	13.4	16.2	-0.3	-	1.0	19.6
Hungary	10.4	14.7	11.4	0.3	231	11.0	32.7
Poland	34.0	17.4	8.0	0.9	77	38.2	28.5
Romania	21.0	19.6	9.5	1.0	70	23.3	42.4
SOUTHERN EUROPE	**132**	**18**	**9**	**0.9**	**77**	**146**	-
Albania	2.3	35.3	7.5	2.8	25	3.3	86.8
Greece	9.1	15.9	8.3	0.8	87	9.7	27.0
Italy	54.9	16.8	9.6	0.7	99	60.0	28.3
Malta [12]	0.3	16.8	9.1	-0.1	-	0.3	23.9.
Portugal	9.8	21.3	11.1	1.0	70	10.7	49.8
Spain	34.2	19.4	8.2	1.1	63	38.1	27.9
Yugoslavia	21.2	18.2	9.1	0.9	77	23.8	48.8
UUSR	**250**	**17.8**	**8.2**	**1.0**	**70**	**286.9**	**22.6**
OCEANIA [16]	**21**	**25**	**10**	**2.0**	**35**	**27**	-
Australia	13.3	20.5	8.5	1.9	37	17.0	17.3
Fiji	0.6	30	5	1.8	39	0.8	-
New Zealand	3.0	22.1	8.5	1.7	41	3.8	16.5
Papua-New Guinea [11]	2.6	42	18	2.4	29	3.6	-

243

FOOTNOTES

1   The *Data Sheet* lists all UN members and all geopolitical entities with a population larger than 200,000.

2   UN, *Total Population Estimates for World, Regions and Countries, Each Year, 1950-1985,* Population Division Working Paper No. 34 (October 1970).

3   Latest available year. Except for North America, estimates are essentially those available as of April 1973 in UN, *Population and Vital Statistics Report,* Series A, vel. 25, no. 2 (1973). Because of deficient registration in some countries adjustments have been made where deemed necessary.

4   Latest UN estimates, except for substantiated changes in birth rates, death rates or migration streams.

5   Assuming no change in growth rate.

6   Latest available year. Derived from UN, *World Population Prospects, 1965-1985, As Assessed in* 1968, Population Division Working Paper No. 30 (December 1969); and UN, *Demographic Yearbook,* 1970 and 1971.

7   Latest available year, in no case before 1960. Derived from UN, *Statistical Yearbook,* 1972 (1973); and Centro Latinamericano de Demográfia, *Boletin Demografico,* vol. 4, no. a (Santiago, Chile, July 1971).

8   International Bank for Reconstruction and Development, 1970 data. In some cases, figures are substantially different from those on the 1972 *Data Sheet* because of a different basis used for computing GNP.

9   Total reflects UN adjustments for discrepancies in international migration data.

10 UN estimates for this country differ from recent census figures by more than 3 percent but are used because of uncertainty about the completeness or accuracy of census data.

11 Non-sovereign country.

12 Kuwait has a rate of natural increase (births minus deaths) of 3.6 percent; Malta's is 0.8 percent, and the Bahamas' 2.2 percent. Their growth rates differ markedly from their rates of natural increase because of migration.

13 Except for population, estimates for Pakistan include data for Bangladesh.

14 Reverted to Japan May 15, 1972.

15 U.S. figures are based on Series E population projections in Bureau of the Census, "Projections of the Population of the United States, by Age and Sex: 1972 to 2020," *Current Population Reports,* Series P-25. no 493 (December 1972); and National Center for Health Statistics. *Monthly Vital Statistics Report,* vol. 21, no. 13 (June 27, 1973).

16 Regional population totals take into account small areas not listed on the *Data Sheet.*

17 Life expectancy for West Malaysia only. East Malaysia estimated to be 55. Dashes indicate data are unavailable or unreliable.

L = Estimated to be less than 5 percent.

GENERAL NOTES

Birth rate: Annual number of births per 1,000 population.

Death rate: Annual number of deaths per 1,000 population.

Population growth rate: Annual rate of natural increase combined with the plus or minus factor of net immigration or net emigration. *(Natural increase* is the birth rate minus the death rate in a given year.)

Infant mortality rate: Annual deaths to infants under one year of age per 1,000 live births.

World Population Data Sheets of various years should not be used as a time series. Because every attempt is made to use the most accurate information, data sources vary and apparently radical changes in rates from year to year may reflect improved source material revised data, or a later base year for computation, rather than yearly rate changes.

Population figures are rounded to the nearest 100,000; thus increases amounting to less than that number do not appear on the *Data Sheet.*

Demographic data for most developing countries are often incomplete or inaccurate. In many cases, therefore, UN estimates are used.

For world urbanization data, see the 1972 *World Population Data Sheet.*

Reprinted by permission from WORLD POPULATION DATA SHEET for 1973, issued by, and copyright by, the Population Reference Bureau, Inc., 1755 Massachusetts Ave., N.W.,

Washington, D.C. 20035. Published annually. (This reproduction is incomplete, some data present on the original sheet being omitted).

www.ingramcontent.com/pod-product-compliance
Lightning Source LLC
Chambersburg PA
CBHW071221290326
41931CB00037B/1601